The Language of the Field

Also from Carcanet

Fly-fishing: a book of words
C. B. McCully

Horse Racing: a book of words
Gerald Hammond

Theatre: a book of words
Martin Harrison

Whisky: a book of words
Gavin D. Smith

The Language of Cricket
John Eddowes

Michael Brander

The Language of the Field

CARCANET

First published in Great Britain in 1997 by
Carcanet Press Limited
4th Floor, Conavon Court
12–16 Blackfriars Street
Manchester M3 5BQ

A CIP catalogue record for this book
is available from the British Library.

ISBN 1 85754 166 9

The publisher acknowledges financial assistance
from the Arts Council of England.

Set in 10pt Plantin by Ensystems, Saffron Walden
Printed and bound in England by SRP Ltd, Exeter.

General Editors' Preface

This series offers a new conception and analysis of the vocabularies used in our sports, pursuits, vocations and pastimes. While each book contains an essential lexicon of words and phrases – explored historically and in depth – each also contains generous quotation, practical reference, anecdote and conjecture. The result is more than a dictionary: specific, inclusive, thought-provoking, each volume offers the past and present through a weave of words, in all their curiosity and delight.

Those intrigued by the language particular to their area of interest will find the relevant book a coherent and challenging treatment of the topic; those interested in the English language itself will find the series yielding significant material on semantic scope and change; and general readers who wish to understand the vocabularies of human endeavour will find the series tracing the necessary but implacable relationships between words and world.

Editors, chosen because of their intimate enthusiasm for their subjects, have been encouraged to be comprehensive in their coverage: vocabularies typically range from the demotic to the esoteric, from slang to the technical and specialised. Within that range, emphasis is also placed on *how* each lexicon developed, and *why* its terms acquired their peculiar descriptive power. These are books to read with pleasure as well as keep on the reference shelf.

Gerald Hammond
C. B. McCully

Acknowledgements

While compiling this book I have learned a great deal that I did not previously know about subjects that have always interested me and about which I have written extensively. As a professional author I found researching and writing it not only interesting and informative, but also rather amusing. I hope my readers will have the same reactions.

My thanks must go primarily to Michael Grose, who first pointed me in the direction of this project. My grateful thanks must also go to Miss Elizabeth Burrard for permission to quote extensively from the work of her uncle, the late Major Sir Gerard Burrard DSO, the three volumes entitled *The Modern Shotgun* published in 1930, which are still the outstanding work in the field, also his less well-known, but still interesting book *In the Gunroom*. I must also thank Dr Frank Holmes for permission to quote extensively from his excellent book *Following the Roe*, published in 1973, which is also generally considered an outstanding work on the subject.

Finally, my thanks and congratulations must go to Professor Gerald Hammond and Dr Chris McCully, of the Department of English Language and Literature at Manchester University, who conceived this series and who as editors worked their way through piles of manuscript and kept me on the right lines.

Abbreviations

AF: Anglo-French
Du: Dutch
Fr: French
Ger: German
It: Italian
L: Latin
LL: Late Latin
ME: Middle English
MDu: Middle Dutch
N: Norse
NF: Norman French
OE: Old English
OF: Old French
ON: Old Norse

References to often-cited sources are given in shortened form; full details may be found in the References at the end. Two that may be puzzling are:

Encyclopedia: The Encyclopedia of Sport; see under Aflalo
LL Shooting: Lonsdale Library vol. iii, *Shooting*; see under Parker.

We thank the Oxford University Press for permission to include material from the Dictionary, cited as OED.

Introduction

While hunting, hawking and fishing are amongst the earliest pursuits of mankind, so that their origins and etymology in Britain go back to the Normans and beyond, shooting and stalking with a shotgun or rifle, rather than a longbow or crossbow, are comparatively modern. It was only in the reign of Henry VIII that it was felt necessary to introduce an Act against the excessive use of 'hayle shotte'. It was only when Drake and Ralegh's gunners returned from the Spanish Main and the Americas and manhandled their cumbersome arquebuses inland to shoot the enormous rafts of wildfowl which were then to be found on our marshes and round our coasts that 'fowling' with guns instead of hawks or nets began to be regarded as a sport. George Turberville in 1576 was amongst the earliest writers to note the changes taking place. Around the turn of the century, Gervase Markham was discoursing on training the 'Water Dogge', but it was only towards the end of the 17th century, in 1686, that the concept of 'Shooting Flying' was first mentioned in print by Richard Blome in *The Gentleman's Recreation.*

As late as 1830 no less an authority than Lt.-Col. Peter Hawker was asserting that only fifty years previously anyone 'shooting flying' had been regarded with amazement. His book, *Instructions to Young Sportsmen in all that relates to guns and shooting* was the first of its kind. In 1838 William Scrope was the first to write on deer stalking. Thereafter books on shooting, and to a lesser extent on stalking, proliferated.

The development of the shotgun was revolutionised by the change from *flintlock* to percussion hammer gun in the first decade of the 19th century. The next two great changes were the development of the *breech-loader* in the 1850s and then the hammerless ejector shotgun in the 1870s. By the late 1870s, with farming at low ebb because of the import of cheap grain from the mid-west of America and frozen meat from the Argentine and the Antipodes, land was readily available for shooting. Indeed the shooting rents and the rabbits were often all that enabled some farmers to survive.

From the 1880s to the present day shooting and stalking have only altered in minor ways, although there has inevitably been a slow and steady change in attitudes as well as in etymology. As an author and word-smith, as well as a keen stalker and shot, the etymology of shooting and stalking holds its own fascination for me. It may come as a surprise to many, for instance, to learn that some of our commonest commands to our gundogs, such as 'Fetch' and 'Hie-lost' stem from Old English and Norman sources. In somewhat different form they may have been used by our ancestors even before 1066. The origins of the command 'Hup', still commonly used by many spaniel trainers, also has an interesting background, probably going back to eighteenth-century musket drill.

There are more modern examples of words developing with the sport of shooting. A word such as *wormburner*, a live pigeon released from the traps and flying away at speed close to the ground, was a term developed in the days of live pigeon shooting, which lasted roughly from the early 1800s until just after the turn of the century, when the obvious cruelty of the sport and the malpractices involved led to its being banned. The term is now already obsolete. *Flash-in-the-pan*, a commonly used expression until the turn of the 19th century, although still sometimes heard, is now becoming almost as obsolete as the flintlocks which inspired its use, but its origins are fascinating.

Since the etymology of these sports is so recent it is of considerable interest to note how the various writers used the terms and their often considerable divergence of views on the correct meaning. Words which were used in hunting and fal-conry, or in shooting with a longbow or crossbow, were often changed almost beyond recognition. Thus *retrive*, a term in falconry used to indicate the second find of game, when the falcon was ready to be cast on, was greatly changed. With the addition of an <e> the *retrieve* became the gundog's familiar task of finding and returning with the shot game. Thus too came soft and hard of mouth and many other terms we now accept as commonplace, but which would have been barely recognisable to our grandfathers.

Included here, then, are the words most commonly used in the sports of shooting and stalking with their origins and the altera-tions that have taken place in their meaning. There are some surprising throwbacks to Old English, Norman French and Norse as well as words of German, Dutch and Italian origins. In some cases the usages in the USA and North America are strangely different. Some words have even crossed and then re-crossed the Atlantic changing their meaning as they did so.

At first sight this may not seem of interest to the practical-minded reader, but this is not just an idiosyncratic dictionary. There is a practical side to it as well. Readers will find, while browsing through the book, discovering the meaning of the words used in their sport, that they will also often learn something useful and which can be put to good effect. Here and there, it must be admitted, for instance under *keeper*, *hare's birth*, *hare's breath* and a *zern*, there may have been some degree of personal intrusion. This is unprofessional, but as Colonel Peter Hawker pointed out over the spelling of *wigeon*, 'lexicographers are not gods, but men.' And as Confucius said; 'Knowledge, however gained, is always useful.'

Acknowledge ON *on* + *cnawan*, 'to know' (by the senses) to recognise, the prefix afterwards reduced as normal to *o-*, *a-*and at length corruptly written <*ac-*> in imitation of *ac-* before *c-*, *k-*, *q-*, in words adopted from L. (OED *acknow*): in present form only used since the 16th century: OED 'to own as genuine'. A hound, when hunting, may be said to *acknowledge* or to 'own' the scent of a quarry, by giving tongue. In the same way a gundog may be said to acknowledge or own scent when hunting ground, by lowering the head and checking briefly when passing where game has been lying, then continuing to hunt. An example is to be found in Brander (*Gundogs*, 69): 'The faint wag of the tail acknowledging the scent of a covey of partridges, which departed as the handler entered the field.' When a gundog is hunting and a bird, or groundgame, gets up downwind, it is said to acknowledge, or *honour*, the *flush*, if it halts and stands or drops, while watching the flushed game depart, without offering to chase. Similarly a gundog should stand, or drop, and mark the flight or the effect of shot, when game is flushed and shot after a point. The importance of a steady dog in such cases scarcely needs emphasising, since a dog which runs in to flush may well itself be shot. The dog which runs in to scent, flushing game out of shot, is, however, merely an unruly nuisance and is probably better shot, which in any event is its likely fate if it continually runs into the line of shot. It is certainly no use as a working dog.

across-eyed stock, or cross-over stock   a *stock* with sufficient bend adjusted to shoot from the one shoulder, either right or left, while using the opposite eye. Its use may be advocated by a gunsmith because of faulty vision caused by weak eyesight in one eye and a very strong master eye. The principle of an *across-eyed stock* was almost certainly introduced by gunmakers only after the advent of the **breech-loader** in the 1870s, by which time gunfitting was becoming more scientific. The first reference in print appears to be in 1889 by Charles Lancaster, a prominent gunmaker, who wrote:

When the left eye is the 'master eye' and the gun is used from the left shoulder, 'cast on' serves the same purpose as 'cast off' does in the normal case of right-eyed shooting. To a left-eyed person who shoots from the right shoulder two courses are open. The first is either to close the left eye, or otherwise screen it from the gun barrels, but this is a serious handicap, throwing as it does all the work upon one eye, and that the weaker of the two. The alternative is to use an 'across-eyed' gun, which is one built to fit the right shoulder, but cast-off

5

sufficiently to allow the rib of the barrels to come opposite the left eye for the alignment. (*Shooting*, 131) It is perhaps not surprising that Lancaster was among the foremost makers of this somewhat uncommon type of stock. Such stocks are rarely seen, since the cost of fitting them is considerable, but some people do prefer them to the much cheaper alternatives of blanking off the master eye with a guard attached to the barrel, or an eye patch, or else using a monocle, spectacles, or contact lenses to correct the defect. Most people whose physique or eyesight require any such aid to shooting usually adopt these cheaper and perfectly effective alternatives. Apart from being expensive to make and fit, such stocks are neither particularly attractive to look at, nor convenient to use or carry.

action   from L *action-em*, a doing. OED: 'the mechanism by which an instrument acts': 'This lever is secured in position by the screw and washer to a pivot passing through the lever, the said pivot being solid with the action' (*The Greener Gun*, 1881, p. 195). Of a shotgun: connects the stock to the barrels and contains the lock, i.e. the mechanism for firing the cartridges. It may be a *box-lock*, or *side-lock* action. The latter is more complex and is used in high-grade guns, but the former is stronger. The outward components are the *safety catch*, the top lever (or under lever in some cases), the strikers, the action face, the extractor cam, the cocking levers, the knuckle, the sideplate, the trigger guard and the right and left triggers. The *action* is a steel housing which connects the barrels to the stock. In 1930 Burrard wrote: 'This connection is effected by means of the "Action," which is a steel housing which contains the mechanism for the attachment of the barrels and the firing of the cartridges and which is fastened in a more or less permanent manner to the wooden stock by screws . . .' (Shotgun, i, 37). See *bar of the action*; *face of the action*.

air scent   not attested in the OED, but see *scent*. It is scent particles carried by the air, as opposed to *ground scent* or *foot scent*; this scent may be followed by a dog with head held high, and is sometimes detected at a considerable distance. Brander wrote: 'Watch the retriever trained to work the ground slowly and methodically . . . as he catches an air scent his tail starts to move' (*Dog*, 11).

airshot   not attested in the OED. A miss. Probably a development of the old shooting saying 'There's a lot of air around a bird', originating perhaps from Lancaster's comment in 1889 (*Shooting*, 11): 'There's a lot of space round a flying bird.' An

early example of this usage is in 1939 by T.D.S. & J.A. Purdey
(*The Shotgun*, 81): 'Two barrels – "airers" – or in other words,
an airshot, or miss.'

alarm gun a device which can be set to fire off a blank shot
at intervals to act as a bird scarer to protect newly sown grain,
growing corn, or storm-damaged crops; alternatively a gun
attached to a trip-wire to give warning of intruders or poachers
in the coverts. See *spring gun*.

albino from L *albus*, white. Originally applied by the Portuguese to the white negroes on the coast of Africa. A condition
in humans distinguished by congenital absence of colouring
pigment in the hair, skin and eyes, so that the former are
abnormally white and the latter pinkish; hence by extension any
animal having a similar condition. Also said of deer; rare, but
not unknown.

ammunition from Fr in the 16th and 17th century, and a
corruption of 'munition', or 'monition'. OED: 'Formerly all
military stores and supplies used in charging guns and ordnance,
as powder, shot, shell and by extension offensive missiles
generally.' For the *rifle*, it is advisable to keep different calibre
ammunition separately in clearly marked containers. There is
nothing more annoying than finding oneself out on the hill,
miles from home, with ammunition of the wrong *calibre* for
the rifle. Most experienced stalkers will remember one occasion
when this has happened. It is also advisable to carry it in slotted
containers so that there is no chance of its clinking at a vital
moment in the stalk. For the shotgun, it is advisable to keep
cartridges of different gauge or shot size separate, since it is
undesirable to shoot at snipe with shot intended for geese, or
vice versa. It has also been known for a 20-bore cartridge to be
loaded accidentally in a 12-bore gun, slipping far enough into
the chamber for another cartridge to be loaded on top and
causing the gun to explode.

anal tush OED gives the etmyology of *tush* as from OE *tusc*,
being an obsolete variant of *tusk*. Of a roe doe: the white tuft of
hair at the lower edge of the *target*, or the white rump patch of
its winter coat. This is one of the ways of distinguishing between
doe and buck during the winter months when the buck has shed
his antlers and there is often very little otherwise to distinguish
the sexes at any distance.

angle of shot the *angle* at which a shot is fired very much
affects the result with both rifle and shotgun. The angle
naturally varies with regard to the angle of stance of the deer or
the angle of flight of the bird. Regarding the rifle, as early as

1830 Hawker wrote: 'For a deer standing sideways take the forelegs, the neck, or the head, but in firing at the latter, be careful not to shoot too forward or too low, as you would then only break his jaw' (*Instructions*, 189). It is seldom as simple as that. When firing steeply uphill, it is desirable to aim your shot low in the body, so that a heart shot will go through the lungs and exit through the top of the opposite shoulder. When firing steeply downhill, it is equally important to aim slightly higher. Thus a shot behind the shoulder may go through heart and lungs, exiting below the brisket. Taking a shot from directly above, as sometimes is the case when shooting from a platform, it is advisable to shoot directly behind the withers, when the bullet should go through the spine, lungs and heart, but this is a very small target and since it probably means leaning awkwardly far out of the high seat, it is usually advisable to wait for a broadside shot if possible. In 1986 Brander wrote: 'It seldom happens in practice that a beast is exactly broadside on and it is more often than not at a slight angle . . .' (*Deer*, 125). With the shotgun, when a bird is approaching it is desirable to **black out** the bird with the barrels, i.e. to fire in front of it. When a bird is going away, it is desirable to fire above it, i.e. once again, beyond it. If a bird is flying away downhill, it is advisable to shoot below it. When a bird is crossing a valley, it is advisable to shoot beyond and above it. With any crossing shot the aim should be through and beyond the bird. The same holds good of an approaching high bird. It is necessary to black out the bird with the barrels before firing. In every case, however, the gun should be swung swiftly and instinctively. Any hesitation or pause for thought inevitably leads to *poking* and a missed bird. 'It will be realised that when a bird gets up, it is, more often than not, flying at an oblique angle' (Lancaster, 84).

anointing post   of deer: a tree, or stump, with a part of the trunk worn smooth and oily as a result of deer depositing gland secretion on it.

antlers   *antoilier* (OF), from the LL. *ante-ocular-em*, in front of the eyes: the 'branch' or tine of a stag's horn in front of the eyes. OED: 'Originally the lowest (forward-directed) branch of the horns of a stag, or other deer; afterwards extended to any branch, the lowest then being called the brow-antler and the next the bes-antler.' A bony outgrowth on the head of the male deer, cast annually in the autumn and renewed the following spring. Deer are described as carrying antlers rather than horns. Langland (*Richard Redeles*, 1399): 'Our hauntelere dere were all y-takyn.'

anti's   from Greek, literally, 'those opposing', but not used before 1600 in conjunction with a noun, e.g. anti-Christ. The term has been commonly used since the 1960s by supporters of field sports for those claiming to be 'anti-field sports'. There has always been a minority in Britain opposed to all forms of hunting since the Forest Laws introduced by Canute were used by the victorious Normans as a means of subjugating the Saxons. Subsequently, the Puritans disapproved of hunting and similar sports on religious grounds. These historical roots, with an admixture of envy and intolerance, nurtured by the hysteria engendered by the slaughter in the First World War, as well as the ever-increasing gulf of ignorance between town and country, produced a 'League Against Cruel Sports' in the UK in 1924, followed belatedly by the formation of the British Field Sports Society (BFSS) in 1930. The *anti's* however, were a phenomenon first widely encountered in the 1960s, styling themselves pejoratively and emotively 'anti-blood sports' and they have become increasingly active since. Their highly organised campaigns aimed at disrupting and discrediting field sports have resulted in increasingly vigorous support for the pro-field sports societies, notably, in the case of shooting, the Game Conservancy, the British Association for Shooting and Conservation (BASC) and the BFSS. By concentrating their counter-arguments largely on the negative quality of the word *anti-*, and refuting the pejorative follow-up phrase, the pro-field-sports organisations have scored a moral victory.

anvil   according to the OED the etymology is uncertain, but the *anvil* is the iron block on which the blacksmith hammers and shapes his metalwork, in this case applied to the interior part of the cartridge beneath the percussion cap, which absorbs the blow of the striker pin. Burrard: 'In one of these [Continental caps] the anvil is made in the cap chamber by raising its base' (*Gunroom*, 62).

at heel or **to heel**   all gundogs should be trained to walk *at heel* or *to heel*. Retrievers generally stay at *heel* when not being used to hunt or retrieve. In 1924, Richard Sharpe mentioned 'The first lesson – to sit down, to walk to heel . . .' in his *Dog Training by Amateurs* (19).

automatic   from Greek, literally, 'self-acting'; of a shotgun, a type of single-barrelled repeater shotgun in which the cartridge is automatically ejected after the shot and the shotgun is automatically re-loaded. All automatic shotguns operate on one of two basic principles, either recoil operated, or gas operated. It is illegal to own an automatic shotgun in Britain.

Back   of a pointing dog. As a verb, to *honour* the point of another dog working with it and to freeze (i.e. stand in a cataleptic state) *on point* as well. 'Some very high couraged dogs are very difficult to make "back;" and indeed I have known many highly-bred ones in which the cataleptic condition was never fully developed' (Walsh, 34). In 1865 *The Encyc. Brìt.* noted: 'A dog which backs another is not aware of the proximity of game at the time otherwise than by inference.'

A method of teaching a young dog to back which is advocated with considerable regularity is to hunt an old dog singly, the backing pupil being meanwhile kept at heel. When opportunity offers the young dog is made to back the older specimen . . . I am unable to subscribe to such a system as it seems to be a positive inducement to blinking . . . there will be a decided risk that when he sees the old dog draw-on game he will go back to the breaker. (Sanderson, 23)

A dog may be trained to *back* when young if taken out and worked freely with an older dog and encouraged to point at the sight of the other doing so. If it is already beginning to point the chances are that it will stiffen at once at the sight of the other dog on point and it should then be soothed and encouraged to remain on point until it is desired to flush the game. It is, however, inadvisable to encourage a young dog to rely too strongly on an older dog for it may then develop hesitancy about working on its own and even develop faults such as *blinking*.

badger   of doubtful origin. The OE term for a badger was a *broc*, from the old Celtic *brocco*, itself derived from Gk 'Grey-white'. Broc is one of the very few words permanently loaned from Celtic to OE. One of the earliest attestations appears to be in 1552: 'Brock, or badger, or grey beaste'. In 1845 St John wrote: 'One of his most favourite repasts is the contents of the nest of the wasp, or wild bee, great numbers of which he must destroy' (*Wild Sports*, 27). 'It is difficult to understand how any person, who is not lost to every sense of humanity and shame can take delight in the cowardly and brutal amusement of badger-baiting – instead of amusement I should have said the disgusting exhibition of a peaceable and harmless animal worried by fierce and powerful dogs' (ibid., 277). A company of badgers is known as a *cete* of badgers. They are rightly a protected species under the 1981 Wildlife & Countryside Act, for the badger is an attractive and interesting mammal, generally harmless to shooting interests. The Royal Society for the

10

Prevention of Cruelty to Animals, however, still has to prosecute occasional badger-baiting cases.

bag   probably from the Old Norse. OED: 'sporting-Gamebag; hence the contents of a gamebag; the quantity of fish or game however large (embracing, e.g. elephants and buffaloes) killed at one time; the produce of a hunting, fishing or shooting expedition.' One of the earliest references is in 1486 (*The Boke of St Albans*, Bk iii): 'Ye most take a partrich in yowre bagge.' In 1842 Charles Dickens (*The Pickwick Papers*) described 'a tall raw-boned gamekeeper, and a half-booted leather leggined boy, each bearing a bag of capacious dimensions . . . "I say," whispered Mr Winkle to Wardle . . . "they don't suppose we're going to kill enough game to fill those bags, do they?"' The *bag* also represents the *head* of game and 'various' shot during a day or more's sport. It is possible, for instance, to refer to the bag for the season shot on a particular shoot, or to detail the bag from certain days, or seasons. The record bag of grouse in this country was obtained on 12 August 1915 by eight guns on the 12,000-acre Littledale and Abbeystead moor in Lancashire. The bag of an individual, shot during one day's shooting, or over several shoots, or during his lifetime might also be recorded, but it is usually considered both invidious and impractical to record an individual's bag during a driven day when there are a team of guns involved, since it is purely a matter of luck in the placing at each drive as to whether a gun is in a position to kill many birds or not. A classic example of a notable individual bag is that of Colonel Peter Hawker, who between 1802 and 1853 is credited by Eric Parker with killing a total bag, including Game, Wildfowl and Various of 17,582 head (notable for only 20 woodpigeons, then scarce in the south, but also for including 3 bitterns, 2 phalaropes and an avocet. N.B. This cannot be taken as entirely accurate, since it is apparent by reference to the original diaries in Yale Library that he freqently included the entire bag when shooting in company.)

Also used as a verb. OED: 'to put game killed into a bag, also to kill game (without reference to the bag).' This latter usage appears to have been introduced in the early years of the 19th century and though still in use is now less common. In 1830 Hawker wrote: 'In 1827 . . . in eight hours, he bagged fifty-one brace of partridges' (*Instructions* 148).

bald face   of deer; having a white blaze covering the face. The OED indicates that whereas *bald* may be ME from *ball*, i.e. 'rounded like a ball' hence 'smooth' and applied to the head 'hairless', in Dutch and many languages the analogy is white, especially that of 'having a white patch on the forehead' as in 'a bald-faced stag'.

bar of the action   of a shotgun: that part of the *action* of a shotgun which projects horizontally beneath the barrels when they are joined to the action. 'If the bar remains absolutely rigid there can be no separation of the barrels from the breech face' Burrard (*Shotgun*, i, 46).

bark   from OE *beorcan*. OED: 'the sharp explosive cry uttered by dogs, or similar sound made by other animals; esp. foxes': also *roe, muntjac, Chinese water-deer* and sometimes also *red deer*: the distinctive sound made by these species, sometimes when calling to each other, but frequently a sign of alarm and warning. The sound has many distinctive forms. The Chinese water-deer is probably the most persistent barker, with the muntjac a close second at times. The roe is inclined to bark more as the *rut* approaches, when both sexes may bark at intruders, or to each other. Red deer are also known to bark on occasions, especially hinds when scenting danger: 'a "bark" from the nearest hind, which had made sure we were an enemy, caused the entire herd to scamper off' (Speedy, 257).

barking, bark stripping   to strip off the bark from trees. *Bark stripping* may be done by various animals. Serious damage may be caused by a deer's, or a hare's, teeth, also sometimes rodents such as mice. *Barking* may result in the tree's dying. It is one of the foresters' complaints about the presence of deer, but is not common with roe. A persistent culprit may, however, have to be *culled*. In 1884 Speedy noted: 'During the heavy snowstorm in December 1882 . . . a great deal of destruction was done by hares to an orchard of young fruit-trees . . . by barking them . . .' (p. 284).

barrels   OED: 'The metal tubes of a gun through which the bullet or shot is discharged.' See *side-by-side* and *over-and-under*. Barrel length has been a particularly vexed question over the centuries. In 1621 Markham (*Fowling*) recommended barrels for the fowling piece 'from five and a half to six feet long', probably to allow the slow-burning powder sufficient time to develop full thrust. In 1806 Thornton had definite views:

> it is necessary for every gentleman who sports much to have two guns; the barrel of one about two feet nine inches to serve in the beginning of the season and in wood shooting, the other three feet three inches or upwards, for open shooting after Michaelmas, the birds by that time being

grown so shy that his shots must be at greater distances. But if he intends one gun to serve all purposes, a three feet barrel, or from three feet six is the most proper. (*France*, ii, 235) In 1807 Daniel, on guns for woodcock shooting, noted: 'The Gun should not exceed *two feet eight* in the barrel and the shot used be No 6 or 7' (iii, 172). Also: 'Mr. Robins procured two barrels of the same calibre, the one *Thirty three* and the other *Sixty six* inches long . . . repeatedly firing them . . . at different distance . . . the Effect was always similar . . . These Trials afford a decisive Testimony in favour of SHORT *Barrels*' (iii, 463). In 1830 Hawker wrote:

It was formerly the custom to make barrels . . . of three or four feet in length; and now that it has been ascertained that two feet six inches will shoot equally well at the short distance of a gunmaker's confined premises, many have gone too much to the other extreme, and cut them to two feet four inches and less . . . To avoid all extremes I should recommend small barrels, never less than two feet eight, nor more than three feet in length. [. . .] I have every reason to believe that we have all, to this very day been completely in the dark about the length of guns . . . a short gun has no chance with a long one in keeping the shot well together at long distances. . . . Fire a fourteen gauge sporting-gun two feet eight inches . . . at a gunmaker's iron door, against one of three feet and there will probably be no difference. But go out into an open field and particularly on a windy day with the two feet eight inch barrel and try it at sixty yards, and . . . the three feet barrel keeps the shot together. (*Instructions*, 16, 17)

A few years later, Walsh stated firmly: 'With a fourteen or sixteen gauge the barrels should be from thirty to thirty two inches in length . . . Single barrelled gun should weigh from five to seven pounds . . . and the barrel should be from thirty four to thirty six inches in length. For covert shooting a difference should be made of about four inches' (p. 21). By 1870 views had changed, and W.W. Greener noted: 'Some gentlemen will not have them longer than twenty-four inches . . . we think it unwise to shorten a barrel to more than twenty-six inches' (*Modern Breech-loaders* 9th edn, 1910, 68). In 1889 Lancaster stated: 'Although barrels are universally made of steel now, there remains considerable diversity in length. Since 1920 the vast majority have been 28 inches long, although more than this length is often required and many hold shorter barrels in favour as quite a number did in 1875. . . . Of course the length of stock must be considered in fixing barrel lengths to give a

properly proportioned gun' (p. 119). In 1930 Burrard took a
measured view: 'For many years the barrels of an ordinary 12-
bore have almost always been made from 28 to 30 inches long
... there is no general best length for shotgun barrels, and the
best length for an individual shooter to select is the length with
which he finds he can shoot best' (*Shotgun*, iii, 226). The fact
remains, however, that a very tall man with a very a short gun
does look as out of place as a very short man with a long-
barrelled gun. In general the principle is sound that the gun
should fit the man.

battue   ultimately from Latin, via French. OED: 'the driving of
game from cover (by beating the bushes etc, in which they
lodge) to point where a number of sportsmen wait to shoot
them. Hence battue shooting.' A term now largely obsolete. In
1816 (*The Gentleman's Magazine*, lxxxiv, 1.414) it was noted:
'The keen Sportsman ... and a favoured few, on the set day,
have a Grand Battu.' In 1849 Cobden mentioned disapprovingly 'That modern innovation of battue shooting, which was
not known in 1790.' Walsh fulminated in 1856:
> It is for the purpose of the *battue* that pheasants are now
> reared and preserved with all the formidable retinue of head-
> keepers, under-keepers, day-watchers and night-watchers.
> None but men of large means and extensive coverts can
> indulge in this amusement ... In the *battue* nothing short of
> hundreds, or, if possible, thousands, of killed, to say nothing
> of wounded, will constitute a successful day. (p. 61)
In 1884 Davenport remarked airily 'Battue shooting and grouse
and partridge driving are as a rule the only modes by which
game can be satisfactorily killed in England in these days'
(p. 122). However in 1897 (*Encyclopedia*, ii, 85) under 'Pheasant Shooting' it was noted: 'The tendency of modern shooting
is undoubtedly towards excess. A great number of birds is
neither conducive to good shooting nor to sport. There must
be a lot of low-flyers and a large proportion are good for
nothing after they are shot.' The word has now been largely
superseded by *driven shooting*. See also *yuppy shooting*.

bay   OED: 'short for *bay-antler*: earlier *be-* or *bes-antler*, from
the Old French *bes* = twice, second, secondary + antler; the
second branch of a stag's horn, formerly also called the *sur-
antlier*, being next above the "antler" proper or (as it is now
called) brow-antler.' In 1884 Richard Jeffries wrote: 'This is a
full horn, brow, bay, tray and three on top, or six points a side'
(*Red Deer*, 69).

BASC   acronym for the British Association for Shooting and

Conservation. Originally formed in the 1930s as WAGBI, the *Wildfowlers Association of Great Britain and Ireland*, but renamed in the 1980s with a greener title, the Association is the largest body representing the sport.

beam   OED: 'the main trunk of a stag's horn, which bears the branches, or "antlers."' In 1576 Turberville wrote: 'When the beame is great, burnished . . . and not made crooked by the antlyers.' In 1862 Collyns noted: 'The "beam" or main horn, increases in size . . . as the stag grows older' (p. ii).

bean goose   *Anser Arvensis*; a darker goose than the other grey geese and less vocal, this goose has a black bill marked with orange-yellow and orange-yellow legs. Its length is 28–35 inches and it weighs about 8–10 lbs. It may be shot from 1 September to 31 January inland and up to 20 February on the foreshore. In 1766 Pennant noted: 'Called the bean goose from the likeness of the nail of the bill to a horse bean' (ii, 234).

beat¹   OED. As a verb, 'to strike (water, bushes, or cover of any kind) in order to rouse, or drive game.' Originally used in hunting and hawking to drive out game to the hounds or hawk. An early attestation in shooting was in 1856, when Walsh on pheasant shooting wrote: 'A man or two, however, should accompany the dogs and beat steadily through the whole length of the plantation to prevent the pheasants running back' (p. 61). In 1872 Sir Samuel White Baker (*The Nile Tributaries*) speaking of larger game, noted that 'I took a few men to beat the jungle.' By 1897, however, driven pheasant shooting was widespread and it was noted: 'Pheasant Rearing and Shooting: Beats; Keepers make a mistake in not having more corners or stands; long waits are fatal to beating and annoying to the guns. The maxim to be impressed on the keeper should be; "little and often"' (*Encyclopedia*, ii, 85). See also *battue*; *driven shooting*.

beat²   As a noun: 'A tract over which a sportsman ranges in pursuit of game' (OED). In 1856 Walsh noted: 'The frauds . . . are enough to make him cautious before engaging a beat.' Also, an area of shooting looked after by a single keeper, usually under the management of a headkeeper, which might be a stretch of moor restricted mainly to grouse, an area of low-ground restricted mainly to partridges, or an area restricted mainly to pheasants, or even a mixture of the three. In 1930 A. Hipgrave wrote: 'The keeper on the partridge beat likes to show his master where his partridge nests have hatched' (*LL Shooting*, 274). Since river keepers were a later introduction, the use of

the term in fishing seems to have stemmed from the shooting
usage. Also, of a forest: an area under the charge of one forester.
beater   OED: 'A man employed in rousing and driving game.'
It is questionable whether beating has ever been restricted solely
to men and certainly today men, women, boys and girls are all
used as *beaters* regardless of age and sex. Before the shooting of
driven game in *battue* shoots which resulted from the development of the *breech-loader*, beaters were mostly used for
driving hares for coursing with greyhounds. In 1856 Walsh
under 'Coursing', wrote: 'The Beaters . . . a line should be
formed, placing one beater at every thirty yards; and proceeding
abreast of one another from one extremity of the field to
another' (p. 150). By 1884 *driven shooting* was widespread
and Davenport under 'Covert Shooting' wrote: 'For a time not
a sound save the gentle tapping of the beaters' sticks is heard'
(p. 133). In the same year Speedy under 'Cover Shooting'
noted:

> Some think that any person can beat. This is a mistake, as
> unless they keep in line with the precision of military drill,
> and have a knowledge of the habits of game, there is a
> tendency on the part of ground and winged game to run
> backwards and thereby defeat the object in view. We have
> frequently seen inexperienced beaters, who rather than run
> the risk of getting their clothes torn, or their hands scratched
> by thorns or bushes, would go round the outside of them,
> thereby affording every facility for the game to get in rear of
> the entire party and be lost . . . Boys, as a rule, do not make
> good beaters . . . are also apt to get unnecessarily noisy, which
> is most objectionable . . . for by such proceedings game is so
> frightened that it is just as likely to run backwards as
> forwards . . . (p. 280)

In 1929 Mackie went a stage further: 'The most important duty
of the keeper on the morning of a shoot is to have his beaters
out early and drive in all the surrounding country so as to have
the birds in the coverts' (p. 308). By 1930 Leslie Sprake writing
on the pheasant felt the subject still merited comment:

> The experienced keeper will endeavour to collect beaters that
> have demonstrated their ability for this work; and he will
> always try to gather together the same team – for there is . . .
> definite evidence of proficiency as the result of regular
> practice . . . the beaters should advance at a slow regular
> pace. (*LL Shooting*, 158)

The greatly increased sums now expected for a day's beating,
irrespective of age, sex or efficiency, are a material factor in the

overall cost of driven shooting today, particularly in the many
areas where beaters are hard to find. Inefficient and noisy
beating by badly organised and untrained beaters cannot be
compensated for by rearing large numbers of birds. Indeed the
combination of the two is inclined rightly to bring shooting into
disrepute. See *yuppy shooting*.

beaters' gun   literally, the *gun*, or guns, walking in line with
the beaters, whose task it is to shoot the birds *breaking back*.
It sometimes happens if there is a long drive, with outlying
strips being driven in to a main covert, that the beaters' guns
have considerable sport. The sound of the beaters' guns shooting more or less continuously can be somewhat irksome to the
waiting guns at a drive when no birds are coming across them
and is indicative of poor *shoot management*. In 1930 Leslie
Sprake noted: 'When a Gun is walking in line with the beaters
he should never fire at a pheasant that is going forward towards
the stand where the other birds are waiting . . .' (*LL Shooting*,
170).

bed   OED: v., of an animal: 'to make its lair; the specific term
used of the roe.' Also v., when retiring to rest, and n., where
it has been resting. First attestation 1470. 'You shall say that
a roe beddeth' – Guillim, *Heraldry*, 1610; 'Bedding: A roe is
said to bed; a hart to harbour' – Abraham Rees, *Cyclopedia*,
1819. In 1939 Hare noted all these under 'Animals retiring to
rest' along with 'A Buck lodges, a Fox kennels, Marten trees,
Hare seats or forms, Otter watches, Badger earths, Coney sits'
(p. 112).

bell   from the OE *bellan*, to *roar*, *bark* or *bellow*. OED: '*spec.*
of the voice of deer at rutting time.' Sir Walter Scott, *Marmion*:
'The wild buck bells from ferny brake.' This is poetic licence.
A stag might be said to roar or bellow, but a buck tends to
groan. Nowadays the usage *bell* may be considered obsolete.

bellow   OED: '1. *prop.* To roar as a bull, or as a cow when
excited. 2. Applied to the roaring of other animals.' Of a stag;
to roar, or bell. In 1576 Turberville noted: 'An harte belloweth'
(*Venerie*, 238). In 1845 St John wrote: 'On the height of the hill
he halted, and stretching out his neck and lowering his head,
bellowed again. [. . .] several times during the night I got up
and listened to the wild bellowing of the deer . . . To an
unaccustomed ear it might easily have passed for the roaring of
a host of much more dangerous wild beasts . . .' (283, 284).

bender   OED: 'that which bends'. In a country sense, literally a
willow stick bent down in a curve under tension, over several of
which a tarpaulin may be spread to make a tent or shelter. For

trapping it is used on a smaller scale with a brass rabbit-snare attached and secured by a simple wooden catch which, on being disturbed, allows the bent willow to straighten and trap the intended quarry suspended in the snare. Generally used for rats and similar small creatures, but seldom seen now with the development of modern traps; one of the earliest and most effective of traps. Brander: 'Bender; A wire snare attached to a hazel wand so set that when an animal is caught in the snare, the disturbance frees the wand, which automatically straightens and leaves the animal dangling.' (*Sporting Terms*, 71) See also *springe*.

bevy   ME. The proper term for a company of maidens, or ladies, of roes, of quails, or of larks. 1486, *The Boke of St Albans*: 'A Bevy of Ladies, a Bevy of Roos, a Bevy of Quaylis.' The OED says that the derivation and early history are unknown. It has been suggested that the ME *bevoy* corresponds to the OF *buvee* or drinking and may have passed from drinking bout to drinking party, hence to party, or company generally, but the OED admits this explanation is 'far-fetched'.

bez or ***bez-antler***   see *bay*. The second branch, next above the brow antler.

BFSS   abbreviation for British Field Sports Society; founded in 1930 to counter the activities and propaganda of the League Against Cruel Sports. Incorporates members representing all spheres of Field Sports: Fox-hunting, Deer-hunting, Beagling and Mink hounds, and Coursing, as well as Game Shooting, Wildfowling, Deer Stalking, Fishing and Falconry. The principal body representing field sports, including shooting, and countering misleading propaganda. See also *Game Conservancy*; The British Association for Shooting and Conservation *(BASC)*.

binoculars   OED: short for binocular glass. A field glass in which both eyes are employed. Essential for *still-hunting*, in woodland deer stalking. They should be light and rubber covered, otherwise any metal parts which might cause a noise in contact with the rifle should be covered with insulating tape to prevent this happening. A telescope may be a positive handicap in woodland. Holmes maintains:

> Binoculars are vastly preferable to a telescope for several reasons; the latter is noisy when being drawn, slow to focus, and performs badly in poor light. Its greater magnification, coupled with its narrow field of view, is more of a hindrance than a help in woodland stalking. I use a telescope only when in search of roe in open hill country, where deer may be

spotted a long way off. Even on these occasions I carry binoculars as well, to enable me to search over a wide area quickly and to be ready to focus quickly on a possibly fleeting target. The telescope is reserved for leisurely identification of distant roe. (p. 28)
See *glass*.

black   of a stag, when it has been rolling in a bog, or peat hag. In 1884 Speedy noted:
on peering through some heather we discovered the object of our anxiety, not within a hundred and fifty yards as we expected, but about four hundred yards off, rolling in a moss-hole, to which he had betaken himself. On emerging from his peaty bath he appeared as if transformed into a black stag and began tearing up the heather with his horns. (p. 243)

blackgame   see *black grouse*.

black grouse   *Lyrurus tetrix*. OED: of which the male is called blackcock and the female greyhen: a game bird, generally known as blackgame and distinguished by sex as the blackcock and greyhen. The cock is a large glossy black bird having a lyre-shaped tail with noticeable white undermarking and white wing mark. The hen is smaller, light brown, like a grouse, except for the white wing bar. Their habitat is the edges of moors, forests and heaths. Now restricted to Devon and Cornwall and from the Border northwards, the black grouse has a remarkable musical gobbling sound as a mating call. Polygamous, they perform spectacular *lek* courtship dances on their lekking, or breeding, grounds, in April. The cocks dance in a circle displaying their tails over their backs to the hens. An early reference in 1678 Willoughby (*Ornithology*, 173) refers some-what uncertainly to 'The Heathcock, or Blackgame, or Grous, called by Turner the Morehen.' In 1807 Daniel seemed little better informed: 'The Grous are fond of wooded and mountain-ous situations and perch like the pheasant' (iii, 101). In 1830 Hawker was the first to write on shooting them:
To shoot a black cock (in the winter) when he becomes wild you should wait near, or in the direction of the larch firs, for which he flies to perch; and send someone round to drive him from the stubble . . . In the North the female of the species is termed *gray-hen* but in the New Forest both male and female are collectively named *heath-poults*. Game shoot-ing on the borders of Hants and Dorset . . . one of the best day's blackgame shooting that was ever known . . . in these parts, I had with the late Mr John Ponton at Uddens on the

25th of August 1825 . . . we killed eight brace without missing a shot.' (*Instructions*, 204)

St John was more interested in their courtship dances: 'Usually there seems to be a master bird in these assemblages, who takes up his position in the most elevated spot, crowing and strutting round with spread out tail . . .' (p. 36). Their nests usually have six to ten eggs. They fly silently and deceptively fast, easily outstripping grouse. In 1884 Speedy noted:

> We have seen first-class blackcock-shooting got on the summits of some of the highest mountain ranges in the south of Scotland . . . In driving blackgame, they, unlike grouse, when once fairly on the wing, will not deviate from their course . . . there are few birds which go at such a tremendous speed and with such impetus as an old blackcock. (p. 207)

Mackie gave sound advice on driving them: 'game will not drive well . . . when the weather is wild and blustering. The best day on which to shoot black game is a dull misty one when there is little wind. The mist hides the "guns" from the fine long-ranged sight of the birds. High wind is apt to scatter the packs' (p. 218). In 1930 Eric Parker was emphatic:

> game . . . should be left to be driven in October . . . They fly great distances and at a great pace; their steady wing beat makes them look a slower bird than grouse, but if the two come side by side in a drive the blackcock soon leaves the grouse behind. Yet in a way they are easier birds to hit than grouse, for . . . when they have made up their minds which way to fly they go straight on without swerving. (*LL Shooting*, 216).

See also *capercailyie*; *red grouse*.

blind   ME: 'Anything which obstructs the light, or sight,' hence 'any means or place of concealment' (OED). In the 17th century this was recognised as any place of concealment from which a sportsman could lie in wait to shoot game. First attested in 1646, a good example was by Dryden in 1696 (*Virgil*, iii, 52): 'The watchful shepherd from the blind, wounds with random shaft the careless hind.' Today *blind* is seldom used in Britain, but has crossed the Atlantic and is still in common use in the USA and Canada to describe a *hide* for shooting wildfowl. After visiting France in 1819, Hawker wrote of the French method of 'Hut-Shooting' at wildfowl by which a man 'may kill ducks while as dry and warm as if by his fireside' (*Instructions*, 397). Some of the blinds used in N. America even include heaters and other luxuries.

blink   almost exclusively in use from late 16th century. OED:

'to evade, shirk, pass by, ignore'. Originally used in a sporting sense of a pointing dog's failure to point game, or alternatively failure to remain on point and returning to the handler. Usually caused by bad handling when young, or when being trained, or through running with an older dog in the early stages and not allowing the youngster to develop its own initiative. It may also be caused by doubtful breeding, e.g. a cross with a foxhound. The term is now becoming obsolete. The earliest attestation is in Fielding's *Joseph Andrews*, 1742: 'There's a bitch . . . she never blinked a bird in her life.' See *back; draw-on*.

block   of a forestry plantation; an area of forestry generally delineated by broad fire-breaks, or rides. For game shooting, it may be possible to drive certain forestry plantations *block-by-block* with guns moving steadily along the rides and the beaters driving the various blocks in turn. However if the rides are not kept clear and if the *canopy* is overgrown, allowing little skyward vision, this is not likely to be very successful. For shooting deer it is often desirable to place a high-seat at a suitable junction of rides, covering various blocks where roe, or other deer, are known to be feeding or lying up. It is important, however, to site a high seat at the junction of a block, or blocks, so that all shots may be taken safely and with the maximum field of fire down the rides.

blood sport   pejorative and emotive phrase, deliberately appealing to the emotions rather than reason, frequently applied to *field sports*, especially in the 1960s and 1970s by the 'Anti-Field Sports' lobby. See *anti's*.

blot out   when aiming a shotgun in certain shots, going straight away, approaching and overhead, the bird should be *blotted out* with the barrels at the moment of firing to ensure a *clean kill*. In 1889 Lancaster advised: 'For the straight-away shot, where the bird flies in a bee-line, the gun should be put to the shoulder so that the muzzles blot out the bird' (p. 65).

blowback   half-burned, or burning, grains of powder after a shot; almost unknown with modern cartridges, but very common in the days of *muzzle loaders* and black powder. It appears to have still been a problem in 1930, for Eric Parker warned that: 'up wind shooting . . . may lead to very bad shooting, for the smoke of the cartridges will blow straight back into the shooter's face and if there is any "blow back" – that is half-burnt, or burning grains of powder – it will probably find its way into his eyes' (*L L Shooting*, 118).

blown pattern   when the shot is widely scattered, leaving large gaps through which a bird might fly unscathed. It may be

caused by faulty loading of a cartridge, i.e. one which is loosely
packed, or by a faulty wad failing to seal the barrel when the
shot is fired. Excessively high velocity cartridges are also liable
to cause *blown patterns*. Not so common today with modern
cartridges and powders, but may arise if cartridges have got wet
and been dried, or subjected to considerable changes in
temperature.

blue   OED v. : 'to make blue, spec to heat (metal) so as to make
it blue.' Of gun parts and barrels: to colour the metal of the gun
black. In 1881 it is noted: 'Any amateur may blue by placing
the pan of charcoal upon a fire and burying the work to be
blued in it' (*The Greener Gun*, 253). In 1930 Burrard was more
cautious: 'Blueing, or blacking, is not an easy process . . . The
metal to be blued is first polished absolutely clean' (*Shotgun*, i,
138).

blue hind   a hind which has not bred in the previous season,
so-called because of the colouring; see also *yeld*.

blue mountain hare   Lepus Timidus Scoticus. OED: 'A less
common species (than the common hare) is the Alpine, or
varying hare. *L. variabilis*.' Cousin to the *common brown
hare* but with blueish fur when young, hence its name. This
turns grey in the adult and white in winter. Found in moorland
and hilly areas it is lighter boned than the brown hare and
generally weighs less, 5–7 lbs. It may have up to eight young,
also known as *leverets*. The blue mountain hare may go to
ground when chased and may be shot throughout the year,
although it may not be offered for sale between March and July
inclusive. In 1769 Pennant described: 'A peculiar species of
hare, which is found only on the summits of the highest hills
and never mixes with the common kind, which is frequent
enough in the vales; is less than the common Hare; its limbs
more slender; its flesh more delicate; is very agile and full of
frolick when kept tame' (*Tour of Scotland*, i, 97).

blue rock   see *stock dove*.

bog-bleater   nick-name for *common snipe* because of
drumming sound made by tail feathers.

bolt action   of a shotgun: a type of single-barrelled shotgun,
generally heavy and slow to use, with a hand-operated *bolt
action*, similar to a rifle, hence the name. Of a rifle: the normal
type of action.

bolt loop or **loop**   in 1830 Hawker noted: 'Bolts; pieces of
steel, which push through the loops to fasten the barrel into the
stock' (*Instructions*, 49). Burrard defined it as 'a projection
from between the underside of the two barrels to a few inches

from the breech end on to which the fore-end fastens' (*Shotgun*, i, 20).

bop, bopping   not in OED. A verb, used of the characteristic action of small animals such as stoats and weasels to stand now and then on the hind legs to scent the air or look out over long grass or cover. In some European sporting circles used more specifically as referring to the action of the hind legs of the hare, another animal often seen sitting or standing erect peering over cover. It may in this sense be applied to pointing dogs, particularly Brittany spaniels. Perhaps derived from a dialect variation of *bob, bobbing* (OED, 'to move up and down'), or possibly from *bo-peep, bo-peeping* (OED, 'a nursery play with a young child, who is kept in excitement by the nurse ... concealing herself ... and peeping out for a moment at an unexpected place'). Dr Johnson: 'The act of looking out and then drawing back as if frighted, or with the purpose to fright some other ...'; William Tindale (*Works*, 1528, p. 214): 'Mark how he plays bo-peep with the scriptures.'

bore   from ON *bora*, 'bore hole'. OED: 'The calibre of a gun'. One of the earliest references appears to be in 1583 by Sir Hugh Platt: 'Beeing of petronell bore, or a bore higher.' Burrard defined it as: 'That part of the inside of the barrel which is sealed completely by the shot charge and wads ... The size or gauge of a gun depends on the diameter of the bore ... denoted by the number of spherical balls of pure lead each exactly fitting the bore which go to the pound' (*Shotgun*, i, 17). Hence, 12 bore, 16 bore, 20 bore etc. In 1972 Geoffrey Boothroyd made the additional point: 'Often used, loosely, instead of gauge when referring to the size of a shotgun. e.g. 12 bore' (Brander & Zern, 114).

bore-sight   to look at a target through the bore of a rifle fixed to a stand and with the bolt removed prior to checking the sights. 'First thing is to bore-sight the rifle by removing the bolt and looking through the bore at a target' (Forrester, 118). This usage is not in the OED. See *sight-in*; *zero*.

bottom lever   of a shotgun: see *lever of the action*.

bottom rib   of a shotgun: see *ribs*.

bouquet   from the Provençal *bouquet* and the Italian *boschetto*; 'a little wood'. OED: 'the flight of a multitude of pheasants breaking covert from the central point at which the beaters meet.' In 1884 Speedy noted:

> When a cover is dense, pheasants as a rule, will, instead of rising, run to the end till within a few yards of the guns

stationed there, and will rise in large numbers on the approach of the beaters. Provision must be made in anticipation of this by several guns being placed forward, otherwise a large number will necessarily escape. (p. 288)

When there is such an explosion of birds over the guns it may nearly always be taken as the result of bad *shoot management*. Yet in 1930 Leslie Sprake seemed to accept it as quite common when he wrote: 'As the beaters approach the end of a particular beat they should retard their rate of progress, and whenever a "bouqet" of pheasants rises, the whole line should stop.' (*LL Shooting*, 159). In 'Points on Driving', Brander declared in 1965: 'When too many birds are flushed . . . in a cloud over the guns it is impossible to shoot more than a few and indicates bad management. It is known as a bouquet' (*Gameshot*, 208).

box lock   synonymous with the Anson and Deeley Action introduced in 1875 and still in general use; fitted into the body of the action rather than behind the action body and let into the side of the gun. See *side-locks*.

brace   from OF; a pair, two, a couple. The term may be both singular and plural; e.g. several *brace* of partridges. OED: 'Two things taken together, a pair . . . In this sense the plural is also two or three brace.' The OED states that it was originally used with reference to dogs, possibly because the couple connecting two greyhounds when coursing was called a brace, and only later applied to other animals. In 1830 Hawker wrote 'These birds [Quail] are so scarce in Britain that to find a bevy of them and to kill three or four brace is considered as something extraordinary' (*Instructions*, 225). On being shot, a brace of game birds are customarily tied by the necks with string, a cock and a hen together, to make for easier counting at the end of the day. Young birds are also generally separated from old, especially grouse and partridges, in order to keep accurate game records.

brace work   of gundogs: to work as a brace, to work together in harmony, esp. pointers and setters or springers, when hunting. In 1920 Sanderson wrote: 'Pointer and Setter work presents very many striking peculiarities . . . Far from being the least of these . . . is the intricate problem of brace work' (p. 23).

brash   Fr. To remove the lower branches of a plantation at the *thicket* stage, to prevent choking and allow free growth.

break, break cover   OED to *break covert* or *cover*, 'to start forth from a hiding place.' A development of the senses of *break*: it is used in this sense in 1859 by Alfred Tennyson (*Enid*, l. 159): 'They break covert at our feet.' *Break field*, or *fence*; said of a

gundog: to enter a field before the handler, or to enter a field
other than the one in which the handler is working him, also to
go through a fence or hedge before the handler. Generally a
sign of loss of control. In 1856 J.S. Walsh dealt with the matter
very clearly:
> Whenever the dog is taken into the fields, which should only
> be allowed where there is no game, he should be called back
> at every fence or stile, if he attempts to pass or "break" it. If
> he does break it he should immediately be called back . . .
> and made to understand he is never to leave the field in which
> his master is. This is easily done by *checking him the moment*
> *he passes the fence.* (p. 29)

Break back, of game being driven to waiting guns, which flies
back over the beaters' heads. *Break line:* of guns walking in line,
failing to keep the line properly, behaviour deserving severe
reprimand as endangering safety of others. See *line.*

breech-loader   OED: 'A fire-arm in which the charge is introduced at the breech.' In 1858 Greener (*Gunnery,* 143) stated:
'Under no circumstances . . . can a breech-loader be as safe as
a solid gun.' With the general introduction of the breech-
loading shotgun in the 1860s and 1870s the practice of *battue*
or *driven shooting* became widespread. The initial *breech-*
loaders were *pin-fire* guns, with an outside hammer operating
the firing-pin which was located on the cartridge, but these
were soon superseded by the centre-fire cartridge and the
hammer gun, which in turn gave way to the *hammerless*
ejector. See *covert shooting.*

brocket   Fr. OED: 'A stag in its second year, with its first horns
which are straight and single, like a small dagger.' Sometimes
incorrectly used to refer to a third-year beast as well. The
earliest reference appears in 1425: 'The hert, the fyrst yere he
is a calfe, the secunde yere a broket.' In 1881 (*The Greener Gun,*
520) it was noted that 'To shoot a staggart, brocket, suckling
hind or calf is unwarrantable.' See *shootable beast.*

brow, brow-antler   OE. OED: the lowest tine of the horn of a
stag, the 'antler' in its original sense; sometimes also known as
the first antler. An early reference is to be found in 1610 in
Guillim's *Heraldry:* 'Skilfull Woodmen . . . do call the Lowest
Antlier the Brow Antelier.'

brown   a verb, used of a covey of grouse or partridges: to fire
into the midst of them, i.e. the brown; hence to fire haphazardly
at a covey without singling out individual birds. Usually the sign
of a novice shot.
   Instructions for shooting at Partridges . . . are here inserted;

So the ambition of the Sportsman lies
More in the certain shot than bleeding prize;
While *Poachers* mindful of the festal hour,
Among the Covey random slaughter pour;
And as their number press the crimsoned ground,
Regardless reck not of the secret wound,
Which borne away the wretched victims lie,
'Mid silent shades, to languish and to die.
O let *your* breast such selfish views disclaim,
And scorn the Triumph of a casual aim!
Disdain such rapine, of your Skill be proud,
One *object* singling from the scattering Crowd! *Pye*

(Daniel, iii, 485)

In 1852 Surtees wrote satirically:

Jog had had many a game at romps with these birds and knew
their haunts and habits to a nicety. The covey consisted of
thirteen at first, but by repeated blazings into the 'brown of
'em' he had succeeded in knocking down two. Jog was not
one of your conceited shots who never fired but when he was
sure of killing. On the contrary, he always let drive far and
near. . . . The dog was now fast drawing upon where the
birds lit . . . Up whirred four birds out of a patch of gorse
behind the dog, all presenting most beautiful shots. Jog blazed
a barrel at them without touching a feather and the report of
the gun immediately raised three brace more, into the thick
of which he fired with similar success. They all skimmed
away unhurt. (*Sporting Tour*, 320)

In 1884 Speedy admonished his readers: 'The practice of firing
at random into coveys of any description is most reprehensible
and should be frowned down by all keepers; and it is a rule
from which there should be no exception amongst sportsmen,
that in every case one bird should be deliberately aimed at'
(p. 271). In 1897 H.F. Phillips was scathing on the subject: 'In
game shooting the sportsman selects one object to shoot at; the
shooter who *'browns'* his birds, i.e. habitually fires at and bags
more than one head of game for each shot is dubbed a pot-
hunter by all true sportsmen' (*Encyclopedia*, i, 499). This
ultimate sin of *browning* a covey of birds is sometimes rewarded
by two or three birds falling, at one shot, generally wounded
not killed. It is not something to boast about. Browning usually
results in several birds flying away *pricked,* to die later, lost to
the shoot and the *bag,* or else failing to breed. It also encourages
coveys to become wild and liable to take flight more readily out

of shot. Anyone habitually browning coveys should give up
shooting.

As a noun, e.g. 'To fire into the brown'. In the days of
muzzle-loading rifles and even into this century, the misleading
advice was often given to deer-stalkers to take their aim, by
'following up the foreleg until they reached the brown'. This
resulted in many wounded deer going off with a broken foreleg.
In 1986 Brander observed that: 'too often the shooter becomes
hypnotised by the size of the beast and fires into the brown,
merely wounding it' (*Deer*, 119). The same phrase may be used
regarding birds, as in Hare: '*Firing into the brown*: Firing into
the middle of a "flock" of birds instead of picking out a
particular one' (p. 66). See also *buck fever*.

browse   from the 16th-century French *brouster*, the English
word probably being formed by analogy with *graze*. OED: 'to
feed on the leaves and shoots of trees and bushes . . . said of
goats, deer, cattle.' Persistent browsing can damage trees
seriously. Almost all deer are likely to browse at times, some
more than others depending on circumstances and availability
(see *feed*). In 1973 Holmes made this point: 'Foresters are
generally agreed that the worst effect of roe on timber production is due to browsing, which can do serious damage during
the first three to four years after planting' (p. 101). This can be
the cause of complaints by foresters, often concerning roe, but
if a master buck is culled it can sometimes have the opposite
effect to that desired as two, three, or more younger bucks take
over the territory and cause even more damage.

browse line   the level up to which a deer has eaten the foliage
from trees and bushes. They can reach a surprising height when
standing on their hind legs and pulling down a juicy morsel. It
is possible to assess the age, size and sex as well as the type of
deer involved from careful examination of the *browse line* and
associated tracks.

buck   from the OE *buc*, meaning a male deer; the correct term
for a male *fallow*, *muntjac*, *roe* or *Chinese water-deer*. Also the
male of the hare and the rabbit.

buck fever   colloquial recognised term for an attack of nerves
when raising the rifle to shoot deer, or other large game. Those
in the grip of acute *buck fever* have been known to shut their
eyes and shoot without even being aware of the fact, let alone
taking aim. It is noticeable that expert shots at small game are
often prone to this phenomenon when first seeing deer, even
experiencing a mild form when unexpectedly faced with a hare
which they may often miss behind, or merely wound. They are

also likely to miss larger birds, such as black cock and capercailzie, behind for much the same reason. In 1800 Major Hazzard, of Beaufort, S. Carolina, noted in a letter:

It is remarkable that the English gentlemen who hunt frequently with us shoot very badly at our large game and yet will kill the smaller sorts with the greatest ease. I have known a gentleman shoot on the wing any of our fleet flying birds without missing a shot, and yet miss five, six and seven shots at deer and turkey in a day. I attribute this to agitation ... and their not being accustomed to them.

A classic example is inadvertently provided in Lt.-Col. Peter Hawker's diaries for 1813:

June 27th. Disastrous ill-luck with 2 ... deer.... one of them ... galloped up within 20 yards of me ... I was obliged to fire through a bough, which so intercepted the sight of my rifle that I had the mortification to see him completely missed ... however ... to our utter astonishment, up sprung ... the other deer, which trotted across me at about 30 yards. I fired both barrels without being in the least nervous, and with the most accurate aim, and (to add to my bad luck) never touched him. Thus had I (who so seldom let anything escape within fair distance) the mortification to miss one deer at 20, and the other within 30 yards, and both from sheer ill-luck and misfortune!!

In 1967 Rex Forrester wrote:

when he has his first shot at a deer his eyes will glaze with fever, his rifle will dance a crazy jig as he tries to take aim, he will miss by yards with his first shot and then empty the magazine at the retreating deer when it is well out of range. That is buck fever ... [...] As often as not buck fever stepped in ... My client's ... rifle would begin to jump about like a flea in a bottle and when he fired he would bracket the escaping animal with a hail of wild shots. One client was so clobbered with buck fever that he couldn't see a 500lb stag standing smack in the middle of a clearing 25 yards in front of him. He wasn't colour blind. And there was nothing else in sight. (pp. 40, 142)

In 1986 Brander remarked that: 'often the shooter becomes hypnotised by the size of the beast and fires into the brown, merely wounding it. The same thing on a smaller scale is often seen with hares. It is all a manifestation of buck fever' (*Deer*, 119). See also *stag fever*.

bulge   gun barrels may acquire a bulge for several reasons: a

heavier than suitable load might cause a bulge. Damage may
also be caused by incorrect use of a cleaning *jag* and tow.

bull   in *target shooting*, the centre of the target.

bull's eye   from the boss of glass formed in the centre of a
sheet of blown glass, hence OED: 'the centre of a target'. The
first attestation is in 1833 (*Regulation Instructions for Cavalry*, i,
32): 'A bull's eye of eight inches diameter.' Another early
attestation is by Charles Dickens (*The Old Curiosity Shop*,
1840): 'This is wide of the bulls-eye.' See *target shooting*.

bunch   colloquially of hinds, a group. See *parcel*.

burr   etymology uncertain; the rough outer edge of the *coro-
net*. In 1730 it was noted in Nathan Bailey's *Dictionarium
Brittanicum* as follows: 'Burr; the round Knob of Horn next a
Deer's Head.'

burrow   origins obscure; commonly thought to be a variant of
borough. OED: 'a hole, or excavation made in the ground for a
dwelling place by rabbits.' Probably subject to many local
dialect variations. As late as 1879 Richard Jeffries (*Wild Life in
a Southern County*) wrote: 'In heavy rain . . . they [rabbits]
generally remain within their buries.' In 1880 Carnegie wrote:
'the chief points of such a dog are that he searches at every
burrow till he finds a rabbit in one' (p.16). See *rabbit*.

bush   a verb derived from the common noun *bush*. OED: 'to
protect (land or game) from net-poachers by placing bushes or
branches at intervals in the preserved ground to interrupt the
sweep of the net.' With the advent of four-wheeled drive motors
and high-powered lamps to dazzle game at night, superseding
the netting of partridges and long-netting of rabbits in the hours
of darkness, *bushing* fields has become more or less obsolete,
although a similar method might be used to prevent motorised
poaching by night. As late as 1930 A. Hipgrave wrote:
> The keeper tries to prevent the netting of partridges on the
> fields by bushing. He places bushes about all over the fields,
> the more prickly the bushes the better. They are let into the
> ground by a small iron bar . . . Where long netting of rabbits
> is suspected, bushes and pieces of dead wood should be
> scattered from the covert side to about forty yards into the
> field. (*LL Shooting*, 280)

butcher's weight   of a deer; the weight of the skinned and
cleaned carcase, minus the head and feet and with only the liver
and kidneys still in place.

butt[1]   of obscure etymology, probably ON. First appears in
15th century. OED: 'The thicker end of anything, especially a
tool or weapon . . . the broad end of the stock of a gun or a

pistol' – comprised of the **heel**, at the top of the *butt*, and the toe, at the lower end. In 1888 W.W. Greener (*Modern Shotguns*) wrote: 'The butt-plate will not be very much rounded and will slope in a little to fit the shoulder – that is to say measured to the *edge* of the heel plate.'

butt²   a mark for archery on a mound – hence transferred to a mound for artillery and rifle practice, from thence transferred to the prepared position for the gun to stand awaiting driven grouse and concealing him from view. Brander noted:

It may be of stones, peat, hurdles, or other suitable material and may be circular, in which case care must be taken that sense of direction is not lost and safety markers are advisable. Alternatively it may be two-sided so that either side may be used. In any event a butt should have good footing and room for a gun to swing and for a loader, guns and cartridges. It is best to fence it off against sheep and cattle. (*Sporting Terms*, 73)

butterfly shooter, b- day   a derisive wildfowling term referring to weather more suitable for butterflies than wildfowl. On 27 January 1823 Hawker recorded in his Diary: 'I to be well to windward of the butterfly shooters, weathered the torrent of rain all day, and (by capital locks and good management) contrived to keep my gun dry for the five shots I got . . .'; and in 1826: 'Jan 12th; A butterfly day! Every jackass afloat with a blunderbuss or a swivel . . .'. Applicable also to 'popgunners', 'popping vagrants'.

buttons   OF *boton*: of stag, or buck; the first signs of growth of fresh antlers. Hence of deer, which thrust out their *buttons* when starting to develop new antlers. In 1576 Turberville (*Venerie*) wrote: 'Hartes . . . beginne in . . . March and Apryll to thrust out their Buttons.' Not often used but not obsolete.

button-head   of a young roebuck, with small first-year antlers.

C **abers** Gaelic. A stag with a *switch* head, with only two points, or at most four.

age trap may be of many kinds, e.g. a semi-permanent *trap* for *corvids*, generally constructed of wire-netting and often set on the lobster-pot principle with an entrance narrowing like a funnel through which the bird cannot return. They may be quite large constructions capable of catching numerous birds, or quite small and movable, only capable of catching one bird at a time like the *Larsen trap*. In either case a *decoy bird* is usually placed inside the trap to attract others. Small cage traps are usually made on the principle of the Larsen Trap with a bait set to operate a trip-lever to close the trap. Suitably baited and well-placed, such traps are very effective in catching undesirable predators of eggs such as jays, magpie, crows, etc. May also be of metal mesh and portable, for catching mink, foxes, etc. alive. Such traps are bulky to transport, but are also very effective. It is desirable that they have handles for carriage since a captured mink can be a vicious beast to dispose of once caught. One method is to immerse the cage in water. A simpler and cleaner death is to insert a .22 barrel and when the mink siezes it in its jaws to pull the trigger, resulting in instantaneous death.

Caldra system a method of long-netting invented *c.* 1950 by the late Sir Eric de la Rue of Caldra in Berwickshire. He mounted several thousand yards of long nets in reels on a rubber-tyred barrow on which he also carried hollow metal supports for the nets, so that when one net was unwound he simply inserted another in the main feed on the front of the barrow and continued on his way. When the rabbits were out feeding at dusk, he could thus surround whole fields at a time with more than a mile of overlapping nets, cutting the rabbits off from their escape to their burrows in the neighbouring woods or cliffs. He would then walk through the fields flushing the rabbits into the nets with a well-trained dog, or trailing a rope between himself and an assistant.(A method known as a *dead dog*.) He was regularly making bags of over a thousand rabbits at a time with this method, which he first evolved while a prisoner of war in Germany, but which took him a full five years to perfect on his return to his country. The perfection of this ingenious method, unfortunately for the inventor, co-incided with the outbreak of myxomatosis in 1952. It was therefore never used as widely as might otherwise have been the case, or as it deserved. It still merits consideration by anyone who has severe rabbit problems.

calf   originally 'the young of any bovine animal' then extended to the young of other animals, e.g. the young of red, or sika, deer. An early example of the usage is in 1486 in *The Boke of St Albans*: 'Ye shall him [a Hart] a Calfe call, at the first yeare.'

calibre   OED: of uncertain origins, possibly from *Caliver*, a type of light arquebus. The use of *caliver* in the sense of calibre in the 16th century seems to favour this. OED gives 'a. the diameter of a bullet.... b. Hence the internal diameter or "bore" of a gun.' First attested in 1588. In 1973 Geoffrey Boothroyd contradicted this: 'The measurement of the bore of a rifle, expressed in decimal points of an inch for British and American guns and in millimetres for continental guns. It is not the measurement of the bullet, but of the inside diameter of the barrel before rifling. The bullet is actually made slightly larger' (Brander & Zern, 115).

call, calling   OED: 'To attract animals by a particular call.' Deer may be brought within range of the rifle by imitating their mating call. Also used of roe, the *call* of the doe to attract the buck; it is advisable when blowing the roe call to turn sideways at each call so that the call seems to be coming from a doe circling excitedly round, as they usually are when calling. Of red deer, the call of the stag in rut to attract either sex. For foxes, stoats and weasels, the imitation of a snared or frightened rabbit squealing will attract them; foxes may also be called by barking in the mating season. For wildfowl: mallard and geese particularly may be brought within range by imitating their feeding call. It is, of course, important to imitate the conversational or excited feeding call, not the alarm call, which is quite distinct and different.

call duck   tame *decoy ducks*, possibly with their wings clipped, kept and fed on a *flight pond*, to attract wild duck. *Call ducks* are often white, to avoid identification problems. In 1830 Hawker wrote: 'three French ducks, like three Frenchmen, will make about as much noise as a dozen English' (*Instructions*, 398).

Canada goose   *Branta canadensis*, introduced into Europe from Canada, hence its name. 'This is a species that has been domesticated and multiplied in many parts of Europe' (Daniel, iii, 254). It is now the largest goose breeding in Europe. It is grey-brown with a black head and long black neck contrasting strongly with its white breast. It has a distinctive broad white patch from throat to cheek. It mainly frequents fresh water and grazes in fields. In 1838 the *Penny Cyclopedia* noted this rather obvious truth: 'The Canada Goose generally builds its nest on the ground' (xi, 208).

canopy   Fr. OED: in a figurative sense 'an overhanging shade', first attested in William Shakespeare's *Julius Caesar*: 'Their shadows seeme a Canopy most fatall, under which our Army lies.' Of woodland; where the crowns of the forest trees meet overhead to form a continuous cover.

capercailye, capercailzie   the OED gives both spellings. *Tetrao Urugallus*, the wood grouse, the largest of the European Gallinaceous birds. OED: 'The male is also called Mountain Cock or Cock of the Woods.' The name is a corruption of Gaelic, *capull coille* or Great Cock (literally horse) of the Wood. The earliest attestation is in 1536 in John Bellenden's *Chronicles of Scotland*. James Dalrymple, transcribing Leslie's 'History of Scotland' of 1596 (in 1885), wrote: 'The Capercailze . . . with the vulgar people the horse of the forest.' Thereafter it is mentioned at regular intervals. In 1630 Sir R. Gordon in *A History of the Earl of Sutherland* noted: 'In these forests . . . there is great store of partriges, pluivers, capercaleys.' Around 1730 Captain Edward Burt, in his *Letters from North Scotland*, wrote of 'The Cobberkelly which is sometimes called a wild turkey.' In the *Statistical Account of Scotland* of 1797 for Inverness it was recorded: 'The caper coille or wild turkey was seen in Glenmoriston about 40 years ago' (xx, 307). In 1807 Daniel wrote: 'Cock of the Wood, Capercalze, or Wood Grous; From the scarcity of this species, the notice of it here may be thought superfluous; as it was however formerly and possibly may still be found in some parts of Great Britain, its History is inserted' (iii, 95). In 1884 Queen Victoria noted in her diary: 'Saw a capercailzie of which there are many here.' In the same year Speedy wrote: 'This bird was some years ago confined almost exclusively to the Breadalbane estates, but it is now . . . scattered throughout Perthshire, and stray birds are . . . in all the surrounding counties. Notwithstanding the heavy, clumsy appearance . . . it is surprisingly swift in flight. . . . These birds . . . rarely drop unless when fired at within a reasonable distance' (p. 287). Mackie advised in 1929: 'In placing the guns for capercailzie driving, knowledge of the usual flight of the birds is of value; in our experience capercailzie generally come out of covert, take a wide sweep round and close to it and then fly in again. They seldom fly out into the open. Guns should be placed quite near the covert' (p. 343). Indigenous to the Scottish Highlands, they were believed to have become extinct by the early 19th century. They were re-introduced in 1837 into the Taymouth estates of the Marquis of Breadalbane by Larry Banville, headkeeper to the Norfolk naturalist and landowner Thomas Fowell Buxton, working in conjunction with the latter's friend, the naturalist Llewellyn Lloyd in Sweden from where the birds were transported by Banville. Whether they were ever actually extinct is open to question. See also *black grouse*.

carrion crow *Corvus corone* from NF *Caronie*, the first attestation in English is in 1225. A species of crow, smaller and more common than the raven but slightly larger than the rook, notable for feeding on carrion and small animals, poultry, poults, eggs, etc. It is best caught by the *Larsen trap*. Also known as 'hoodie crow' and 'corbie' in Scotland. It interbreeds with the *hooded crow*, where their habitats overlap. With its habit of eating the eyes out of sickly but living lambs and sheep, it has never been a popular bird. An early somewhat sombre reference is to be found in 1528 in Sir Thomas More's *Heresyes*: 'We fare as do the rauens and the carein crowes yt neuer medle with any quicke flesh.' In Goldsmith's *Natural History* of 1774 it is solemnly noted: 'The Carrion Crow is less favoured by mankind' (iii, 122). Continuing on a similar theme, in 1811 John Leyden in his dramatic poem *Lord Soulis* wrote: 'And they heard the cry from the branches high of the hungry carrion crow.'

cartridge from Fr, a corruption of *cartouche*, 1579. For a shotgun, the case, of waxed cardboard or plastic, containing the powder and shot. One of the earliest references is in 1644 by Nathaniel Nye (*Gunnery*): 'Canvas, or strong paper, to make Cartredges.'

cartridge adaptor a cylindrical metal tube inserted in the chamber of a shotgun to allow the use of a smaller bore cartridge; e.g. 4.10 adaptor for a 12-bore gun to enable it to be used for shooting rabbits at close range, as when ferreting. These seem to have been first introduced around the turn of the 19th century.

cartridge bag a bag, generally of leather, or canvas reinforced with leather, with a reinforced open mouth, capable of holding 50 to 150 cartridges. Generally only used in driven shooting for a handy supply of cartridges. It is important to have one that has a wide enough opening to insert the hand when required and that will stay open so that access to cartridges is quite simple. Such *cartridge bags* only came into use in the heyday of driven shooting, from the 1880s onwards, and the design has changed little since then.

cartridge belt   a belt of leather, cloth, or fibre, with loops, or clips, generally for carrying up to 25 cartridges. Spring clips very quickly become worn and may easily catch in branches, bushes, or similar obstacles, resulting in loss of cartridges. In wet conditions it should be worn under the shooting coat to keep the cartridges dry. An obvious adaptation of the military cartridge bandolier, these were probably in use comparatively early, from around the 1870s onwards.

cartridge cap   the primer which ignites the powder. Originating from the explosive mixture of fulminate of mercury inside a copper cap which replaced the flint to ignite the charge in the old *flint-lock muzzle-loader*. It was subsequently incorporated in the cartridge when the *breech-loader* was invented. It contains the substance known as the detonator compound and is generally inserted in the centre of the brass head of the cartridge, where the impact of the striker-pin acting on the cap and that part of the interior of the cap known as the *anvil* causes the flash which ignites the powder. In 1889 Lancaster noted: 'Directions to be observed by gentlemen using detonating guns: 1. Load with the cocks down, which prevents the powder from being forced out of the pegs that receive the copper caps.' See *centre-fire cartridge.*

cartridge case   the outer covering, either plastic or stiff paper, which contains the charge, usually stamped with the maker's name, and details of charge.

cartridge dispenser   a device slung round the body which provides two cartridges to hand when required for re-loading. Useful for loaders, at grouse drives or for driven shooting, when the birds are coming very fast, otherwise of no particular value. A comparatively modern invention of the 1950s.

cartridge extractor   a device which grips the base of the cartridge and enables a swollen cartridge to be extracted when jammed in the chamber. Although seldom needed, it can prevent a drive, or even a day, being spoiled by a recalcitrant cartridge stuck firmly in the gun. Not often seen nowadays as modern cases are mainly impervious to damp, but still useful.

cast¹   of antlers; when shed by a male deer, antlers are said to be *cast.*

cast²   of a shotgun: the degree of bend of the stock. It may be *cast on*, or *cast off.*

cast off   the degree of bend in the stock of a shotgun required by someone shooting from the right shoulder. Amongst the earliest references is that in 1830 by Hawker: 'Casting off; Inclining outwards of the but, so as to bring the line of aim

inwards, and more ready to meet the eye'; 'The length, bend
and casting off of a stock, must, of course, be fitted to the
shooter who should have his measure for them as carefully
entered in a gunmaker's books as that for a suit of clothes on
those of his tailor' (*Instructions*, 49, 31). An authoritative
modern reference in 1930 by Burrard reads:

> Cast off is given by the perpendicular distances from the
> comb and heel of the butt to a vertical plane through the top
> rib of the gun when the gun is held horizontaly . . . Cast off
> always means that the central plane of the stock is situated
> wholly to the right of this vertical plane when the gun is held
> in the normal position . . . The man who shoots from his
> right shoulder requires Cast Off. (*Shotgun*, i, 131)

cast on   the degree of bend in the stock of a shotgun required
by someone shooting from the left shoulder. An authoritative
description in 1930 is by Burrard: 'In the case of a man who
shoots from his left shoulder the gun is given "Cast On," the
stock being bent to the opposite side of the vertical plane
through the ribs' (*Shotgun*, i, 130).

catch up   of deer, to trap deer for removal to another area, for
injection, examination, or identification, etc. Of game birds, at
the end of the shooting season: to trap game birds in cage traps
for breeding, etc. A keeper *catches up* the hen pheasants at the
end of the shooting season to provide eggs for future breeding
stock.

centre-fire cartridge   the fore-runner of the modern cartridge, these were first introduced into Britain in 1861 and the
centre-fire *hammer guns* soon followed, sweeping away both
muzzle-loaders and *pin-fire* guns.

cete   of badgers; a group. Now 'Obs.' according to OED, but
'Cete (Set)' is quoted in 1939 by Hare (p. 152). First attestation
1486 *The Boke of St Albans*.

challenge   OED: 'To assert one's title to'. Of a stag in rut; to
roar at a rival while protecting a *harem* of hinds. In 1845 St
John wrote: 'The red deer had just commenced what is termed
by the Highlanders roaring; i.e uttering their loud cries of
defiance to rival stags and of warning to their rival mistresses'
(p. 279).

chamber   from Fr *chambre* and ultimately L *camera*: OED:
'that part of the bore of a gun in which the charge is placed.' In
1830 Hawker wrote 'Chamber: Centre, or principal tube in
breeching. The *Ante-chamber* is the smaller tube, leading from
this to the touchhole' (*Instructions*, 49). A modern definition

was provided by Burrard: 'That part of the inside of the barrel that receives the cartridge' (*Shotgun*, i, 19).

chamber cone   Burrard defined it as 'That part of the inside of the barrel which connects the front end of the chamber to the rear end of the bore. There is a tapered connection between the two visible as a dark ring thrown by the chamber cone which does not receive any direct light when seen from the breech end. It gives the illusion of a ridge.' (*Shotgun*, i, 19)

chamberless gun   in 1930 Burrard wrote:
The term "chamberless" is not strictly accurate as all guns must have chambers to receive the cartridges, but in these special guns the diameter of the bore is the same as that of the chamber and they are chamberless in that they have no chamber of larger diameter than the bore. Thin brass cases can only be used in such guns, for if ordinary paper cases were used the wads would be too small to seal the bore during the passage of the shot charge down the barrel. Owing to the absence of any form of chamber cone, brass cases of different length can be used with equal efficiency and consequently different loads can be fired effectively from the same barrel. . . . The very fact that thin brass cases must be used must prevent such guns from ever coming into general use, but in wildfowling the brass cases are an advantage and for this form of sport these chamberless guns are undoubtedly excellent. (*Shotgun*, iii, 265)

charge   OED: 'the quantity of powder (or more loosely, with sportsmen, etc.) of powder and shot, with which a fire-arm is loaded for one discharge.' Hence by transference of a shotgun cartridge: the powder and shot in the cartridge – really the 'discharge'. Burrard noted:
When a true 2¾ inch cartridge is fired in a 2½ inch chamber the pressure is increased . . . the actual powder and shot charges are heavier than those of the 2½ inch cartridge . . . The nominal charge for a 2½ inch 12-bore cartridge is 26 grains of No 60 powder and 1½ oz of shot. That for a 2¾ inch cartridge 20 grains of the same powder and 1¼ oz of shot. (*Shotgun*, ii, 153)

chase   under the Forest Laws, a *chase* was similar in many respects to a *park*. In 1807 Daniel wrote:
A Chase, is the same liberty as a Park, save that it is *not* enclosed, and also that a man may have a Chase in another man's grounds, as well as his own, by prescriptions . . . The Beasts of Chase are the Buck, Doe, Fox, Martern and Roe. The Buck attains that appelation in his sixth year, being

progressively a *Fawn*, a *Pricket*, a *Sorel*, a *Sore*, a *Buck of the first head*, and lastly a *Great Buck*. The Doe is first year a *Fawn*, secondly a *Pricket's Sister*, or a *Teg*, and the third year a *Doe*. The first year a Fox is called a *Cub*, the next a *Fox*, and after that an *Old Fox*. The Martern is so called in his second year; in the first he is termed a *Martern Cub*. A *Kid* is the name which the Roe bears in the first year, the second a *Girl*, the third a *Hemuse*, the fourth a *Roebuck* of the first head, and lastly, a *fair Roebuck*. (i, 261)
Also of a gundog: it is highly undesirable for it to *run in* on ground game or, worse still, flushed birds, and *give chase*.

cheek wind   when the *wind* is coming from one side or the other it is known as a *cheek wind*; game or deer upwind will not be disturbed, but those down wind will be. A pointer quartering the ground will have to work its ground at an angle across the wind.

cheeper   apparently dating from the 16th century. OED: 'that which cheeps, a squeaker: applied especially to the chicks of partridge and grouse.' The verb *cheep* 'to utter shrill feeble sounds like those of young birds' is first attested in 1513, but the first usage of *cheeper* appears to be 1611, in Cotgrave's *Dictionarie*: '*Pioleur*: a puler, cheeper, chirper.' In 1863 John Atkinson (*Provincial Names of Birds*) wrote: 'Cheeper . . . a young partridge or grouse . . . whose cry of alarm is acuter than that of the full grown bird.' See also *squeaker*.

Chinese pheasant   *Phasianus torquatus* or ring-necked pheasant; introduced to this country during the 18th century. As its alternative name implies, it has a notable ring of white round the neck of the cock bird and is common throughout the country today.

Chinese water-deer   mainly escapees from Woburn Park, but now established in Bedfordshire, Buckinghamshire, Hampshire and Shropshire and over into East Anglia. They stand slightly higher behind, but are graceful looking deer, although without antlers. The male, known as a buck, has prominent tusks about 2 inches long, protruding well below the jawline. The females, known as does, have very short upper canines. The young are known as fawns. They are a reddish brown in summer and greyer in winter. They have a tail nearly 3 inches long, but there is no trace of white visible in the tail region. The bucks stand about 20 inches at the shoulder and weigh about 25–30lbs. The doe stands 19–20 inches and weighs 20–25lbs. The gestation period is about 180 days and fawns are mostly born in June and July. Twins and triplets are common,

more have been recorded. They are fast movers and can jump
well, but have a habit of squatting in the open after running a
short distance. The alarm cry is a harsh repeated bark. They
will also bark repeatedly to each other and at an intruder. A
considerable amount remains to be learned about this species
of deer.

choke   OED, a constriction. The OED also has a somewhat dated
entry for *Choke-bore*: 'The bore of a fowling-piece which
narrows towards the muzzle thus tending to keep the shot
together and increase the range of the gun.' Burrard defined it
in a shotgun thus:

> Choke in a barrel is really a constriction of the bore at the
> muzzle . . . the usual plan is to start tapering the bore at a
> point *about* 1 to 1¼ inches from the muzzle. [. . .] Theoreti-
> cally choke is any constriction of the muzzle of a gun; but in
> actual fact a smaller constriction than 3 thousandths of an
> inch is seldom if ever adopted . . . any gun is choked which
> has its barrels bored with constrictions at the muzzle which
> may vary from 3 to 40 thousandths of an inch . . . 1
> thousandth of an inch is always known as a "point" so the
> smallest constriction . . . is one of 3 points. An Improved
> Cylinder is one in which the constriction is from 3 to 5
> points. (*Shotgun*, iii, 20, 24)

See *full choke*; *half choke*; *modified* or *quarter choke*.

clap, clapped   from ME *clappe*. OED: 'to press, get, "stick", or
lie close, (to, in, etc anything).' Of game, especially groundgame: to lie close to the ground unmoving, hoping to escape
observation by immobility. An example of this usage is in the
Pall Mall Gazette, of 29 October 1885: 'The young deer clap in
their forms and rise only when the eye is directly upon them.'
Almost any game caught by surprise may remain *clapped* to the
ground, or in cover, hoping to escape observation. Rabbits and
hares are both notable for lying clapped down in cover, or open
ground, hoping to escape being seen by lack of movement.
Hares tend to rise after they have been passed; they also back-
track and then break their trail by leaping sideways before
clapping down in their form. Speedy noted of a hare:

> During the heavy snowstorm in 1882 . . . After following the
> track for about three hours . . . we came within range of it
> . . . Four times it had turned and run back exactly on its own
> track for a distance of about one to two hundred yards, and
> then making a bound of eight or ten feet off to the side had
> started in a new direction. This in all probability would have
> thrown the dogs off the scent; but the depth of snow made

the tracks easy to be discerned . . . young hares a few weeks
old . . . display the power of instinct in this particular. We
have . . . ascertained this by following the footprints of small
leverets after a snow-shower in . . . April. (p. 284)
Brander remarked:
The hare clapped in its form can often be extremely difficult
to see. Without a pointing dog it will often be hard to find
and he knows the virtue of absolute stillness, none better. He
has only his protective colouring and speed to save him. I
once looked down from horseback and saw a hare clapped in
its form below the horse's belly, immediately beneath me.
Even though it had been ridden across it had not moved.
(*Sport*, 86)
See *common brown hare; hare myths; hare's breath;
puss.*

clay-pigeon   OED: 'a saucer of baked clay thrown into the air
from a trap, as a mark at shooting matches.' A small circular
bowl-shaped target of compressed compound, generally coloured black, but now often orange, or other colours, to show
up in artificial light. Fired from a concealed trap by a specially
designed machine, or sometimes by a hand thrower, the 'clays'
may be presented in pairs or separately, from almost any angle,
and present extremely testing targets. Originating from the use
of coloured glass balls, often filled with feathers, used as targets
in the early 19th century, the first clay targets were made from
baked clay similar to that used in making clay pipes. Although
primitive *clay-pigeons* were used as targets at shooting matches,
it was not until live-pigeon shooting was declared illegal just
before the First World War and not really until after 1918 that
clay-pigeon shooting was first developed and gradually became
popular. Initially referred to as 'clay pigeons', or 'clay birds',
now in general usage referred to as 'clays'. An early example is
by Purdey in 1936: 'there is no doubt that the demand for clay
bird shooting is greatly on the increase' (p. 128). See *down-
the-line; skeet.*

clean   of antlers; when the *velvet* has dried up and been
discarded. It is largely a misconception that the velvet is
removed by *fraying*. Although some remaining fragments of
velvet may be removed in this way, by and large the antlers in
velvet are much too tender for such treatment. Making this
point in 1973, Holmes noted: 'I have seen bucks virtually clean
within half-an-hour of seeing them in velvet' (p. 78).

clean delivery   of a gundog; to deliver freely to hand without
attempting to *mouth*, or retain the game, or dropping the game

at the handler's feet. Such common faults are frequently
disregarded by amateur dog-trainers, but in a field trial would
be severely marked down. There is all the difference between a
well-trained dog and a slovenly performer. Few things are more
irritating than a gundog dropping a *runner* at the handler's
feet, out of reach of his hands, and allowing it to run off. This
is simply a question of care in training. *Clean delivery* to hand is
important and should be inculcated from the very beginning.

cleaning jag   see *jag*.

cleaning rod   the rod, usually jointed, to which a cleaning
jag, or *turks head* mop, or other fitting for cleaning the barrels
may be attached, usually by a brass screw. The *cleaning rod* is
generally in two parts, screwing apart to fit in the gun case.
Burrard wrote:

> The ordinary wooden rods are quite satisfactory, but it is
> essential that the female screw at the end into which the
> various brushes, etc., screw should be of a standard size. This
> is most important as few things can be a greater nuisance
> than the inability to transfer any standard brush or other
> appliance to any particular rod . . . It is wise not to economise
> on the number of rods as it is a great convenience to have a
> different rod for every type of brush, etc., which is used and
> thus avoid the bother of unscrewing and screwing on different
> appliances to one rod. For this reason two rods should always
> be included in every guncase – there is seldom space for more
> – while half-a-dozen is not too many to have ready for use in
> the gun cupboard. The initial cost is not heavy . . . and the
> convenience is great. (*Shotgun*, iii, 280)

clean pick up   of a gundog; to pick up shot game without
hesitation, mouthing, pouncing, or seizing it in a manner likely
to damage it. Throwing a dummy in the open where the
youngster can see it is often responsible for this sort of reaction.
After the very early retrieves with a puppy, it is always advisable
to throw the dummy so that it lands in long grass or cover
where it is not in full view, and where the pup has to work with
its nose to find it. Otherwise it may develop the habit of
pouncing and damaging the game, even developing the beginnings of *hard mouth*.

clean weight   of a deer; after the lungs, stomach and intestines
have been removed; the liver, heart and kidneys, being edible,
are usually included, but customs vary.

cleave   from OE *cliofan*, *cleofan* hence *cliefen*, and *clofen*
divided, and then transferred to cloven foot(ed). First attestation in 1200: of deer; the toe; the two cleaves make a cloven

hoof common to deer and most ruminants. In the *track* of deer the spread between the cleaves indicates the speed of movement, while the size and depth indicate sex and age.

close season   of game. OED: 'Closed for the purposes of sport, during which the killing of certain kinds of game is illegal.' That part of the year when game may not be shot: the converse of the *shooting season*. Of deer; that part of the year when deer may not be shot, or hunted, also known as *fence month*. In 1814 Sir Walter Scott (*Waverley*) wrote: 'Though close-time was then unknown, the broods of grouse were yet too young for the sportsman.'

Clumber spaniel   the OED notes that the origin of the name is from Clumber in Notts, a seat of the Duke of Newcastle. A gun-dog breed generally regarded as the oldest of the spaniel sporting breeds. French in origin, it is also the heaviest of the spaniel breeds and, it has been suggested, was at one time crossed with the basset hound. They have large heads, long and heavy bodies, broad backs and powerful hindquarters. They are slower than most spaniels, but have excellent noses and are fine retrievers. Now out of fashion, they were at one time amongst the most popular of the spaniel breeds, especially when worked in teams. The average height at the shoulder is, dogs, 16–18 inches, bitches, 13–15 inches. In 1856 Walsh recommended:

> Dogs for Cock Shooting . . . The Clumber spaniel is the best I have ever seen, being hardy and capable of bearing wet with impunity. His nose is also wonderfully good, which its full development, in point of size, would lead one to expect. They are bred so much for hunting cocks that they own the scent very easily, and seem to delight and revel in it, giving generally a very joyous note on touching upon their trail. The true Clumber may easily be kept strictly to feather, and though they will readily hunt fur when nothing else is to be had, they do not prefer it as most other dogs do . . . I should always prefer hunting two couple at a time. (p. 64)

coat   OED: 'an animal's covering of hair, wool, feathers; rarely, the skin, or hide.' It is, however, commonly used to describe the skin of deer, e.g. a dark/spotted coat.

coccidiosis   a disease common to all game birds, caused by a parasite, *Coccidium avium*, in the alimentary canal producing listlessness and white diarrhoea in young birds. Generally fatal, unless immediate action is taken in the case of reared birds, the disease has spores which lie dormant in infected ground and so can repeat itself. It is undesirable therefore to rear game chicks in the same field as poultry, or on the same ground year after year. See also *gapes*.

cock¹ from OE *coc*. OED: 'The male of the common domestic fowl', hence of other birds. Among game birds used especially of pheasants, or as a shortened version of *woodcock*. The cry of 'Cock' is used by the beaters when a woodcock is sighted; the same cry may be used on a *cocks only day*. Hawker noted in his Diary for 4 November 1811: 'I bagged 10 partridges, 4 hares, a pheasant, a rabbit and a woodcock! besides a quantity of game that I only wounded, from the gun not coming well to my shoulder. The cock was fired at by the keeper, but it was evident that he fell to my gun.' And on 28 October 1822, 'Just before I left the river I had a snap shot at what I took for a cock, just topping the elders, and it proved to be a long-eared horn owl!' But on 1 October 1852 he wrote: '*One* old cock was the only pheasant seen or heard of on the estate! I had the luck to bag this said pheasant with 7 partridges 2 hares and a rabbit; which performance, under all circumstances, we considered an excellent day's sport.'

cock² as a verb, OED: 'To put (a loaded firearm) in readiness for firing by raising the cock, or hammer. To draw (the cock) back. To full cock, half cock.' To prepare a hammer gun for firing by pulling back the lock, or locks.

cocker spaniel OED: 'A breed of spaniels trained to start woodcocks, snipes and similar game; a cocking dog.' A breed of gundog whose name is derived from 'cocking spaniel', or spaniels used primarily for flushing woodcock. There was undoubtedly a small breed of setting spaniel common in the 17th century, but the breed as such was not recognised officially until 1892. It remains amongst the most popular of the show breed, although no longer so common in the shooting field today. The average height is from 12–14 inches at the shoulder for dogs and for bitches 11–13 inches. Colours vary from golden, yellow and liver to strawberry roan, blue roan and red. Their distinctive working characteristic is their merry working temperament.

cock over the cry of the beaters when a woodcock is seen, or alternatively when a cock pheasant is seen on a *cocks only day*.

cocks only day a shooting day when it has been agreed that only cock pheasants will be shot and all hens spared. It is often advisable to hold such days early in the season, before the cocks have become wily and learned to keep out of sight on shooting days. Too many cocks left at the end of the season is undesirable, since they are likely to fight amongst themselves for the available hens and they may also disturb hens wishing to nest. Brander advised that 'the back-end cocks only days should be conducted vigorously' (*Gameshot*, 208).

collared dove   *Streptopelia decoacta*. Only around 11 inches in length, the *collared dove* has a narrow black half-collar round the back of the neck. The upper parts are dusty brown with pale blue-grey shoulders and red eyes. It has an unpleasing, short, harsh flight call. It crosses with the *turtle dove*. Although a comparative newcomer, only arriving in the British Isles in 1952, it already shows every sign of becoming an unattractive pest which should be shot whenever possible. It is not as hard to shoot as the woodpigeon and does not 'carry' as much shot, but it quickly adapts to circumstances and when shot at it soon becomes wary.

comb   OED: 'The upper corner of the stock of a gun against which the cheek is placed in firing.' The part of the stock of a shotgun rising at an angle behind the hand, or *grip*.

combination gun   a gun which has a shotgun and rifle barrels combined; where there are only two barrels, the rifle barrel usually on the left. Inevitably such guns tend to be heavy and cannot have the balance of either a shotgun or a rifle. In both these respects a *combination gun*, or *drilling*, with a rifle barrel usually above, or below, the side-by-side shotgun barrels, which was developed subsequently to the side-by-side combination, is likely to be preferable, as it is better balanced although still heavy. Both are generally equipped with a sling for easier carriage. Combination guns were common in the latter half of the 19th century with sportsmen going abroad, to Africa in particular, but also to India and South America, who wanted a gun with which they could shoot any game from game birds to leopards, or even larger game. They are no longer common and even when popular amongst foreign-going sportsmen, they were seldom seen in use in Britain. In 1888 W.W. Greener noted: 'The combination of a rifle and shotgun in one double-barrelled weapon is much esteemed by South African sports-men. The rifle-barrel, usually on the left, may be rifled on any system' (*Modern Shot Guns*, 107). This was amplified in 1897:

> The Combination, or Shot and Ball Gun: A weapon which has been found to be exceedingly useful in foreign countries is a combination shotgun and rifle. This has two barrels side by side as in an ordinary shotgun, but with a rifle barrel on the top taking the place of the usual top rib. This rifle barrel

is useful for shooting deer and other small game . . . A gun of
another type is the "Paradox" which is a double gun bored
to shoot shot or ball. (*Encyclopedia*, i, 498)
common brown hare   *Lepus europeaus;* OE and Norse. OED:
a rodent quadruped of the genus *Lepus* having long ears and
hind legs, a short tail and a divided upper lip: a brown-furred
and four-legged mammal with long ears, generally tipped with
black, of great speed and timid nature. Found as *ground game*
throughout the British Isles below a certain level, its size varies,
with the district and the feeding available, from 6–12 lbs. They
will eat most herbiage, greens, roots and similar vegetables and
like deer are often guilty of *barking* trees and damaging young
trees in plantations. The *common brown hare* lives in the open
and lies up in a scrape known as a *form*. Unlike the *blue
mountain hare*, *Lepus Timidus Scoticus*, the common brown
hare does not normally take refuge in holes, or under stones
(although known to take refuge in a drain in a walled garden
when hard pressed by dogs). Its litters are born with their eyes
open and fully furred, usually from 2 to 5 in number; and the
young are termed *leverets*. They are soon carried by their
mother to different forms, where they are left by themselves
and fed at intervals. See *hare's birth*. They may be shot
throughout the year, but may not be sold between the months
of March and July inclusive. They are polygamous and breed
throughout the year and a double oestrus, or second rut,
resulting in a second fertilisation, is not uncommon. The male
is termed a buck and the female a doe. Hermaphrodite hares
are occasionally found.

   Associated over the centuries with witchcraft and widely
credited with magical powers, they have long been the subject
of country lore and myth. In *c.* 1327 William Twyci, or Twiti,
huntsman to the king, wrote: 'The Hare . . . she is the most
marvellous beast which is on this earth . . . at one time it is male
and at another female' (*Venerie*). In 1674 Cox observed: 'If
when a Hare riseth out of her Form she couches her Ears and
Scut, and runs not very fast at first, it is an infallible sign that
she is old and crafty' (p. 142). In 1806 Thornton suggested:
'When a hare starts up at a distance, it is often advisable to
follow her with the eye, because she will sometimes squat down
and the sportsman may soon afterwards approach and shoot
her on her form' (*Tour of France*, ii, 236). In 1830 Hawker gave
rather more sporting advice: 'Always endeavour to shoot a hare
crossing and consider the head as your object. Withhold shooting at her when coming to you until she is very close, or her

skull will act as a shield against your charge. If a hare canters
past and you are behind a hedge at feeding time, she will often
stop and sit up if you whistle. This I name to facilitate a shot
for a schoolboy' (*Instructions*, 207). In his Diary for 10 December 1840, he recorded interestingly:

> Got a hare for my larder which was an animal novelty! Mr.
> Sleet the master of Squire Legh's yacht, saw something at sea
> which he thought was a dog, or a fox; he lowered his boat
> and chased it; and it swam so fast he could hardly row fast
> enough to catch it; and on coming to close quarters, (he said)
> it dived like a water-rat; and in short he killed it with an oar,
> and it proved to be a fine fat *hare!*

In 1852 Surtees, more interested in hunting than shooting,
wrote satirically of hare shooting:

> Jog raised his wide-awake hat from his eyes and advanced
> cautiously with the engine of destruction cocked. Up started
> a great hare; *bang!* went the gun with the hare none the
> worse. *Bang!* went the other barrel, which the hare acknow-
> ledged by two or three stotting bounds and an increase of
> pace.
> "*Well missed!*" exclaimed Mr Sponge.
> Away went Ponto in pursuit.
> "P-o-n-t-o!" shrieked Jog, stamping with rage. (p. 330)

Walsh, more interested in coursing hares than shooting them,
indicated that the hare provided poor sport for the gun: 'The
hare . . . is usually shot in covert except when preserved for
coursing; but it is poor sport, as, while in covert, she never goes
faster than a canter and may be killed with certainty by any
tyro. It can only be for the pot, or for increasing the list of the
slain that this game is shot' (p. 65). In 1884 Speedy revealed a
naturalist's interest:

> Before settling for the day in the open field, the hare, as a
> general rule, doubles back upon her own track for a distance
> of some thirty to sixty yards, and then immediately before
> settling down, makes a spring directly to the right or to the
> left to a distance of some six to nine feet . . . She will . . .
> unless when rising wild . . . allow the person or dog to pass
> on two or three yards beyond the point at which she has
> doubled and will often slip off immediately in their rear
> unperceived, by this means gaining a considerable start and
> not unfrequently saving her life. (p. 284)

As late as 1938 Tennyson confirmed Peter Hawker's diary
entry: 'Another characteristic of the hare is its readiness to take
to the water when in danger and the large distances which it can

swim . . . Early one spring a party of about fifty hares *and stoats*
were seen to ford a flooded Yorkshire river, fully 60 yards wide
and flowing fast' (p. 58). A further observation on their habits
is to be found in Brander, *Sport*:
> the hare, after a moment's hesitation, turned and bolted
> towards us at full speed . . . running apparently blindly . . .
> Yet he was not running without purpose. Less than five yards
> from us he stopped suddenly and clapped down in the grass
> pushing up another hare that had been lying there all the
> time unnoticed . . . Having moved this hare on, the first hare
> then calmly lay down in the newly vacated form, while the
> second hare continued over the hill in apparently headlong
> flight . . . A greyhound coursing by eye might well be
> confused into following the second hare . . . after the rapid
> changeover. (p. 85)

This could well be the explanation of why William Twyti was
convinced that hares often changed their sex, since he might
well have seen an obvious old doe start up in front of his hounds
and then discovered them hunting a buck instead. See *clapped,
hare myths, hare's breath, puss, trace*.

common partridge   see grey partridge.

common pheasant: *Phasianus colchicus*; of Roman origin. Not,
as often thought, a native game bird, but introduced, probably
by the Romans, around Colchester, and now widespread in the
British Isles. The male is highly coloured, with a glossy green
head, variable brown plumage and a long tail. The female has
grey-brown markings with a shorter tail. The average size of
the male from beak to tail is 30–35 inches, weighing about 3
lbs, of the female 21–25 inches and about 2½ lbs. Its call is a
strident 'Cock-up.' It is polygamous and its nests have from
8–16 eggs, which generally hatch from May to June. Season
from 1 October to 1 February. There are many other varieties
of pheasant, see *Chinese pheasant*; *melanistic*. As early as
1830 Hawker was writing: 'Besides the common pheasant, there
are now in preserved coverts as well as aviaries, other beautiful
kinds which have mostly been brought from China; viz. the
golden pheasant; silver, or pied pheasant &c . . . In a small
covert of my own I had one nide of twelve, in which were
hatched nine common and three white pheasants . . .' (*Instructions*, 212). In 1856 Walsh noted: 'the Pheasant (Phasianus
Colchicus) is the grand foundation the *pièce de resistance* of the
covert shooting in this country' (p. 58). By 1884 Speedy was
writing:
> In general bags at cover-shooting, the pheasant bulks most

prominently and though falling an easy prey to the experienced sportsman in the open, they require sharp practice amongst trees. At the same time, pheasant shooting requires a certain amount of practice, from the circumstance of their often rising almost straight up, when they often escape unscathed, or injured only in the lower extremities, in consequence of the aim having been too low. Notwithstanding the shortness of their wings, they fly with great velocity when once in the air, and afford excellent shooting as they pass overhead. (p. 288)

common pochard *Aythya ferina*. The OED states that the name is of uncertain origins. Possibly derived from *poacher*, since the bird is a keen fish-eater, unwelcome in fish-ponds, but more probably from *poker*, since in flight its head and neck poke forward distinctively. William Yarrel wrote in his *History of British Birds* (1843): 'The Pochard, or Dun-bird, for this species is known by various names, as Red-headed Poker, and Red-eyed Poker . . . is a winter visitor to this country.' Generally found in lakes inland, not often on the sea. The drake has a dark chestnut head and neck, a black breast and a grey body. The beak is black with a pale blue band. The duck has a brown head and front with a pale patch round the beak and chin. Its size is about 18 inches from beak to tail and the season is as for other wildfowl.

common scoter *Melanitta negra*. The origins of the name are obscure. The drake is entirely black and the bill has a bright orange patch with a knob at the base. The duck is brown with white cheeks and throat, generally found near the sea except in the breeding season. It measures about 19 inches from beak to tail. It is now protected.

common snipe *Capella gallinago*; ME *snype, snyppe*; the origins are obscure, possibly Scandinavian. A common game bird found throughout the British Isles, generally in boggy or moist patches. About 10½ inches from bill to tail and weighing about 6 oz, it has black and rufous plumage, striped with buff on the back, while its tail shows white at the edges. Its flight is distinctive, zig-zag and towering, or rapidly rising. Its call sounds like cloth tearing, a dry 'Scaap', and its season is from 12 August to 31 January. The nests generally have four eggs, which usually hatch in March to April. Its feeding is similar to that of the *woodcock*. The *snipe* is notable for the drumming, or bleating, sound made by its tail-feathers, generally during the breeding season, for which it is known as the 'blog-bleater', or 'heather-bleater'. It is surprising how far and fast a snipe will

run when being shot over pointers. A dog will often have to
draw on for a hundred yards or more on a zig-zag trail before
the bird is flushed. *Runners*, though not often encountered,
since if hit by more than one pellet it is usually killed or disabled
because of its size, may be hard to find and may go a surprising
distance. In 1807 Daniel noted:

Snipes are in winter very usual inhabitants of all our wet and
marshy grounds, where they shelter themselves in the Rushes
&C . . . Snipe Shooting, when the birds are plentiful is an
excellent diversion; they are said to puzzle the Marksman by
the irregular *twistings* of their Flight when first sprung; but
this difficulty is soon surmounted if the birds are suffered to
reach a certain *distance*, when their flight becomes steady and
easy to traverse with the Gun: there is no reason to be
apprehensive of their getting out of the Range of the Shot, as
they will fall to the ground if struck but slightly with the
smallest grain. *Snipes*, like *Woodcocks*, and many other birds,
always fly *against the Wind*; therefore, by keeping the Wind
at his Back, the Sportsman has this advantage of the bird
when it first rises, that it presents a fairer mark. These birds
are scarcely good until *November* when they get very fat; in
hard, frosty, and more particularly in *Snowy* weather, Snipes
resort in numbers to warm Springs, where the rills continue
open, and run with a gentle Stream; these, on account of
their long Bills, are *then* the only places where they can hunt
for food. Snipes will generally lie well to a *Pointer* and some
dogs have a singular knack at finding and standing them. (iii,
174)

In 1929 Mackie wrote authoritatively under the heading Snipe:

1. Snipe are markedly affected by the moon. Choose, therefore, for shooting, a day after a clear night. Then they will
have fed well and will lie well to the guns. Like woodcock
snipe feed mostly at night-time; but after dark nights they
feed during the day and are very much on the alert..

2. The best time to shoot snipe is during the thaw after a
frost. At such time they get a plentiful supply of worms,
which always come near to the surface of the earth after
frost.

3. Snipe lie best in muggy weather; with a gentle breeze and
a barometer which shows a tendency to fall, and after a
moonlight night.

4. Snipe lie worst in bright, fresh weather, with a high breeze
and after a dark cloudy night.

5. In the generality of cases, for finding the birds, the guns should walk *downwind* – this is unusual with other game
  a. In a thaw – when the birds will be lying well.
  b. When the birds are lying badly during a strong wind.
On the other hand the guns should walk *upwind*:
  a. During a sharp frost, when the birds will be lying badly.
  b. When there is only a light breeze (but not during a thaw) after a dark night.
  c. In approaching a bird for the second time after flushing.
6. The best hours to shoot snipe are those immediately following daybreak and the hours just before dark.
7. Snipe-shooting should not be commenced on 1st August as is commonly done. The end of September is the earliest time that they are likely to be found in good condition.
8. Better shooting is obtained in big grass-fields soaked with water, or in bogs that have only shallow pools, than in large flooded bogs and extensive marshes. In the latter case a single shot may cause a whole flock to rise in 'wisps' and thus offer poor sport. In these cases it is perhaps better to drive the birds. If suitable arrangements can be made a rope may be drawn across the bog or 'moss.' In most cases, where mallard and teal are also present capital sport can be obtained with good guns.
9. It is wise to remember that, after being shot at, snipe may fly, or be blown, long distances and then fall dead.
10. The best dogs for snipe-shooting are Irish water spaniels and red Irish setters, the latter being used for shooting over bogs or large marshes and the former for smaller and drained marshes. (p. 348)

compartment   of forestry; an area used for purposes of management, usually about 20–30 acres.

compass   though not often thought of as an invaluable adjunct to shooting, a compass may sometimes save a life if carried by wildfowlers on a strange foreshore, or by anyone venturing to the high tops to shoot ptarmigan, or even sometimes on a grouse moor, should they be overtaken by thick mist as may easily be the case. It is also an essential should anyone be unwise enough to stalk on strange ground in the Highlands without a stalker who knows the ground intimately. A mist can come down without warning in a deer forest and may result in the stranger to the ground soon becoming completely lost without both a compass and a map. In 1884 Speedy noted:

It is not an unusual thing for sportsmen, while engaged in grouse-shooting, to lose their way among the volumes of mist which settle down among the mountains, dense and wellnigh impenetrable to the human eye. During the long days in August and September when the weather is genial no serious danger is to be apprehended. It is, however, very different when those out hind-shooting become enveloped in one of those impenetrable fogs with a heavy fall of snow, while the piercing north-east winds, charged with frost, threaten to congeal the blood when active exercise becomes no longer possible. (p. 258)

Mackie advised his readers:

It goes without saying that there is no use taking out the guns on a misty day. In all forms of sport, where there is a thick mist there should be no firing, and when on a fine day, the guns being on the 'tops' mist begins to collect, shooting should cease. On this account it is recommended that in ptarmigan shooting the keeper and each of the guns should possess a pocket compass. (p. 220)

coney, cony   derived from OF *conil* and L *cuniculus*, pronounced to rhyme with honey, i.e. cunni. The old word in general use for rabbit, but now largely obsolete, except in some country districts. In 1576 Turberville wrote: 'The coney beareth her rabbettes xxx days' and as late as 1846 Bulwer-Lytton (*Childe Harold*) still wrote: 'You might see . . . the hares and conies steal forth to sport and feed' but by the late 16th century the word had developed vulgar and indecent connotations, as an example by Philip Massinger in his play the *Virgin Martir* (1662) makes plain: 'A pox on your Christian cockatrices! They cry, like poulterers' wives; No money, no coney.' As a result of the widespread use of this alternative meaning the word was gradually discarded and was replaced by the word **rabbit** which was formerly the name for the young only.

core area   term used by naturalists of the home range which an animal frequents. Often used in Game Conservancy studies of game behaviour.

coronet   OF: of an antler; the base above the pedicle.

corrie   Gaelic, *coire*, a cauldron: a term used in the highlands to denote a cleft, gulley, or bowl in the hills where deer are likely to find shelter and grazing. The wind in such places can often be fitful and flukey, bouncing off sides of the hills and making for difficult stalking conditions which favour the deer rather than the stalker. Knowledge of local conditions and the way the wind may carry scent is one of the advantages the local

stalker has over a visitor. Once the chance of a shot has been
lost because the wind carried the scent unexpectedly towards
the deer, the circumstances are unlikely to be repeated. Like the
use of an echo, however, the use of scent to move deer in the
required direction may be well worth trying on occasions when
the wind is right. (See *driving*.) An early example of the usage
is in 1884 by Speedy: 'in some of the deep round-shaped
corries, the wind not unfrequently whirls round like the water
in an eddy. This fact is well understood and taken advantage of
by the deer. Hence the explanation why they are so often found
in these corries' (p. 226).

corvids   L: members of the corvidae, or crow, family: ravens,
carrion crows, hooded crows, jackdaws, jays and magpies.
Mostly enemies to all nesting birds and avid egg thieves.

couple   from OF. OED: 'that which unites two': of dogs, a leash
to join two together. Speedy declared: 'When two or more
young dogs are under training, they must, as a matter of course
be taught to go in couples' (p. 41). Also used as a noun. OED:
'A union of two, a pair': a brace of dogs used in hunting, e.g.
spaniels; also a brace of rabbits. In 1725 Richard Bradley
(*Family Dictionary*) noted: 'Couple; In respect to Conies and
Rabbets, the Proper term for two of them.' Used as a verb: to
join two together. Of groundgame: after *harling*, or *legging* it
is customary to couple them by interlocking the hindlegs of two
harled or legged carcases, this operation is known as *coupling*.
The coupled and legged carcases are then hung each side of a
pole for convenience of carriage and counting: a brace of
gamebirds, if possible of different sexes, i.e. cock and hen, may
be hung over a pole in the same way, coupled by string around
their necks. Also of animals; esp. deer, dogs, to mate.

cover   OF. OED: 'Wood, undergrowth and bushes, that serve
to shelter wild animals and game = Covert.' The two words are
often regarded as virtually synonymous and interchangeable,
but *cover* is probably wider ranging. In 1719 Daniel Defoe
wrote: 'Never frighted hare fled to Cover . . . with more terror
of mind than I to this retreat' (*Robinson Crusoe*). In 1802 Peter
Beckford wrote: 'You hunt a cover that is full of foxes'
(*Hunting*). Also of male animals; to mate with female.

covert   OF. OED: 'a place that gives shelter to wild animals and
game.' The same meaning as *cover*, but possibly more
restricted and more commonly used in foxhunting and driven
pheasant shooting. As early as 1494 an Act of Parliament under
Henry VII decreed: 'It is ordained that no Man . . . drive them
out of their Coverts.' In 1897 it is noted: 'Coverts vary very

much in their adaptation, natural as well as artificial for the
purposes of pheasant shooting. Amongst the natural advantages, we place first a good supply of water, which tends to keep
the birds at home, and second position on the side of a hill,
which ensures good sporting shots' (*Encyclopedia*, ii, 84). 'The
best age for moving the young birds to covert will depend on
certain circumstances. In theory we should not start until the
pheasants are eight or nine weeks old, but we may find that
when the young birds have made very good progress and are
well grown, they will, at seven weeks, start wandering' (*LL
Shooting*, 151).

covert shooting   synonymous with *driven shooting*. In 1887
it was noted: 'In a big day's covert shooting retrievers are not
much used, but there should be some out with under-keepers
in order that every wounded bird, if possible, may be collected'
(*Encyclopedia*, ii, 85). In 1930 Leslie Sprake wrote: 'The term
"a covert shoot" may convey to the mind of "the man in the
street" the vision of pheasants fluttering around like poultry . . .
But actually the ambition of the majority of shooting men is to
show (as a host) and shoot (as a guest) pheasants that fly so
high and fast that they offer a really severe test of marksman-
ship' (*LL Shooting*, 156). See also *yuppy shooting*.

covey   from OF *covee*, 'a hatching,' going back to the Latin
cubare 'to sit'. OED: a brood or hatch of partridges. A family of
partridges keeping together during the first season. Sometimes
also of grouse and ptarmigan. An early example is in 1486, *The
Boke of St Albans*: 'Let yowre spanyellis fynde a couey of
partrichys.' In 1768 Pennant noted: 'A partridge followed by a
large covey of very young birds' (i, 365). Dubious sporting
advice was provided in 1830 by Hawker: 'When distressed for
partridges, in a scarce country at the end of the season, take a
horse and gallop from one turnip-field to another, instead of
regularly slaving after inaccessible coveys' (*Instructions*, 149).
In 1835 Sir James Ross in his *Narrative* of his Voyage in the
Arctic, wrote of seeing 'A covey of ptarmigans.' In 1845 St
John wrote: 'Our next cast took us up a slope of hill, where we
found a wild covey of grouse . . . Another covey on the same
ground gave me three shots' (p. 31).

creek crawling   the act of crawling, or stalking, through the
mud channels and creeks of a salting or foreshore after wildfowl.
See *wildfowling*.

cromie   see *crummie*.

cross-pin   Burrard gave an authoritative definition:

The Cross-Pin, or Action-pin is the large screw through the front end of the bar on to which the barrels are hooked when the gun is put together. On the majority of cheaper guns a cross-pin is not used, the joint being cut out of the solid action. A cross-pin is, however, an advantage since it enables the gunsmith to tighten the gun up should the fit between the barrels and action became slack in course of time. (*Shotgun*, i, 38)

crottels   Fr. OED: 'The globular dung, or excrement, of hares.' Now virtually obsolete.

crotties or **croties**   of roe and fallow deer; droppings. Again nearly obsolete.

crown   ME. OED: the upper part of a deer's horn. Of red deer antlers, if the three topmost points are in the shape of a crown, or cup, they are so-named.

crummie   OED: 'Scottish and N. Country diminutive of *crum*, "crooked" (OE)'. Having crooked, or crumpled horns. Of red deer antlers; stunted and goat-like; said to be not uncommon on the Isle of Jura, perhaps from inbreeding.

cryptorchid   of male animals, inc. deer and dogs: when the testicles have not dropped into the scrotum, but remain in the abdomen; the animal is usually infertile. See *havier, monorchid, rig*.

cull   ME. OED: 'To choose from a number or quantity, to select.' Also 'early form of kill'. Of deer, game or wildfowl; selective killing of the surplus, aged, sick, weakly, or bad breeding stock. This is one of the basic principles of good stockmanship and the full-time year-round task of any worthwhile gamekeeper, or game-preserver.

cup   of antlers; see *crown*.

curly coated retriever   one of the oldest of the gundog breeds, having evolved, like most others in its present form during the late 19th century. With a thick curly coat, colour of black or liver, height about 25–27 inches at the shoulder, it was thought to have been the result of a cross between the Newfoundland and the Irish water spaniel. Now scarce, it was at one time amongst the most favoured of retrieving breeds.

cut off   Burrard defined it as: 'A Cut off or Separation, is a separation of the paper tube (of the cartridge) from the brass head, which occurs on firing, with the result that the brass head only is ejected on the gun being opened and the paper tube is left ... in the chamber' (*Shotgun*, ii, 96). This is a rare occurrence with modern cartridges.

D **arne action gun**   a type of shotgun or sliding breech gun, made in France and notably light and strong. The barrels are fixed to the stock and the breech is removable.

dead dog   not in the OED. A term for a weight on the centre of a rope dragged between two handlers through a field of grass or stubble to flush groundgame into nets; used with long nets, esp. the *Caldra system*, originally used by poachers at night to flush game into nets. Brander: 'In beating out uneven or overgrown ground . . . a "dead dog" is not enough' (*Groundgame*, 82).

deadfall   any trap working on the principle of a heavy weight, such as a slab of slate, or stone, delicately poised to fall on the quarry and crush it when a bait is disturbed. The first attestation is in 1611 by Markham: 'Some do use to take them with hutches or dead-falles set in their haunts' (*Country*, i, xvi). In 1880 Carnegie wrote: 'Deadfalls such as the figure of 4 trap arc easy to make and useful for killing small animals' (p. 59). See *figure-of-four trap*.

decoy   OED gives originally *coy*, with variants such as *decoye*, *dequoy*, *de quoi*, *duckoy*, with later Dutch *de koi*, but the origins are now lost and the derivation and history unknown. Meanings include a tame duck used to entice others to come to it; similarly a decoy deer. In modern usage, a live or dead bird, or dummy, set out in a lifelike manner to attract others of the same species. Generally only used for shooting pigeons and wildfowl, ducks and geese, there is however no reason why they should not be used for any species, including *corvids* (see *cage trap*, *Larsen trap*). Good dummy decoys are made of rubber, plastic, fibre and other materials and can be bought at most gunsmiths or sporting shops. Cardboard silhouettes are also effective and light to carry, but liable to blow away in a high wind even when well pegged down. It is desirable to ensure that all artificial decoys are as lifelike as possible, and shiny paint or any similar obvious defects are to be avoided. Movable decoys with flapping wings or other movements are sometimes also used. Solid carved wooden decoys, made in the 19th century or earlier, are recognised as valuable antiques as well as works of art. Almost any materials can be used for making decoys. Pigeons have been decoyed to patches of iron filings and to roof slates with chalk wings marked on them either placed flat on the ground, or stuck in on one edge. Suitably shaped pats of mud with feathers may be used to decoy ducks. In every case, however, dead birds of the species set out in a suitable pattern and

adjusted in lifelike poses, with a stake supporting the head and
neck, will prove as good as any other decoy and better than
most. Live decoy ducks with clipped wings kept and fed on a
flighting pond, are also known as *call ducks*, since their call
may entice wild birds to join them. As early as 1822 Hawker
wrote in his diary: 'At night took some decoy birds and waited
at the river for some hours and though a beautiful moonlight
and white frost, I never saw or heard but one duck, which the
call-birds brought round several times, but too high to shoot
at.' An early mention of decoys for pigeon shooting is given in
1884 by Speedy:

> When they have acquired the habit of feeding in a field, if a
> few stuffed ones are stuck in the ground as decoys, directly
> any fly over and perceive them, they are almost certain to
> circle round and settle beside them. We have killed large
> numbers in this manner even without the use of stuffed ones,
> by simply propping up the heads of a few dead ones with
> pieces of stick and making them as lifelike as possible. We
> never went out of the ambush to pick them up as they were
> shot; and though we have had as many as thirty or forty dead
> ones strewn around, still it did not in the least deter others
> from alighting. (p. 313)

Hence also v. *to decoy*: to set out decoy birds to attract others of
the same species within range of the gun.

decoy bird   a bird used to attract others of the same species
either within range of the gun, or into a *cage trap*. It is rightly
illegal to use live birds tethered by the foot as *decoy birds*. *Call
ducks* (see also *decoy*), may be used with clipped wings on a
flight pond. Live birds may also be used in cage traps as decoy
birds to bring in others into the trap, which may be built on the
lobster-pot principle, allowing access, but not egress, as with
the small and easily moved *Larsen trap*. The latter, however,
should be moved daily to fresh ground and be provided with a
perch and fresh food and water, so that the decoy bird does not
have to languish on fouled ground. Such a practice is both cruel
and self-defeating, since a contented decoy bird will be more
effective than a listless beast crouched in miserable conditions
beside several old carcasses on dirty, muddy ground. This may
not be illegal but should be.

decoy run   used to describe the actions of a wild bird of either
sex indulging in the *wing-trailing* and wing flapping imitation
of a wounded bird to lead intruders or possible predators away
from its nest or young. See *winged bird*.

decoy shooting to shoot birds over decoys, see *decoy; flighting.*

deer the OED gives: '1. A beast, usually a quadruped, as distinguished from birds and fishes: 2. The general name of a family (Cervidae) of ruminant quadrupeds.' It is today accepted as the generic term for all the *cervidae* of either sex, but it is interesting that the original meaning given by the OED dates back to the 10th century, when wild cattle, boar and wolves would have been commonly hunted as well as deer. It became confined to deer in the later medieval period as hunting became similarly restricted.

deer fencing fencing erected with the intention of limiting the movement of deer, usually to protect plantations of young trees, but sometimes used on the *marches* of a *deer forest* in an attempt to contain the deer, a misguided policy which can lead to undesirable results such as overstocking and deaths in hard weather.

deer forest in the Highlands this implies an area inhabited by deer, although generally devoid of trees and possibly looking at first glance like stony, inhospitable mountainside. *Deer stalking* is a sport developed in its modern form only since the 1840s and the term does not appear to have been used before then, by which time most of the mountains had been deforested. The Scottish terminology is usually *on the hill* and it may be simply that the English expected deer to be found in forests, hence the usage. In 1856 Walsh wrote: 'The Deer Forests are confined to Scotland and are only to be obtained by those whose purses are long enough to pay large sums for them. Indeed it is seldom that any are on the market as the fashion of the day has made this sport more eagerly sought after than any other' (p. 86). In 1884 Speedy noted 'While in a number of the high-rented deer-forests in the Scottish Highlands no great exertions are required to discover deer, it is in many other places very different' (p. 228). The use of a stalker with local knowledge is essential until the ground is thoroughly known. Anyone who ventures on unknown ground in the Highlands and attempts to stalk deer is asking for trouble. A mist can come down without warning and without a guide who knows the ground it is easy to become totally lost and even to have to spend the night on the ground. *Deer forests* can be dangerous ground for the novice and a *compass* and map would be essential for anyone venturing on ground they do not know.

deer leap raised ground, outside or inside an enclosure, allowing deer entrance, or egress; commonly used outside deer parks to allow wild deer easy access, for one-way traffic only. Under the old *Forest Laws* the installation of an unauthorised *deer leap* was regarded as a poaching offence.

deer park   an enclosed area, fenced, or walled, intended to retain a herd of deer. Originated under the *Forest Laws* in the early Middle Ages as an area reserved for hunting on which tax was duly payable to the Exchequer (see *park*). They remained an adjunct to large estates throughout the Tudor period for hunting and to provide meat for the household. They were largely broken up during the Civil War, when many deer escaped into the countryside and formed feral populations. Brander observed:

> With the development of an aesthetic taste for landscape gardening deer parks also became a feature of many country estates. The number, which had increased from 32 in 1086, probably reached its peak of over 700 around the accession of Charles I, prior to the Civil War, when many were destroyed. Then after the Restoration in 1660 the numbers began to build up again until by the year 1800 there were around 300. It is an interesting point that whereas they had previously been kept with a practical viewpoint in mind, either to provide meat, or sport, they were now kept largely for aesthetic reasons to improve the view, or perhaps as an aristocratic version of keeping up with the neighbours. (*Deer*, 15)

Today they are still to be found around some large houses to provide a tame herd of deer as an adjunct to the view and also providing venison as a source of food and income.

deer pass   a favourite route in the hills which red deer are known to follow regularly. A rifle may often be stationed in such *deer passes* when driving hinds at the end of the season in order to cull the necessary numbers. In 1884 Speedy wrote: 'As deer are much easier driven up hill than otherwise it is desirable that the rifles should be placed in the "passes" on the rising ground' (p. 248). See *deer stalking*.

deer stalking   in woodland this may be by *still-hunting*, or from a high-seat; in the open, or *on the hill* in a *deer forest* generally by stalking. Some early and rather dubious advice on deer stalking was provided in 1830 by Hawker:

> If you have an outlying deer . . . go out in a summer morning just before sunrise, while the dew is on the grass . . . and look with caution into every enclosure and particularly among young peas . . . if you go carefully and silently, you will see him feeding, and most likely at no great distance from a

hedgerow. If ... you can approach without being smelt, (There is a remedy to obviate this ... that is to carry before you an armful of very sweet hay) seen, or heard ... you will probably get a good shot ... To approach a buck in an open field crawl as low as possible on the ground and hold before you a green bough which if there is a hedge of wood behind, will appear so confused with it that he will often suffer you to come within rifle shot. (*Instructions*, 190)

By 1856 Walsh wrote rather more knowledgeably, but still without obvious personal experience:

It may readily be supposed that for the pursuit of deer-stalking a hardy frame and plenty of pluck in the deer-stalker are required ... The *model* deer-stalker, however, should be of good proportions, moderately tall, narrow hipped to give speed and with powerful loins and well-developed chest for giving endurance and wind. No amount of fat should be allowed ... The foot should be sure, and the eye keen and long seeing as the telescope cannot always be applied to that all-important organ. He should be practiced in running stooping, in crawling on his belly or on his back, by means of his elbows and heels; and should care neither for business, nor cold, nor wet ... The stalker must be full of plans and resources, yet cautious in putting them into execution ... (p. 89)

Writing from personal experience, Speedy noted:

Deer-stalking has very appropriately been designated 'sport of princes.' In order to obtain its full enjoyment, grouse-shooting must have been prosecuted and enjoyed in mountainous regions, where difficulties and even hardships, could only be overcome by the perseverance of an enthusiastic sportsman. The training thus acquired, by the scaling of precipitous rocks and the traversing over miles of moorland, whereby the limbs and lungs are alike tested, is indispensable as a preliminary to make deer-stalking either enjoyable or successful. We should as soon expect to find a good English scholar who had not passed through the preliminary standards as to find a gentleman a successful deer-stalker, who had not previously been an ardent and somewhat successful general sportsman, and more especially, as we have indicated, among grouse, and we may add, mountain hares and ptarmigan. (p. 223)

Some years later, in 1897, Augustus Grimble also sounded a warning note:

This sport as now carried on in the Scottish highlands is one that has changed but little since guns and rifles, bullets and villainous saltpetre, first made their appearance on the hills; the weapons themselves have been improved, and have been coupled with the later advent of the telescope, or spy-glass, but these are the only alterations that have taken place in the manner of carrying out the sport ... With regard to personal condition, if plenty of golf and lawn-tennis has been played during the summer months, and hill walking be not an entire novelty, most shooters will find themselves fairly fit at the commencement of the season, while each day on the hill will make them more so ... when soon after setting out, a long and steep hill has to be negotiated, stop to admire the view the moment nature warns that too great a strain is being placed on the pumping powers of the heart. Many a good man has seriously injured himself by trying to 'live' with a practiced and well-trained walker during the ascent of a high and severe hill ... (*Encyclopedia*, i, 301)

Further on he gave the then current advice on taking aim: 'if the stag is standing broadside on, put the rifle-sights on the inside of the nearest foreleg; raise them slowly till they meet the body, and squeeze the trigger gently when you "see brown."' (ibid., 305). Much more to the point and all-embracing are Mackie's comments:

Deerstalking Notes ... the following points should be observed by the young stalker:

a. Never attempt a *downwind* stalk.

b. Always try to stalk *down hill*, as deer seldom look up the hill; and always try to have the sun at your back, and shining in the eyes of the deer.

c. Remember the general rule – that deer move upwind when they are feeding.

d. In fine weather the bigger stags are on the highest hills; in wet and stormy weather they are on the lower ground.

e. Do not stalk, or be very careful, on days when there is a very high wind, as the deer are apt to dash about from place to place without any obvious reason.

f. Remember that whatever wind may be blowing across the hills, there is always a current moving *up and down* the narrow glens. It is therefore wise to carefully spy out the ground near to where the deer are grazing, notice the movements of the grass in their vicinity and then make your stalk accordingly.

Mist is the bugbear of the stalker, but the times of

enforced inaction resulting from its presence are not wasted if you watch carefully and note the drift of the mist as showing the different currents of air, many of them contrary to the general direction of the wind. Constant observation is the making of a good stalker. Never try to stalk in a thick mist. You will do much harm and no good.

g. The distance one may approach near to a herd varies. When here is a strong wind it is not safe to pass within a mile of the herd.

h. In making a stalk, be particularly careful to avoid any outlying herds of deer; if these see you they may scamper over the forest and upset all your calculations. (p. 270)

See also *glass*.

delayed implantation   of a roe doe; the delayed growth of the foetus after fertilisation; generally for a period of 4½ months; one of the interesting and still little understood features of the roe's life cycle.

dental pad   of deer, the hard pad in front of the upper jaw against which the lower front teeth bite.

dew claws   of deer and dogs: vestigial toes, two above the cleaves on the back of the leg in deer and one inside the leg above the pad on dogs. The OED suggests rather poetically that they may be so called because while the rest of the foot contacts the ground, they merely brush the dew. Turberville gave the first attestation in 1576. On working gundogs, especially fast movers such as pointers and setters and the HPR breeds, it may be advisable to remove these claws soon after the litter is born, since if left *in situ* they can become torn during hard work and may prove a source of trouble in an older dog.

Dickson's round action
The Dickson Patent Round Action, which is the descendant of the old Macnaughton Trigger Plate Action is ... the connecting link between box and side locks. The name is derived from the rounded shape of the body as well as from the absence of square or sharp edges. The original Patent was obtained in 1880 and the locks are carried entirely on the trigger plate and are inserted from underneath; but they occupy a space *behind* the body of the action as do sidelocks. (Burrard, *Shotgun*, i, 146)

dish faced   of dogs and horses. The OED gives W. Gordon Stables' definition of 1884 (*Our Friend the Dog*, Chap. vi, 50): 'having the nose higher at the tip than the stop.' Since this condition is also found in hounds, gundogs, horses and deer, it might be better described as a concave-shaped frontal appearance to the face.

dislodge   OF. OED, of hunting: 'to drive (a beast) out of its lair.' Of roe deer particularly, to rouse from its bed. An early example is by John Guillim (*Heraldrie*) in 1610: 'You shall say, Dislodge the Buck.'

doe   OE: the female of *Chinese water-deer, fallow, muntjac* and *roe*, also of *hare* and *rabbit*. The first attestation is in 1000. For rabbits there is an interesting example of the usage in 1607, Edward Topsell (*Historie of Four-Footed Beasts*), noting the phenomenon of *double-oestrus* common to both hares and rabbits: 'One that kept tame Conies . . . had Does which littered three at a time and within fourteen daies after they littered four more.'

dog   late OE. The first attestation was in 1050, but the generic OE name was *hound*: the difference seems to have been that hounds were kept solely for hunting, but *dogs* were used for other purposes, viz. guard, herding, etc., as well as certain types of hunting, e.g. falconry and fowling, i.e. shooting birds with a bow, generally sitting, although 'shooting flying' was probably quite common with expert bowmen. Also used as a verb, to work dogs over a specific piece of ground to find game, possibly to move it in a required direction, e.g. to *dog-in* ground, or, with guns in attendance, to shoot game, e.g. a moor may be *dogged*, rather than driven; hence *dogging*: e.g. 'a good moor for dogging'. In 1939 Stephens wrote: 'I do not propose to enter here into the arguments about dogging and driving' (p. 23). See *pack*.

double-barrelled over-and-under   see *over-and-under*.

double-barrelled side-by-side   see *side-by-side*.

double barrels   generic term for all double-barrelled guns. Initially there were doubts about these innovations. In 1804 Thornton wrote: 'September 15 . . . I now gave up my double-barrel gun for the season; and here I must remark, that I look upon all double-barrels as trifles, rather nick-nacks than useful' (*A Sporting Tour*, 163). In 1807 Daniel noted:

> In double Guns the stoutness of the Barrels is indispensable if the Shooter has any regard for his own Safety: for in light *double Barrel* Pieces the firing of the *one* will invariably loosen the Charge in the *other Barrel* and should the Shot be shaken so as to leave the Powder a few inches and the second barrel be fired with the Muzzle pointing downwards, most likely it bursts. [. . .] With *double* Guns a danger arises from the Shooter who fires but *one* barrel and kills his Bird, forgetting

to *uncock* the other previous to his reloading that which has been discharged; to obviate this, let him invariably *uncock* the *second* barrel before he sets the *Butt* of the Gun upon the ground . . . After discharging one Barrel be careful to secure with the *Ramrod* the Wadding of the other, which from the *Recoil* usually becomes loose. (iii, 467; 480) In 1830 Hawker was more concerned with the results: 'From one who professes himself an adept with a *double-gun* it is expected he will kill a bird with each barrel, almost every time the covey rises within fair distance; unless impeded by the *smoke of his first barrel*, or *other obstacles*, which he should *endeavour to avoid*' (*Instructions*, 132). As late as 1856 Walsh was still concerned with safety, and also weight: 'The usual weight of a double-barrelled gun is now from 5½ to 7½ pounds. The former *may* be safe, but it is scarcely to be recommended, especially if not made by a perfect artist' (p. 21).

double brows   of antlers; with brow and bay tines.

double head   said of a buck, when carrying the previous year's antlers along with those of the current year. 'Double head. In this condition one or both antlers are not cast and are held in position by the new growth for the following season . . . found only in young bucks and does not recur with later heads' (Holmes, 85).

double-oestrus   of rabbits and hares; a second rut, or heat, resulting in a second fertilisation, followed by a second litter born some time after the first: a not uncommon occurrence. See *doe*.

double snipe   see *great snipe*.

down-the-line   method of *clay-pigeon* shooting in which the shooter fires at a series of 'birds', or clays, flying away from him, thrown from a central trap or traps at 16 yards from a number of evenly spaced stands in turn, in a line from the trap, providing different shots at different angles, hence the name. This is a test of quickness as well as accuracy, as the clay is a long way out before it is hit by the shot charge. It is general practice to shoot with the gun at the shoulder before giving the word 'Pull' to the trapper who releases the bird. See *skeet*.

downwind   the area towards which the wind is blowing is known as *downwind*: game or deer downwind will scent the approach of man or dog; see also *cheek wind*, *up wind*. A pointer or setter working downwind will make a long sweep away from the handler and quarter the ground towards him, thus making good its ground *into the wind*.

draw, draw on   of a gundog, esp. pointer or setter, on point, to advance steadily towards where game is lying, or running in front, after first pointing. In 1830 Hawker rightly warned: 'When birds run (but are not visible on the ground and the dogs keep drawing across a whole field) as they will do, most particularly in a dry easterly wind, they are almost certain to get up at a long distance' (*Instructions*, 143). In 1852 Surtees described a typical spectacle: 'The dog was now fast drawing upon where the birds lit; and Mr Sponge and Jog having reached the top of the hill, Mr Sponge stood still to watch the result' (p. 331). In *The Field* for 1892 there are two instances of the usage: 'Musa pointed and drew on, but could not locate the birds' (7 May); 'The setter must often draw on and draw on, not unlike a cat creeping on its prey' (19 November). A pointing dog should be allowed to *draw on* until freezing solidly on point. If game is moving steadily in front, the dog may be allowed to draw on until the game is flushed within shot. It is a mistake to encourage a dog to draw on too fast, i.e. at a run, when game is wild. This will simply result in the game being flushed out of shot. After drawing on, however, and when the game has been flushed, the dog should be allowed to *road-out* the scent thoroughly.

drilling   noun from Du *drille*; a version of the *combination gun* common in Europe, usually with a rifle barrel under, or over, the twin barrels of a side-by-side shotgun, but there are many variants, both in bore, or gauge, of the shotgun and the calibre of the rifle, as well as their combination, e.g. it might be sixteen bore and .22, or twelve bore and .243, or any preferred choice, above or below the barrels. The object of such *drillings* is to enable to the user to shoot deer, wolves, or wild boar as well as game birds, which may be encountered in the same drive, or ground available for shooting, in parts of Europe. To the average sportsman in the UK there is a touch of *Alice-in-Wonderland* about them: ''Twas drilling and the slithy toves . . .' They have never been very common in this country, simply because there are not a great many occasions on which they are useful; one would be for gamekeepers who may encounter foxes out of shotgun range. They usually have a sling attached for ease of carriage, since, inevitably, they are heavy to carry any distance. Another objection to them is that their firing mechanism is likely to be somewhat complex. They may have three triggers, or alternatively an arrangement whereby one trigger is pushed forward for use with the rifle.

drive   OE: n. a single *beat* in a day's *driven* or *covert* *shooting*. Also used as a verb, to move game towards waiting guns.

driven game   game driven towards waiting guns by beaters. Grouse driving appears to have begun not long after the start of the 19th century, although not really prevalent until the 1850s. Driving partridges and pheasants towards waiting guns followed with the development of the breech-loader.

driven shooting   see *covert shooting*.

droppings   OED: 'Dung of animals. (Now only pl).' The faeces of game birds, or beasts. Has now generally displaced the old special names; see *crottels*, *crotties*, *fewmets*.

drumming   used to describe the distinctive sound made by a snipe's tail feathers vibrating, most often heard when mating. See *common snipe*; *jack snipe*.

Ejector gun   one in which the cartridges are automatically ejected by an *extractor* mechanism fitted to the breech-end of the barrel and working when the gun is opened after being fired. An *ejector gun* can be told from a *non-ejector* at a glance by noting whether the extractor is in one piece or two. In 1888 W.W. Greener wrote: 'Modern sporting breech-loaders, like perfected military firearms, eject the fired case. This principle is certain to obtain popularity. There are difficulties in the way; but it should be remembered that every cartridge case after being fired contracts, and consequently is, or should be, comparatively loose in the chamber, requiring but little force of the right kind to effect its dislodgement' (p. 22). By 1930 Burrard wrote: 'From the point of view of efficiency, which is after all the most important, there is really little to choose between these two types of ejector . . . The Southgate is certainly more commonly fitted, but this may be on account of the greater simplicity of its design; for it is undoubtedly superior to the Deeley in this respect' (*Shotgun*, i, 118). See *hammerless-ejector*.

English pointer   OED: 'A dog of a breed nearly allied to the true hounds, used by sportsmen to indicate the presence of game, especially birds; on scenting which the dog stands rigidly with muzzle raised towards the game and usually one foot raised.' A breed of gundog originally introduced into this country by officers returning from the continent after the War of the Spanish Succession in Queen Anne's reign. The original deep-chested, slow-moving breed were crossed with English foxhounds and other blood to give them dash and pace. It has since developed into the breed we know today. Trained to *quarter* the ground to find game and to *point*, by standing rigidly with their head towards the game, English pointers, up to the introduction of the *breech-loader*, were also expected to retrieve game. Today they are expected to point only. The average height of the dogs at the shoulder is 26–28 inches and of the bitches 24–26 inches. Having only been introduced in the reign of Queen Anne, Pennant in 1768 could write: 'The Pointer, which is a dog of foreign extraction, was unknown to our ancestors' (i, 54). In 1837, on the other hand, Thomas Bell wrote: 'The Spanish pointer was formerly known as a staunch, strong and useful, but heavy and lazy dog. The English breed, however, is now very much preferred' (*History of British Quadrupeds*, 217). In 1859 no less an authority than Charles Darwin noted: 'The English Pointer has been greatly changed within the past century' (*Origin of the Species*, i, 25). By 1938 the Duke of Montrose could write more fully:

66

The type of pointer favoured in Britain today is a fine dog, somewhat taller than a foxhound, and keen and alert in expression and bearing. The head is carried well up, and is wide between the ears, with the nose square tipped and the nostrils soft and moist. The eyes are bright and full, and the ears, which are rather pointed, lie close to the head. The long sloping shoulders, the long back an the large straight legs all combine to give the pointer and air of symmetry and harmonious development. The feet should be pointed, like those of the hare or greyhound and not upstanding and round like those of a terrier. The tail should be fairly short but nicely pointed, and should be carried level, not dropping like a collie's or carried over the back like a foxhound's. (Sanderson)

See also *English setter*.

English setter   although setting dogs have been known for centuries and were used both for *hawking* and *netting* game, their descriptions closely resembling the *setters* of today, the breed as such was not established until the early 19th century. A beautiful dog with a coat of silky hair, a pronounced feather on the legs and a flagged tail, like the *English pointer* they were expected to retrieve in the early 19th century, before the introduction of the *breech-loader*. Thus in 1832 in *The Sporting Magazine*, the following appeared: 'A Pointer or Setter, to deserve the name should hunt high, but steadily; quarter his ground with truth and judgement; turn to hand or whistle; drop to hand, bird and shot; back at all distances; be steady from a hare, yet follow a wounded one if necessary; and recover a dead or wounded bird well.' Latterly they were expected only to *point*, or *set*, game. An instinctive reaction to lie down is still sometimes seen when they scent game, as a result of being trained for generations to lie to allow the net to be drawn easily over their backs, but this is now regarded as a fault. The average height of the dogs at the shoulder is 24–27 inches and of the bitches 23–25 inches.

English springer spaniel   this breed was probably the original type of setting spaniel trained to *spring* game for falconry and for coursing, as well as being used for *netting* from the 16th century onwards. The type, however, was not defined until the turn of the 19th century. Of black and white, liver and white, or any variation of spaniel colouring, it is the longest-legged of the land spaniel breeds and probably the most popular of the spaniel breeds today. Dogs should stand at the shoulder 17–20 inches and bitches from 16–18 inches. Unfortunately there is a clear division prevalent between working dogs and show specimens.

entire   of male animals, including deer; with both testicles dropped in the scrotum and functioning.

entry   of deer; a gap in the edge of a wood made by deer through which they are in the habit of moving.

Euston system   now generally obsolete. A method of hatching partridges by removing the eggs and replacing them with dummies, until those on the point of hatching under broody hens were then replaced. Although laborious, and requiring many underkeepers working on a large estate, the system had the advantage of bringing in fresh blood and that the parent birds reared the young in entirely natural circumstances. It also ensured that any nests laid in positions vulnerable to predators were saved. In 1938 Julian Tennyson wrote:

> Undoubtedly the Euston system, *if* it is successfully carried out, is an excellent way of maintaining and increasing the partridge stock, and the rough shooter may benefit enormously from it. But it is useless to think of trying it unless your time is your own . . . The Euston system is a wholetime job . . . On the rough shoot it is not necessary to practice the Euston system in full; in fact it need only be used with outlying and foolish nests. (p. 31)

Named after the Suffolk estate of Euston where it was claimed, incorrectly, that it was first practised, the system fell into disuse simply because of the labour involved once incubators were generally used instead of broody hens. Attempts to release partridges reared in incubators failed, because they formed packs and lost their territorial instinct. Today partridges can be reared in incubators and the territorial instinct can be retained by releasing up to sixteen or so young birds, one at a time each day, from strategically placed release pens, round which the released birds congregate until after a fortnight or three weeks all have been released, thus inculcating the requisite territorial instinct and ensuring that they remain in the chosen area. This method has replaced the Euston system entirely.

extractor   in 1930 Burrard described the extractor thus: 'A movable part of the breech end of a barrel which slides backwards when the gun is opened and withdraws the fired cartridge case from the chamber. In ejector guns which automatically throw out the fired case when they are opened, there is a separate extractor for each barrel' (*Shotgun*, i, 19). See *ejector gun*.

eye   once erroneously used in place of *nye*, for 'a brood of young pheasants', but this usage is now obsolete. See also *across-eyed stock; master eye.*

Face mask   netting or similar material covering the face and preventing its paleness showing up to incoming birds; generally used when wildfowling, pigeon decoying, *flighting*, or in similar pursuits. The principle of obscuring the face from full view by camouflaging it with mud, woad, etc. is one of the oldest known to man and common still amongst primitive tribes. It is probably preferable to wearing a face mask, which can be hot and sweaty. In 1964 Charles Coles wrote: 'When it grew shadowy under the trees I thankfully pulled off the face mask' (*Pigeons*, 58).

face of the action, action face   Burrard defined it thus: 'the smooth vertical portion which rises at right angles to the flats; Also sometimes called the Standing Breech' (*Shotgun*, 37). See *action*.

face of stock   the body of the *stock*, behind the *comb* of a shotgun, sometimes with a special rubber, leather, or wooden cheekpiece, or pad, added.

fag   of obscure etymology. Said of red deer; a small stag accompanying an older beast, generally to act as look-out. The word possibly results from transference of usage of fag (i.e. public school junior boy of service to a senior) by ex-public-school stalkers. See also *squire, stooge*.

fairweather shot   one who finds an excuse not to shoot when there is foul weather in the offing. Sometimes combined with *foreshore cowboys* as a derisive term.

fallow   fallow deer, *Dama dama*. The original park deer, introduced to this country by the Normans. The male is known as a *buck* and the female as a *doe*; the young are known as *fawns*. The fallow buck sheds his antlers in April/May and they are usually free of velvet by September. The antlers are *palmated*. Midway in size between the roe and the red deer, bucks stand about 32–38 inches and does about 32–34 inches at the shoulder. The average weight of bucks is 9–10 stone and of does 7–8 stone. The variations in colouring are considerable, from reddish brown in the common fallow, to black, white, blue grey, sooty dun, sandy and menil. Without their antlers it can therefore often be very difficult to tell them apart from other deer. Their gaits vary, like red deer, but they are particularly notable for their *pronking*. Like the red deer they jump extremely well. Like red and sika deer they are gregarious and form herds, the bucks forming bachelor groups for much of the year. During the rut the bucks do not have to herd the does in the same way that red deer stags have to herd their hinds, as the does are content not to wander. The gestation period is about seven and a half months and fawns are usually born about mid-May. Does are often followed by a fawn and yearling. Normally a forest dweller, but will live in the open as well if forced to do so through lack of cover. They are remarkable for their ability to lie concealed in minimal cover.

false point   of a pointing dog; to *point* where no game lies; a common mistake of young dogs not fully acquainted with the meaning of the different scents. They may point mice nests, or mole hills or other interesting smells. Such youngsters are often found to *false point* at larks. This is also sometimes a fault of more mature dogs, who should know better; hence possibly one source of the saying 'Stop larking about', although not one given by the OED. Youngsters should certainly be discouraged when they do so and should soon learn to ignore larks and other distractions. An older dog which consistently false points, however, is a nuisance and may even have to be discarded. See *pointer*.

fat buck   of fallow deer; a buck in prime condition.

fawn   OF. OED: a young fallow deer, a buck or doe of the first year. In this sense first attested by Chaucer *c.* 1369. *In-fawn* may be said of a doe when pregnant. Also of *Chinese water-deer* and *muntjac*; the young of either sex in the first year.

feather   verb, of a gundog: to wave the tail eagerly, usually with the head down and questing while attempting to find a scent. Also used as a noun, of long-haired gundogs, esp. *setters*, a plentiful supply of protective hair on the back of the legs or tail; see *flag*.

Also often used as a loose generic term, signifying all forms of gamebirds as opposed to *groundgame*, i.e. hares and rabbits; in this usage the latter are generally termed simply *fur*: The total *bag* for a day's shooting may thus be said to include both fur and feather. Similarly, a gundog may be said to be steady to feather, but not fur, or have a *soft mouth* on feather but not on fur, signifying that it will retrieve game birds with a soft mouth but with groundgame has a *hard mouth*, the latter usually being the result of poor introduction to groundgame. 'The true Clumber may easily be kept strictly to feather . . . though they will readily hunt fur when nothing else is to be had' (Walsh, 64).

feed   of game: n. a feeding place with *feed hopper* or *feed stack*; v. to provide feed for game.

feed hopper   a container holding grain, or pellets, for feeding game. Of many kinds; may be automatic, providing feed at regular intervals and even providing a recognised feeding signal;

may be a container with feed available on a gravity system
whenever the gamebird wishes to help itself. These are often
made from old oil-cans and similar containers and placed at
strategic positions within the *coverts* to encourage birds not to
stray. Placed in *rides*, or similar spots, gamebirds soon learn to
feed from them during the winter months when natural feed is
scarce. See also *feed stack*; *Warfarin*.

feed stack   usually consists of a heap of *tailings* on a straw
base, placed under a hurdle, or piece of corrugated sheeting,
resting on bales of straw to act as protection from the weather.
This provides a place for birds to rake about for feed and is
easily replenished as required.

feep   a sound made mainly by roe does. In 1974 Holmes
declared: 'Another sound by which roe communicate is so soft
that it is either missed or associated with a bird, rather than an
animal of the size of roe. The Germans call it "fiepen" and
because I find this word onomatopoeic I decided to adopt it for
the purpose of this discussion as "feep." The sound is uttered
by both sexes in various situations, but only rarely by mature
bucks' (p. 93). See also *peep*.

Fenn trap   an approved humane type of spring trap for small
predators such as rats, stoats and weasels. There are the Mark
IV for small ground predators and the Mark VI general purpose
trap for small ground predators, rabbits and mink.

ferret   OF *fuiron* going back to the L *furon-em*, 'robber', hence
the French diminutive *furet*, i.e. 'little robber'. OED: 'A half-
tamed variety of the common *polecat* (*Puterius foetidus*) kept for
the purpose of driving rabbits from their burrows, destroying
rats, etc.' A small furred mammal, a near relative of the polecat,
which it resembles, it is trained for the sport of ferreting rabbits
and also rats, and is of two distinct kinds; the larger cream
coloured type and the smaller darker brown polecat-cross,
generally known as a *fitchet*. The male is known as a *hob*, the
female as a *jill*. They are inserted in the burrows to bolt the
rabbits into *purse nets*, or for shooting. An early reference is
in 1616 by Markham: 'Good hunters will never put their ferret
into any earth, whose mouth they see stopt' (*Farme*, 647). In
1768 Pennant noted uncertainly, if accurately: 'Warreners assert
that the Polecat will mix with the ferret' (i, 78). In 1847 in the
Penny Cyclopedia it was sensibly stated: 'Ferrets should not be
fed before they are taken to the warren.'

fetch   OE. OED: 'To go in quest of, and convey or conduct
back.' First attested in 1000. Also, 'To fetch and carry; lit:

chiefly of dogs.' Shakespeare, 1591 (*Two Gentlemen from Verona*, iii. i. 274): 'Her Masters-maid ... hath more qualities than a Water Spaniell ... Imprimis, Shee can fetch and carry.' In 1621 Markham, well ahead of his time, described how to train such a dog to *retrieve*, using the word *fetch*:

> The Water Dogge: Traine him to fetch whatsoever you shall throw from you, as Staves, or Cudgels, Bagges, Nettes, Instruments of all kindes, and indeed anything whatsoever is portable; then you shall use him to fetch round cogell stones, and flints, which are troublesome in a Dogges mouth, and lastly, Iron, Steel, Money and all kindes of metall, which being colde in his teeth, slippery and ill to take up, a Dogge will be loth to fetch, but you must not desist, or let him taste food till he will familiarly bring and carry them as anything else whatsoever. (*Fowling*)

'Fetch' is therefore one of the oldest commands to a retriever and is often still used as a command to retrieve as an alternative to the possibly even older command *hie lost*.

fewmets   AF. OED: or *fumet*, from *fumer*, archaic word for dung, itself now a semi-obsolete term for droppings of a deer.

field-craft   knowledge of nature and the ways of wild animals, enabling the hunter to find and get close to game; 'No-one ... expects to fill his bag save by "field-craft"' (*Pall Mall Gazette*, 26 September 1887).

field spaniel   a breed originally developed as a heavier version of the *cocker*, about 1870. It was ruined by breeders who developed the long low body, which reduced the animal to an absurdity. Although uncommon they are still to be seen and are nowadays a more sensible size, resembling the *Sussex spaniel*, but larger, the dogs standing 15–18 inches at the shoulder and the bitches about 12–15 inches.

field sports   the OED gives 'Outdoor sports, esp. hunting.' 1674: 'Field sports of wch I have ever bin a lover' (*Essex Papers*: Camden:I:210). 1812: 'Field-sports..the chief pleasure of his own youthful days' (Scott, *Waverley*, iv). Today *field sports* is a term generally accepted as embracing hunting, shooting, fishing, coursing and falconry. See *anti's*; *sport*.

field trial   the OED gives 'a trial in the open field esp. of hunting dogs.' There is a little more to it than that. In 1865 the first *field trials* for gundogs were held at Southill near Bedford on the estate of S.M. Whitbread, for *pointers* and *setters* only. After the formation of the Kennel Club in 1873, field trials eventually became organised under their jurisdiction. To start with they consisted of Field Trials for Pointers and Setters or for Retrievers, the only two categories of gundog the Kennel Club then recognised. With the belated acknowledgement of *spaniels* as a third category of gundog in the first years of the 20th century, field trials also came to be accepted for them. Finally, in the 1950s a fourth category of gundog was acknowledged, 'Those breeds which Hunt, Point and Retrieve', generally known as the HPR breeds. Field trials were introduced for them too. The Kennel Club is now the final authority in any authorised field trials. Dogs which run in unrecognised field trials outside the Kennel Club's jurisdiction run the risk of being disqualified from running in field trials authorised by the KC. The Kennel Club also appoints recognised judges who are authorised to judge at KC-approved field trials. See *labrador*; *pointer-retriever*.

figure-of-four trap   a simple form of *deadfall* trap. In 1880 Carnegie described it thus:

> The materials required are simply three ordinary pieces of wood and a large, heavy, flat paving stone, or slate . . . The upright is usually cut about half an inch wide, shaved to a thin edge at the top. The slanting stick has a notch cut in it half an inch from its upper end to receive the upright, while its lower end is shaved off to fit in a notch on the upper surface of the front of the stretcher. Lastly the stretcher has this notch in front and another notch cut in its side, by which it is caught by the upright and held in its place. A bait being tied to the external end of the stretcher and a stone placed so that it will lie flat on the ground . . . Raise the stone and support it by the notched end of the slanting stick held in the left hand, the notch . . . downwards, then place the upright with one end on the ground and the other in this notch and let it carry the weight of the stone . . . finally hitch the middle notch of the stretcher in the upright, with its front notch facing upwards, then bring the lower end of the slanting stick down to this front notch, drop it in and the trap is set . . . In setting the figure of 4 trap the height of the upright and the size and weight of the stone will be proportioned to the animal for which it is set. (pp. 59–60)

As late as 1929 Mackie writes: 'Where stoats and weasels abound, it is most desirable to have a few flat stones or flags in suitable places, propped up by pieces of stick, set with the old figure-of-four trap. The slightest disturbance fetches the flag down, and the victim is at once crushed to death' (p. 131).

finish   of a gun, the result of the gunmaker's attention to every detail in the manufacture. In 1888 W.W. Greener (*Modern*

Shotguns 54) defined it thus: 'The well-finished gun will not only have a beautiful exterior, but the barrels, every piece of the mechanism, every bolt, pin and screw, will not only be perfectly fitted and well polished, but so placed as to be of actual service . . . Finish in this sense cannot be over-rated.'

firearms certificate   first introduced in 1914–18 War as temporary measure; issued by the police to those wishing to possess and use any firearm and ammunition after they have satisfied themselves as to the applicant's background and suitability. Full details of firearms and ammunition bought must be included. This covers all rifles used for sporting purposes or for target shooting. See *gun cabinet*.

fitchet   OF. OED gives *fitchet* (and *fitchew*) as diminutives of *fitch*, all meaning a polecat/*ferret* cross. In 1607 Topsell (*Historie*) wrote: 'They say "they stink like an Iltis", that is a fitch or poul-cat.' In 1772 Thomas Simpson listed: 'The Polecat, Fitchat, Fitchew, Formet' (*The Complete Vermin Killer*, 23).

flag   OED: 'The tail of a setter, or Newfoundland dog. Also of a deer'. 1859 J.S. Walsh (*Dog*, i, iv, 97): 'The stern, or flag (of the setter) . . . is furnished with a fan-like brush of long hair.' See *English setter*; *Gordon setter*.

flankers   OED: 'One posted or stationed on either flank': only used in a sporting sense for shooting since the introduction of driven game shooting in the mid-19th century. In 1897 it is noted:

> flankers . . . are most important and should be men with an intimate knowledge of the moors and of the usual flight of the grouse. Their duties are to act in advance of the driving line on either side and to prevent the grouse from breaking away and thus not going over the guns. A good 'flanker' will not put up his flag till the exact moment arrives, otherwise he might head the birds back instead of sending them forward, or turn them so much that they would break away over the flankers on the far side. (*Encyclopedia*, i, 490)

Mackie recommended coloured flags: 'In a first rate drive there should be from sixteen to twenty drivers, the best men being on the flanks . . . Different coloured flags should be used . . . plain white for the rank and file, red for the centre or head man, and red and white for the flank men' (p. 209). In 1930 their importance was again stressed: 'there should be two flankers, men who know the ground and can follow a signal intelligently. Nothing will turn back a covey of partridges that really means to fly home, but a good flanker can often steer a covey by a timely use of his flag' (*LL Shooting*, 88); 'flankers, men specially selected for their skill and knowledge of the moor and of grouse . . . showing themselves and waving their red flags to try to turn this or that lot of birds . . . trying to break out at the sides instead of coming forward to the guns' (ibid., 15). Brander defines them as: 'Experienced beaters with flags on poles, whose job is to walk on either flank of the beating line, probably well in advance of the others and to wave a flag to turn back any covey of grouse or partridges attempting to break sideways' (*Sporting Terms*). See **beaters**.

flapper   OED: one who, or that which, flaps, e.g. a young wild duck; young mallard. Gilbert White recorded in 1776: 'I saw young teals taken alive . . . along with flappers, or young wild duck' (p. 99). Hawker, in his *Instructions*, wrote somewhat contemptuously: '*Flappers;* to find a brood of these, go, about July, and hunt the rushes in the deepest and most retired parts of some brook . . . When once found the flappers are easily killed as they attain their full growth before their wings are fledged; and for this reason the sport is more like hunting water rats than shooting birds' (p. 193). In 1856 Walsh only mentioned them briefly: 'When the shooter seeks the wild duck in the shape of flappers he should go to the brook or pond where they are supposed to be in July' (p. 71). Speedy indicated that they were a poor quarry: 'Ducks when young – or "flappers" as they are termed – attract the attention of the sportsman early in August. . . . From their reluctance to fly and their slow, awkward, movements on the wing, they are at best but poor sport' (p. 293). In 1897 it was declared: 'Thanks to the "Wild Birds' Protection Acts" the abominations of what used to be termed "flapper shooting" are at an end' (*Encyclopedia*, ii, 343). Lord Malise Graham thought that 'A day spent in the early part of the season by the riverbank, shooting an occasional flapper, is excellent for teaching the young and inexperienced retriever' (Mackie, 327). In 1930 J.C.M. Nichols warned: 'The First of August marks the opening date for wild duck shooting – which is however subject to local variations . . . In a backward season a large proportion of ducks flushed on the opening day will be only immature "flappers"' (*LL Shooting*, 326).

flash   OED: possibly of onomatopoeic origin from MDu *plasch*, which seems to imitate the sound of 'splashing' in a puddle. The synonymous Fr *flache* may have influenced the English word. A pool, a marshy place: obsolete except locally.' In the *Anglo-Latin Lexicon* of *c*. 1440 it is noted: 'Plasche, or flasche, where reyne water stondythe.' Brander defined it as: 'A small pool, or pond, possibly the result of heavy rain, or floodwater, to which wildfowl are often attracted' (*Sporting Terms*, 84).

flash-in-the-pan still in occasional usage, this saying dates from the days of the *flint-lock* gun, when a miss-fire resulted in the flint sparking off the priming powder in the 'pan' but failing to ignite the main charge, because the touchhole leading to it was blocked, or the charge damp. The OED gives, 'See quotation 1810', and quotes Charles James's *Military Dictionary*: '*Flash in the pan*; an explosion of gunpowder without any communication beyond the touchhole.' The OED also gives: '*To flash in the pan*: literally; said of a gun when the priming powder is kindled without igniting the charge. *Figuratively;* to fail after a showy effort; to fail to go-off.' An example cited was William Jerdan (*Autobiography*, 1850, 237): 'Cannon attempted a joke which flashed in the pan.'

flat-coated retriever a gundog breed evolved during the latter half of the 19th century from a cross between a setter, possibly **Gordon**, or **Irish**, and the **Labrador**, or Newfoundland dog. Originally known as the wavy coat, it was amongst the most popular of retriever breeds at the turn of the century. Its colour is liver or black, and its coat dense, flat and fine textured. The average height of the dogs at the shoulder is 24–26 inches and of the bitches 22–24 inches. Of good *nose* and endurance, it is generally a *soft-mouthed* and useful working retriever.

flats of the action OED: in a breechloading gun, the piece of metal projecting from the breech to support the barrel. 'When the barrels are forged, the flats are formed on the underside of the breech ends' (*The Greener Gun*, 1881, 230). Burrard wrote: 'The Flats of the action comprise the flat upper surface of the bar and come into contact with the flats of the barrels when the gun is put together' (*Shotgun*, i, 37).

flats of the barrels see *flats of the action*.

flehman of deer, horses, and most ruminants; the behaviour reflex of males often after savouring the scent of the female urine, or some strange or unusual tastes; the head is raised and the upper lip curls back baring the teeth, while the lower lip droops.

flighting, flight-shooting OED: 'Shooting wildfowl, ducks and geese, or pigeons on their line of flight at dawn or dusk.' As early as 1815 Hawker wrote: 'Warren Farm has excellent flighting when the wind is from S. to W' (*Diaries*, 14 January). In 1830 he noted:

For shooting woodpigeons ... some hide themselves among
the trees, where they come to roost after sunset ... the most
effectual way is to shoot them when they come to the turnips
in snowy weather. If you make a place in the hedge, it is
preferable to the common plan of putting up hurdles covered
with straw, as the woodpigeons are apt to notice and feed out
of reach of them. [...] In some, though now very few retired
places the diversion of what is called flight shooting is
excellent to those who are neither prepared nor disposed to
follow wildfowl in a more scientific manner ... Flight shooting is always followed with most success in very boisterous
weather ... as this not only obliges them to fly low, but
doubles them well together. (*Instructions*, 221; 307)
In 1845 St John recommended flighting mallard in the evening:
'As the corn ripens they fly to the oat fields in the dusk of the
evening, preferring this grain and peas to any other. They are
now in good order and easily shot as they come regularly to the
same fields every night' (p. 146). Speedy advised on the habits
of the wildfowl: 'Resting all day in the sea or large lakes, ducks
at dusk repair inland to feed on the stubbles, potato fields, small
lochs, brooks and marshes. ... If a hedge or wall be at the side
of the field, where the sportsman can conceal himself, he will
get shots at them as they fly overhead' (p. 295). In 1929 Lord
Malise Graham noted: 'It is about sunset that some of the best
sport ... may be obtained. The wild duck will congregate at
dusk in some pond, and if the right spot be found the air will be
thick with them flying to and fro for about twenty minutes.
This period of flighting, as it is called, rarely lasts for more than
half an hour' (Mackie, 324). J.S. Henderson observed:
> This form of sport, which is annually becoming more popu-
> lar, is, in the writer's opinion, before all other forms of
> shoulder gun-shooting ... The evening, for about half an
> hour just at twilight, is the most suitable time. ... A good
> moon and lots of white fleecy clouds are by far the best
> conditions for showing up the birds to advantage ... At dawn
> the birds may be intercepted returning from their feeding-
> grounds (ibid., 331).
Eric Parker is even more specific:
> Morning flighting: By getting out to your shooting ground
> before daybreak and waiting for the ducks to come to it at
> dawn ... two or three guns may very well bag twice or three
> times the number of fowl obtainable ... during the daytime
> ... mallard, teal and wigeon, will be arriving in pairs and
> small bunches from daybreak to perhaps eight o'clock of a

winter's morning giving a plentiful series of shots at fair ranges[...] Evening flighting: Rather more prolonged sport can be got by heavily baiting a secluded pool ... It is best to post yourself with your back to the wind, for whatever direction the ducks may be coming from they are sure to turn into the wind before alighting. (*LL Shooting*, 237; 238) See also *face mask*; *greylag*; *white front*; *wildfowling*; *woodpigeon*.

flight pond   a natural or artificial pond used for the purpose of *flighting* wildfowl.

flint-lock   OED: 'a. A gun lock in which a flint, screwed to the cock, is struck against the hammer and produces sparks, which ignite the priming in the flash-pan: b. a gun fitted with this lock.' All such guns were inevitably *muzzle-loaders*, as the *breech-loader* was only introduced in the 1850s long after the introduction of the *percussion cap* in the first decade of the 19th century. 'It were therefore good that for half of the Muskets (if not for them all) flint-locks were made' (Sir James Turner, *Pallas Armata*, 1683, p. 176). See *flash-in-the-pan*.

flush   etymology obscure, perhaps onomatopoeic. OED, v: 'to cause to fly or take wing; to put up, start.' To cause game to take flight or break cover. This may be the result of a shot, or sudden sound, or the movement of hunting dogs, spaniels or pointers, or as a result of beaters beating a covert, driving to the guns. An early example of the usage is in 1450 in the *Boke of Hawkyng*: 'Let the spanyell flusch up the covey.' Also n., a number of pheasants breaking cover together are called a *flush*. See also *acknowledge*; *bouquet*; *honour*; *sewelling*; *sewin*.

flushing point   a place where birds are forced to take flight from a covert when being driven forwards, due to the presence of either *sewelling*, or wire netting. Care should be taken with the siting of *flushing points* that they are suitably placed in relation to the waiting guns to provide the highest possible shot, also that there is sufficient clearance to encourage the birds to take wing and enable them to attain maximum height and speed before reaching the guns. At the same time, flushing points should not be so far back that a pheasant is likely to pitch back into the covert before reaching the guns. If the flushing point is placed so that the guns can be stationed behind a river, the birds will rise very much higher at the sight of water in front of them. Pheasants will also tend to be rising if a flushing point faces a hill well covered with trees towards which they are forced to fly. Guns placed between a flushing point high on a slope in front of them and with a similar tree-clad slope behind

them are ideal for showing **high birds** rising to clear the trees
they see facing them.

followers   of deer; young beasts following a mature female.
Deer are largely matriarchal and an old hind will usually be the
leader of any group, except during the rut.

foot scent   the OED only gives: 'Foot-scent: *Hunting*: the scent
of a trail,' but see *road*. Of a gundog: it is the *scent* left on the
ground by the feet of game, esp. wounded game: 'take the
picture of a pointer working out the scent of a covey of
partridges that have been flushed. Then the air scenter is clearly
following a foot scent' (Brander, *Dog*, 11). See *air scent*,
ground scent.

fore-end   OED: the forepart of the stock of a gun which
supports the barrel. In 1881 it is noted: 'The finisher . . . has to
file up and shape the stock and the fore-end' (*The Greener Gun*,
250). 'All that is required is a sufficient grip to keep the fore-
end to the barrels' (ibid, 256). 'Grasp the gun . . . close to the
fore-end tip' (ibid, 487). The wooden addition beneath the
barrels of a shotgun, clipping on to the *barrel-loop*. The
concave steel fitting at the rear end of the *fore-end* rotates on the
knuckle of the action when the gun is broken, and this customarily operates the mechanism of the lock and ejector mechanism. The fore-end may be tapered for lightness, or deepened
into beaver-tail shape for convenience and ease of grip and as a
protection against hot, or freezing, barrels. It is commonly held
in place by a snap spring bolt, but three varieties are common:
  1. the Anson, where the bolt is released by a stud beyond the
apex of the fore-end – also known as the push-rod fore-end;
  2. the Deeley, where the bolt is released by a metal lever in
the forward part of the fore-end;
  3. the simple 'snap' variety which snaps into place.

foreshore   that part of the shore between the low and the high
water marks, where wildfowl shooting is legal throughout the
shooting season from 1 September until 20 February. Hence
foreshore cowboy, a derisive wildfowling term first used in the
1950s for those novices who patrol the *foreshore* in full view of
all the wildfowl, letting off their guns at any bird whether within
range or not. They are a nuisance to everyone; see also
fairweather shot.

forest   OF. OED: an extensive tract of land covered with trees
and undergrowth, sometimes intermingled with pasture, but see
deer forest.

Forest Laws   instituted originally by King Canute and later
appropriated by the Normans after the Conquest in 1066 as a

means of control and taxation, their authority degenerated in the wars of the Middle Ages and finally the Dissolution of the Monasteries, until eventually they became, under the Tudors and subsequently, the basis for the modern Game Laws. The Forest Laws named the Beasts of the Forest, and as late as 1807 Daniel lists:

five Beasts, which are properly Beasts of Forest, or venery, viz., the Hart, Hind, Hare, Boar and Wolf.

The Hart is so named when in his sixth year, being called in the first year, *Hind-calf*, or *Calf*, in the second a *Knobler*, in the third a *Brocket*, or *Spayard*; in the fourth, a *Staggart*; in the fifth, a *Stag*; in the sixth, a *Hart*; after being chased by the King or Queen, if he escapes, he is a *Hart royal*. The Hind in the first year is called *Calf*; in the second year a *Hearse* or *Brocket's Sister*; in the third an *Hind*.

The Hare is a *Leveret* in the first year; a *Hare* in the second, and a *great Hare* in the third.

The Boar in the first year is a *Pig of the Sounder*; in the second a *Hog*; in the third an *Hog Steer*, in the fourth a *Boar*; at which age, if not before he leaves the *Sounder*. (i, 260)

fork   of antlers; the two points on top of the antlers, forming a *fork*.

form   OED: 'the nest, or lair, in which a hare crouches; also, rarely, of a deer.' An early example of the usage is *c.* 1386 from Chaucer in *The Shipman's Tale*: 'As in a fourme sitteth a very hare.' In 1576 Turberville wrote: 'When a hare ryseth out of the fourme' (*Venerie*, 161). In 1616 Markham foreshadowed Mrs Beeton: 'The first point . . . for the killing of the hare consisteth in finding out her forme' (*Farme*, 695). In 1799 James Robertson noted of deer: 'The young keep close to their form, until the dam return to raise them' (*General View of the Agriculture of Perth*, 29). The word *form* implies the scrape in which a hare lies: this may be no more than the impression caused by its body weight wriggled down in the mud of a field, or amid stubble, or grass. A hare will often reach its form only after elaborate back-tracking and precautions, leaping some six to nine feet sideways to reach it, in order to mislead possible enemies following its scent trail; the hare relies on absolute stillness in the form to escape observation. The OED also gives 'v. of a hare: To take to her form; to seat.' Significantly, no later example is given than 1801; this usage is now obsolete. See **common brown hare, ground game, hare myths, hare's birth, hare's breath, puss, trace.**

forward   warning cry sometimes used by beaters when game has been *flushed* and is flying towards the guns. This probably originated from the fox-hunting cry 'For'ard on!' when the fox has gone in front. Alternatively, it might have originated from the golfer's cry of 'Fore' when a golfball was in danger of hitting the players in front, both sports pre-dating shooting.

forward allowance   the theoretical amount allowed in front of a crossing bird when swinging the gun and pulling the trigger. This must vary from individual to individual and the important point is never to cease swinging before pulling the trigger as this leads to *poking*.

The period of time which must elapse between the shooter's mental decision to fire and the arrival of the shot charge at the bird . . . (is) divisible into three distinct periods; namely:

1. The time taken for the brain's decision to fire to the actual pressing of the trigger, which can be called the 'Sportsman's Time.'

2. The time taken from the pressing of the trigger to the exit of the shot charge at the muzzle, which is known as the 'Time up the Barrel.'

3. The time taken from the exit of the shot charge at the muzzle to its arrival at the target, perhaps 40 yards or more away, which is the 'Time of Flight.'

The first of these periods cannot be measured and must vary not only with individuals, but with individuals at different times and even at different times on the same day. It can be overcome by 'swing', that is by shooting with a moving gun. (*Shotgun*, iii, 177)

fouling   the deposit left in the barrels after the gun has been fired. It should be removed with a *cleaning rod* and *jag*.

fox   OE. OED: 'An animal of the genus *Vulpes* having an elongated pointed muzzle and a long bushy tail, usually *Vulpes vulgaris*, preserved in England and elsewhere as a beast of the chase.' A familiar russet-furred, bushy-tailed predator of game birds and their young, leaving obvious signs of its presence in the shape of the wings of its kill neatly shorn off and sometimes a half-buried, half-eaten carcase. In a non-hunting country the game-preserver should shoot, trap, or in the last resort kill foxes by gassing, if he must, whenever possible. Foxes are extremely adaptable and cunning predators and scavengers, now adapting themselves readily to urban and semi-urban life. Whereas a few foxes may be beneficial to the balance of nature, it is very easy to have too many.

fray   of a deer; v. to rub its antlers against a tree, post, stone or bush, to rid them of the *velvet* and also on occasions during the rut to relieve aggressiveness and frustration. This can cause damage to trees, especially with fallow deer during the rut, but usually less so than *browsing*. Since antlers in velvet are tender and easily damaged, it is only after it is hanging *in tatters* that any damage is likely to be caused to trees. Usually this is quite a brief period, lasting merely a matter of an hour or so. The greatest damage to forestry is caused by deliberate *fraying*.

The term fraying means deliberate use of the antlers, and it is this that seriously damages trees because the bark is stripped off. [. . .] Aggressive fraying is an activity of dominant bucks and expresses displaced antagonism. The aggressive mood is brought on by threats to the territory, and therefore aggressive fraying is more common when there are many roaming non-territorial bucks. It has been called display fraying, presumably meaning threat display. The buck usually chooses a small scrub tree or bush on which to vent his feelings and he often attacks the branches more than the stem [. . .] In contrast the frustrated buck attacks numerous trees, sometimes an almost unbelievable number. Perhaps the reason is that frustration is a more lasting mood than aggressiveness . . . Frustration fraying is an activity of non-territorial bucks which are hounded from pillar to post and it is most conspicuous near a fence because the animal's progress was impeded by it. The frustrated buck usually attacks trees about three to four years old and attacks the stems rather than the branches, leaving the bark hanging in shreds and thus often killing the trees. (Holmes, 104)

fraying post, or **stock**   of deer; any post, tree, stone or bush against which a deer rubs off the velvet and also sometimes used during the rut to express aggression, irritation, frustration, or warning. See *fray*.

Frenchman   long accepted nick-name for the *red-legged partridge*, first imported from France during the reign of Charles II after the Restoration in 1660.

full choke   a *choke* of 40 points.

fur   of game, signifying *groundgame*, i.e. hares and rabbits, as opposed to *feather*, i.e. gamebirds. Walsh on the Clumber: 'they will readily hunt fur when nothing else is available' (p. 64).

G **adwall** *Anas strepera.* OED: 'A freshwater duck; of the north of Europe and America; the grey duck, or grey.' An early reference was in 1777 by G. Forster (*Voyage Around the World*, i, 157): 'A small brown duck, which is nearly the same size as the English gadwall.' In 1884 Lord Malmesbury noted, 'We also killed a great many wild duck, gadwalls and snipe, by walking through the marshes' (*Memoirs*, i, 26). The drake is grey with chestnut wing coverts and a black stern, a grey bill and orange-yellow legs. The duck resembles the *mallard* but has a white speculum and more pointed wings than the mallard. The size is about 20 inches from beak to tail and the season as for other wildfowl.

gait the OED gives the original spelling as *gate*, with this form only becoming common in the mid-18th century. Of deer, their paces when moving; walk, trot, gallop. See *pronking*.

gallery shot from 'playing to the gallery' of an actor playing to the spectators in cheapest seats, hence to the least discriminating audience. A particularly spectacular shot killing a high pheasant, or sporting grouse or partridge which had flown down the line, towards the end of a drive in full view of beaters and guns, is sometimes wrongly classified as a *gallery shot*. A gallery shot would in fact be a simple one, taken in front of a group of wives and less knowledgeable spectators, for example at a clay-pigeon shoot, as is shown by this usage in the *Pall Mall Gazette*: 'It is a gallery shot in a sense ... for the bird is flying level' (November 1897).

game OE. OED: '10. The object of the chase; the animal, or animals, hunted'. The first attestation in this sense is in *The Boke of St Albans*, 1486. An interesting example of the usage is in William Shakespeare's *Cymbeline*, Act III Scene iii: 'Hearke, the Game is rows'd ... the Game is up' (1611). In this latter sense it is exactly opposed to common usage today. Also: '11: Collectively: Wild animals or birds, such as are pursued, caught, or killed in the chase.' The first attestation in this sense is in 1290. A wide-ranging example of this usage, although still not all-embracing, is to be found in the Act of 1862, Victoria Regina, 25 & 26: 'The word "Game" in this Act ... shall be deemed to include any One or more Hares, Pheasants, Partridges, Eggs of Pheasants and Partridges, Woodcocks, Snipes, Rabbits, Grouse, Black or Moor Game, and Eggs of Grouse, Black or Moor Game'. Also '11 b. The flesh of such animals used for food.' An example of this usage is to be found in 1848, in William Thackeray's *Vanity Fair*: 'What good dinners you have – game every day.' Although pheasant *cocks* might be

84

included as *game* in this sense, game-cocks were only regarded as game in the sense of being stout fighters, not wild birds. The *Game Laws* dictate to a large extent which birds and beasts are regarded as game. Any bird or beast named in the Licence to shoot game, may be classified as game, but there are still many anomalies. For example a Game Licence is not required for shooting wildfowl, woodpigeons, hares and rabbits. Yet wildfowl, woodpigeons, hares and rabbits could certainly be included in a game-pie and are generally entered in any *game book*. Hares and rabbits are also classified separately as *groundgame*.

game bag   OED: 'A bag for holding the game killed by a sportsman.' All that glitters is not gold, and all game is not killed by sportsmen. A *game bag* is used for carrying game and is generally fitted with a broad strap for carrying comfortably over the shoulder. Waistcoat types of game bag are sometimes favoured, especially by American sportsmen: these fit over the shoulders and buckle at the waist like a waistcoat. Any game bag should be washable, in order to remove blood and feathers, and should be kept clean. It should be large but not too large, a point emphasised by Brander '*Gamebag*: This should be roomy enough to take a large pair of hares at a pinch. That will probably be as much as most people will want to carry any distance . . .' (*Roughshoot*, 24). A good early example of the usage is in Mary Russell Mitford's *Country Sketches* (1826): 'Powder horns, shot belts and game bags scattered about.' See *bag*.

game bird   the birds listed as game birds are as follows: blackgame. i.e. black cock and grey hen; capercailzie; grouse; partridges; pheasants; ptarmigan; snipe; woodcock. Wildfowl and waders, though they may be included in the bag during the shooting season, and may be included in the loose generic term *feather* as opposed to *fur*, are in separate categories of their own: see *game season*.

game book   a book containing a record of each shooting day, including a list of the *bag* and relevant details of the guns, weather, drives, etc. The more detail of each day included the more interesting reading in later years. Mackie recommended:

> The keeper's game-book should be kept correctly, regularly and methodically. Details of the day's sport should be filled in every evening and on no account left over until the following day. The facts entered should include the number of guns, the details of the bag, the number of hours the guns were shooting, the state of the weather, the part of the ground

shot over, and any particular and interesting circumstances relating to the day's sport which may have appealed to the keeper. (p. 509)

One of the earliest game books extant is probably that kept by the Cokes of Holkham, the Earls of Leicester, in Norfolk. It is said that the politician Charles James Fox, a friend and frequent visitor, who enjoyed shooting, first suggested keeping a record of the sport, then an entirely novel idea. The earliest book is a folio volume bound in vellum, in scrawling handwriting covering the period from September 1793 to 9 October 1798, recording only the amounts of game killed each day and its disposal: on 21 October 1793, for instance, Mrs Fitzherbert (the Prince of Wales's mistress) was given a hare and a brace of pheasants. The second game book is a quarto volume, bound in vellum and neatly kept in copper-plate writing, with the names of the guns recorded as well as the bag. It runs from 1 September 1797 to 1 December 1798. Fox and Sheridan the playwright were frequent visitors and seem to have been good but erratic shots. In the 1830s an element of humour appears for the first time: '23rd October 1830. General Ferguson killed a cat big with young. How barbarous!' 'January 29th 1834: Sir Ronald Ferguson was too gallant to shoot at a pheasant of the female sex.' An interesting entry for 16 November 1837 reads: 'General Ferguson shot a *two legged* fox' (presumably a poacher).

Game Conservancy   originally formed in the 1950s as a small off-shoot of ICI's Ely-Kynoch cartridge-making subsidiary, with a view to providing a helpful advisory service on game for its major customers, it became extremely successful and sought-after, eventually branching out on its own under the leadership of Charles Coles. Although only founded as a charity in its present form in 1961, the Game Conservancy is now internationally recognised as a leading authority on conservation and research into wildlife. A body devoted to the interests of shooting, particularly game shooting, it provides a unique service to all interested in rearing and preserving game and shooting on however small or large a scale. Its advisory service is second to none in the world and it is deservedly widely supported by most keen game shooters in Britain. An interesting early usage of conservation in the 'green' sense.

gamekeeper   OED: 'A servant employed in take care of game, to prevent poaching etc.' One who is employed to preserve game, to keep down predators and poaching and organise the management of a shoot in conjunction with the owner or shoot manager. The first attestation appears to be in Acts of Charles II, 1670–1: 'Act 22 & 23: Bee it enacted ... that all Lords of Mannours ... may ... authorize one or more ... Gamekeepers ... who ... may take and seize all such Gunns, Bowes, etc.' Mackie declared that: 'knowledge, skill, perseverance, discrimination, firmness, order, courtesy and enthusiasm – these are the eight primary requirements for a good keeper' (p. 29). A notable review by Ed *Zern*, editor of *Field & Stream*, on a book purporting to cover the life and times of a gamekeeper named Mellors reads:

> this fictional account of the day-to-day life of an English gamekeeper is still of considerable interest to outdoorminded readers, as it contains many passages on pheasant raising, the apprehension of poachers, ways of controlling vermin, and other chores and duties of the professional gamekeeper. Unfortunately one is obliged to wade through many pages of extraneous material in order to discover and savor these sidelights on the management of a Midland shooting estate, and in this reviewer's opinion this book cannot take the place of J.R. Miller's *Practical Gamekeeping*. (Reprinted in Zern, *Hunting and Fishing from A to Zern*, 1985, p. 311)

game larder a means of keeping game cool, fresh and free from flies. It should be provided with hooks to hang the game, allowing free access for air currents. It should be large enough to hang whatever quantity of game is likely to be shot.

Game Laws OED: Laws enacted for the preservation of Game. They were a natural follow-on to the *Forest Laws*. Charles I's attempt to revive the Forest Laws to 'enforest' or take over large tracts of country as a means of raising revenue was a contributory factor in his downfall. After the Restoration in 1670 and throughout the following century, right up to the accession of Victoria, the Game Laws were chaotic. It was only by the Edwardian era that the Game Laws began to achieve their present state and radical revisions have continued from the Firearms Act in 1914 to the present day. An early reference is in Sir William Blackstone's *Commentaries on the Laws of England* (1769): 'Though the Forest Laws are now mitigated ... yet from this root has sprung up a bastard slip known by the name of the game-law.' By 1823, when veterans of Waterloo and the Napoleonic Wars were being hung and transported for poaching game to support their starving families, Sydney Smith complained: 'The game laws have been carried to a pitch of oppression which is a disgrace to the country' (*Works*, ii, 32). By 1830 Hawker wrote: 'Nothing has yet been done with the

Game Laws!' (*Instructions*). As late as March 1845, he noted in
his Diary: '13th ... I was busy all morning ... among other
things sketching some amendments to the game laws on which
a committee has just been appointed in the House of
Commons.'

Game Licence   it is illegal to shoot game in Britain without a
Game Licence, obtainable at the Post Office. A bona-fide gamekeeper is entitled to a gamekeeper's licence at reduced rates.

game predators   enemies of game birds, which prey on
gamebirds and/or **groundgame**. The list includes amongst
winged predators, hooded and carrion crows, rooks, greater
black-backed gulls, lesser black-backed gulls, herring gulls,
magpies, jackdaws, jays, hawks, harriers, buzzards, owls and
eagles. Amongst ground predators are foxes, wild cats, feral
cats, rats, stoats, weasels, badgers, hedgehogs, mink, feral ferrets
and polecats. Many of the above are only occasional predators
and are in any event scarce or non-existent in some areas. Many
are also protected species and may not be shot, trapped or
persecuted. Others, such as rats and mink, should be trapped,
shot and otherwise dealt with whenever possible, as they are
enemies of all birds and of many domestic animals as well.

game preserve   OED: 'A wood or other ground set apart for
the protection and rearing of game: Areas chiefly devoted to the
preservation of game, and the rearing of game birds, where one
or more game keepers are employed.' In 1812 William Wind-
ham stated: 'They preserved them as country gentlemen do
the game in those places near their houses, which by an odd
misnomer are sometimes called "the preserve", where the game
are indeed preserved but only until some circumstance ... shall
furnish an occasion for falling on them with redoubled fury'
(*Speeches*).

game preserver   OED: '1. One who preserves game, fish etc.,
for sport.' One who preserves game, breeds game birds and
protects them from predators. Hence game preservation, the
breeding of game birds, their protection and care, not necessarily only on game preserves. While a gamekeeper is a game
preserver first and foremost, not all game preservers are necessarily gamekeepers, or even professionals. Many keen amateurs
are excellent game preservers. OED: '2. One who preserves the
bodies or stuffed skins of animals; a taxidermist.' Hence in
Hawker's *Instructions*, under 'Preservers of Birds, etc.', is
inserted: 'Leadbetter, Mr., 19 Brewer Street, Golden Square,
who stuffs for the British Museum' (p. 479).

game season   the periods during which game may be shot, as follows:

grouse and ptarmigan: 12 August to 10 December

snipe: 12 August to 31 January

blackgame: 20 August to 10 December

wildfowl: (geese and ducks) and woodcock in Scotland: 1 September to 1 February

partridges: 1 September to 1 February

capercailzie and woodcock in England and Wales: 1 October to 31 January

pheasant: 1 October to 1 February

groundgame, i.e. hares and rabbits: throughout the year.

game shot   one who shoots game birds either driven, or walking-up, or over dogs: see *gun*.

gapes   OED: a disease in poultry, etc. of which frequent gaping is the symptom. A disease common in the rearing field amongst young pheasants, but also virulent amongst young partridges, hence the inadvisability of rearing pheasants on good partridge ground. The disease is caused by a nematode worm, *Syngamus trachealis*, colloquially termed the red, or gape, worm. This causes choking in the young bird because of infestation of the throat, or trachea. The disease can now be readily treated with modern drugs, but infected ground should be ploughed up and limed. This is another reason for not rearing young birds near poultry, which are also subject to the disease. One of the earliest references appears in 1799 in *The Medical Journal*: 'There is a disease prevalent among the gallinaceous poultry in this country called the gaps' (ii, 204).

garganey   OED notes: '(Taken from Gesner *Hist. Anim.* 1555 Volume III 127. who gives *garganey* (sic) as the Italian name used about Bellinzona; the diminutive, *garganello*, he says was in Italy applied to various other birds of similar appearance.) A species of teal: *Anas querquedula*'. In 1678 Ray Willoughby noted: 'The Garganey . . . in bigness it something exceeds the common Teal' (*Ornithology*, 377). In 1766 Pennant stated: 'Garganey . . . in many places these birds are called the Summer Teal' (ii, 512). A small duck only slightly larger than the teal. The drake has a brown breast, a white belly and a pale grey forewing. The duck also has bluey-grey shoulders, but is otherwise similar to the teal. The size is about 15 inches and the season is as for other wildfowl.

garron   from Gaelic, *gearran*. OED: 'a small and inferior kind of horse bred and used chiefly in Ireland and Scotland.' This is incorrect. It is a heavily built, but very sure-footed, Highland pony trained to carry the carcases of the deer off the hill strapped to a specially designed deer saddle. The first attestation is in 1540. In 1897 Augustus Grimble advised:

Should your host place a forest pony at your disposal to carry you to and from your stalking ground, never on any pretence gallop it, for these ponies are as a rule entirely grass-fed and are therefore in no condition for such violent exercise and are easily made broken-winded. These animals can always be relied on implicitly on the darkest of nights, and however bad the track may be, if the rider will but trust them, he is sure to be brought safely home. (*Encyclopedia*, i, 302).

gauge see *bore*.

gaze, at of deer; when a deer stops feeding to look around, especially when staring at something or some movement which has made it suspicious. Also when startled and after a short run it stops and turns to look back at what has startled it; see *stand at gaze*. An early example of the usage is in 1759 by John Lily: 'I haue read . . . that the whole heard of Deare stand at the gaze if they smell a sweet apple' (*Anatomy of Wyt* 78). The term is now becoming obsolete.

German shorthaired pointer the Group IV HPR breeds are termed by the Kennel Club 'German Shorthaired Pointers and those breeds which hunt, point and retrieve.' These were the first of the HPR breeds to be recognised by the Kennel Club after the 1939–45 war. They originated in Germany in the 1870s, when they were deliberately bred for the pointer-retriever role then filled on the continent by the *Gordon setter*. A cross of the old Spanish pointer with indigenous strains, they were firmly established by the turn of the century and were first introduced to this country by servicemen returning from Germany after the war. They have proved very popular with roughshooters for their all-round ability as pointer–retrievers able to work in cover and water with equal facility. Liver and white, or pure liver, the dogs stand 23–25 inches at the shoulder and the bitches 21–23 inches.

gillie from Gaelic *gille*, a lad or personal servant. OED: One who attends a sportsman in hunting or fishing in the Scottish highlands; particularly an assistant to the stalker on the hill; often incorrectly spelled <ghillie>. An early example is in 1839 by William Scrope: 'And now the gillie, who had a clear view of all these things, began to set to work in earnest. He passed forward rapidly still out of sight of both parcels of deer . . .' (*Days of Deer Stalking*). In 1856 Walsh noted of 'Gillies or Hillmen,' that 'Nothing leads to more success in deer-stalking than having two or three thoroughly good and experienced hillmen to aid and assist in the work. In most cases the whole management is confided to them, because they from long experience are better able to know the exact currents of air for the confined vallies, and also can foretell the precise effect of all their stratagems' (p. 85).

gin from *engine*, i.e. mechanical trap. Also v., OED: to catch in a gin, or trap, to ensnare. Now obsolete. An example of the usage as a verb is to be found in 1781 by Peter Beckford: 'I would not gin him though – too good a sportsman for that' (*Hunting*, 340).

gin trap under 'gin' the OED gives 'a contrivance for catching game etc; a snare, net, trap, or the like.' The first attestation given in this sense is in 1220. It would seem logically to have been a corruption of 'engine,' or apparatus, for which the OED gives the same definition, but the first attestation given in this sense is in 1481. The term 'engine' appears to have been more all-embracing, covering anything from traps to stalking-horses, to judge by Cox in 1686: 'Partridges are . . . most easily to be deceived with any Train, Bait, Engine, or other Device' (iii, 141): 'Make an Engine in the form and fashion of a Horse, cut out of Canvas and stuff it with Straw or such light matter' (ibid., 145). As late as the 19th century, 'engine' and 'gin' appear to have been interchangeable: 'He discovered the defendant setting gins or engines to catch hares' (*The Sporting Magazine*, xlvi: 4, 1815). The *gin trap* was a once popular and widely-used form of spring trap, common throughout much of the 19th century and first half of the 20th, a smaller version of the old spring man-trap, designed to hold by the legs rather than kill instantly. It was eventually banned in the 1950s, following widespread condemnation of its inhumane effects on both domestic and wild animals when carelessly set. If set in the open, outside a *tunnel*, it was also often responsible for game birds losing their legs. As early as 1814 Colonel George Hanger, that reprehensible friend and sycophant of Prinny, the Prince Regent, wrote disapprovingly with reference to gin traps: 'It is absurd to permit any farmer to set rabbit traps . . . A rabbit trap (gin) will catch a hare . . . They catch also a great number of partridges and pheasants. A gamekeeper, this season, assured me that one day he shot four brace of partridges and two brace of pheasants; three of the partridges had but one leg and one brace of the pheasants only one leg' (*To All Sportsmen*, 103). The gin trap is now rightly illegal and has been replaced by the humane *Fenn trap*.

give tongue   OED: 'of a hound: to give tongue.' This does not get us very far. The phrase implies: to bay, yap, whine or make a similar noise, while in pursuit of a quarry. First attested in 1832. A highly undesirable trait in a gundog, which should preferably remain *mute*, but some spaniels, especially in search of woodcock, were encouraged to bark when *flushing* a bird. See *noisy*.

glass   OED: 'A telescope or other instrument for distant vision': 'As a man . . . Taketh a glasse good and true, By which things most remote are full in view' (W. Browne, *British Pastimes*, 1613–16, ii, 1). Of stalking, the term applied to a telescope, the *glass*: hence 'to glass the hill' or 'glassing the hill' when the telescope is used to search for deer. It is customary to use the telescope with both eyes open and its use requires considerable practice to pick out the deer at a distance of over a mile. An early example of the usage is in 1845 by St John when stalking 'The Muckle Hart of Benmore'. 'We . . . began to search the valley below with our telescopes..I had almost given up seeking, when Donald's glass became motionless, and he gave a sort of grunt as he changed his posture, but without taking the glass from his eye' (p. 234). Another example of this usage is in 1884 by Speedy 'the keeper surveyed all the ground within sight of the telescope . . . He called to the gentlemen . . . and one after another looking through the glass, distinctly saw the . . . head and horns' (p. 229). It is sometimes also used to include binoculars, for example by Holmes: 'Perhaps I should not leave the subject of observation and identification without a few general remarks about that indispensable piece of equipment, the glass . . . The glass must perform well in a poor light and if it is light and compact this will be an additional advantage. It is often essential to get the subject in focus quickly and for this reason only centre-focusing is suitable for our purpose' (p. 28). It is interesting that this somewhat archaic form has still survived in the sport of stalking.

going back   of a deer's antlers, when they are deteriorating owing to old age, or disease. It is desirable when a stag is seen to be *going back* to cull him for the general good of the stock.

golden eye   *Bucephula clangula*. OED: 'a sea duck of the genus Clangula.' In 1768 Pennant stated: 'Goldeneye . . . These birds frequent fresh water as well as the sea' (ii, 460). The drake is black and white, with a notably large circular white spot between the bill and the eye on a black head, orange legs and obvious white squarish wing patches. The duck has mottled grey upper

parts and a brown head with a white collar, as well as square
white wing patches. A diver, the golden eye has wings which
emit a whistling sound in flight. The size is about 18 inches and
the season as for other wildfowl.

golden plover   light brown spotted plover, generally flying in
flocks. Once so common that plovers' eggs were an accepted
delicacy, readily available each spring; old countrymen can still
recall as boys being paid for collecting the eggs which were sent
to London. The birds themselves were also considered as quite
a sporting bird to shoot, but are now so badly affected by
modern farming methods, notably spraying, that they are
comparatively rare and are rightly protected.

golden retriever   a gundog breed evolved by Lord Tweed-
mouth in the late 1860s, when he found two yellow long-coated
retrievers, dog and a bitch, which he crossed with black flat-
coats, or wavy coats, and kept only the yellow pups. The breed
is therefore an off-shoot of the *flat-coated retriever*, which it
closely resembles. It is affectionately known as 'the goldie'.
(N.B. They should not be termed 'yellow retrievers', although
some are very light coloured, nor should *yellow labradors* be
known as golden labradors.) A handsome and popular breed of
retriever, the dog's average height at the shoulder is 24–26
inches and for bitches 23–25 inches.

Gordon setter   a black and tan breed of setting dog, mentioned as early as the 17th century, but greatly improved by the
Duke of Richmond and Gordon in the early 19th century,
hence the name today. They were much used in Germany as
pointer–retrievers prior to the development of the *German
shorthaired pointer* there in the 1870s. Strong and hardy
dogs, they are still excellent workers, although by no means
common today. With well feathered legs and flagged tail, their
black colouring with tan markings makes them very striking and
they are fully capable of performing in the pointer–retriever
role, although mainly restricted to setter work only. The average
height of the dogs is 25–27 inches and of bitches from 23–25
inches. In 1938 Captain L.C.R. Cameron wrote:

> In appearance the Gordon Setter is a slightly larger and more
> heavily built dog than other breeds of setter. It has a bigger
> head, broad at the top and with skull slightly rounded. The
> nose is moderately long, broad and free from snipiness, the
> eyes show a slight flaw, and should be very dark. The flag
> should be shorter than in other setters, but with plenty of
> feather and the legs should also be well feathered and, of
> course, straight, with plenty of bone.

As to colour there has probably been more controversy on this subject than there has been about the colour of all the other breeds of dog in creation. The British Gordon Setter Club has now rightly decided that this must be definitely black-and-tan, without any stain of white; and there can be no doubt that, however they may have arrived at their decision, they have by it returned to the original colour of the breed. (Sanderson)

gorget OF. OED: A patch of colour on the throat of a bird: hence of roe; a white throat patch.

gralloch from Gaelic *grealach*, intestines. OED: 'the viscera of a dead deer.' Hence of deer, v. to remove the entrails, stomach, heart and lungs. The liver and kidneys are usually retained, but may be removed to a plastic bag to ensure they are not lost in carriage. To prepare the deer for the *gralloch* it is advisable to place it with the head downhill, or else hung by the *harled* hindlegs from the branch of a tree, or fence post. After bleeding by inserting a knife in the jugular and if necessary working the hindlegs to assist the flow of blood, Brander writes:

A fold of skin at the base of the stomach should then be slit, and by inserting a hooked finger and the knife, the skin can be slit, clear of the intestines, right up to the rib cage. The same cut can be extended down to the anal passage, but it is first desirable to cut carefully round the anus and ease the contents inwards. If a buck, or stag, the sheath and scrotum should both be cut round at the same time. The aim is to remove the bladder and its contents along with the rest of the intestines without any of them bursting and tainting the meat of the carcase. If the hole cut for bleeding is then widened it is possible to reach in and cut the trachea and oesophagus so that the entire intestines are free at each end and can be tipped out onto the ground. It may be necessary to reach in and haul them out. . . . (*Roughshoot*, 133)

Prop the chest wall open with a stick to cool the flesh rapidly. Remove to the *game larder* as soon as possible. It is significant that, deer stalking having begun to grow popular in the 1840s, the first attestation of a garbled version of the verb is in 1848.

grass of deerstalking; v. to cull a deer. This appears to have originated in the slang of the prize-ring, *to grass* an opponent, hence by transference game. First noted in 1814: 'A terrific blow on the mouth, which floored, or grassed him' (*Sporting Magazine*, XLIV 70). H. O'Reilly, in 1889 declared: 'I lost no time in grassing another [antelope]' (*50 Years on the Trail*, 21).

grave from OE *groef*, which comes from *grafan*, to dig: hence to bury. A colloquial term for a hole dug by a wildfowler on or near the sea wall on the *foreshore*, in which to lie awaiting wildfowl. It is generally shallow, by nature of the conditions, hence the name.

greater black-backed gull   a winged predator of game-bird eggs and chicks, now commonly found inland. It should be discouraged wherever possible.

great snipe   *Capella media.* Also known as the double, or woodcock snipe. A migratory bird, protected in this country and rarely seen, although it may be shot in Eire. About 11 inches long, it weighs 8 oz.

greedy (shot)   one who takes a shot which should be left for the guns on his right or left, or who shoots across a neighbouring gun when shooting in line, blatantly stealing his shots: one who takes every opportunity to shoot at game, even when it would provide a more sporting shot for another. He may be an excellent shot, and often is, but he is not a sportsman and probably does not understand the meaning of the word. See *poacher; poaching shot.*

greyhen   OED: the female of the black grouse. The male is called the *blackcock*, also known as *blackgame*. An early reference is to be found in 1427, in Sir James Balfour's *Practicks*: 'Wyldfoulis, sic as pertrickis, pluvuris, black cockis, grey hennis.' As far back as 1787 they were very rare in Sussex, as Gilbert White noted: 'Within these last ten years one solitary grey hen was sprung by some beagles in beating for a hare' (Letter vi). In general, greyhens should be spared even where blackgame is numerous. In August and early September they are easily enough shot, whereas the blackcocks are usually much more challenging.

greylag   OED 'Grey Goose', first attestation 1000. OED: 'grey lag goose; (Orig. three words (still often so written); the use of the word Lag a. is supposed to refer to the bird's habit of remaining longer in England than other migratory species of the genus.) The common wild goose of Europe.' *Anser anser*; one of the commoner geese encountered by *wildfowlers*. The greylag has pink legs and feet like the *pink-footed goose* but is distinguishable by its large, orange-yellow beak and larger size. Their weight is about 7–10 lbs and length 30–35 inches. They may be shot inland from 1 September to 31 January and on the foreshore from 1 September to 20 February. In 1807 Daniel noted the following details:

The Grey Lag or Wild Goose weighs ten pounds; the length is two feet nine inches, the breadth five feet and is one of our

largest species of wildfowl ... The bill is long and elevated,
of a yellowish flesh-colour, with the nail white; the head and
neck are cinereous, mixed with dusky yellow., the hindpart of
the neck a pale grey rather than striped and at the base of a
brownish grey; breast and belly whitish, clouded with grey or
ash-colour, back and primaries grey; the last tipt with black
and edged with white ... the legs flesh-coloured, claws black.
(iii, 242)

In 1830 Hawker was more concerned with shooting them in the
south of England.

Common Wild Goose; Greylag; Anas anser: These birds
instead of repairing to the coast like other geese, prefer
keeping inland, where they feed on the green wheat by day,
and in the flooded water meadows by night. You have
therefore no means of getting near them unless they are very
tired from having just arrived after a long flight ... The
surest way, therefore, to kill them, is to let anyone who works
in the water meadows ascertain what parts they have used
(which he will see by their dung and feathers) and then wait
for them at dusk in some ambush that commands the fresh
places adjoining. (*Instructions*, 200)

In 1845 St John also mentioned the difficulty of approaching
them in Morayshire, but approved their edible qualities: 'The
grey goose appears to select the most open and extensive fields
in the country to feed in, always avoiding any bank or hedge
that may conceal a foe. [. . .] The common grey-goose, after
having fed for some time in the fresh-sown corn-fields is by no
means a bad bird for the larder' (pp. 173, 177). In 1897 there
was some more concrete advice on shooting them:

In districts much frequented by grey geese excellent sport
may at times be obtained with the shoulder gun. By waylaying
them as they take morning and evening flights to and from
the feeding ground, some geese may now and again be killed,
particularly when a head wind keeps them near the ground
... Driving ... is the most successful plan to adopt ...
inland ... both gunner and driver will, perforce, have to
undertake many long and arduous stalks. (*Encyclopedia*, i,
470)

By 1929 J.S. Henderson, under the heading 'Wildfowling',
revealed the increasing interest in this form of sport and in the
greylag goose:

There are three recognised means whereby the sportsman
may get to the windward of the wily goose – *Stalking, Driving
and Flighting* ... everyone who has any experience of wild

goose shooting will admit that *Stalking* is by far the most
interesting, although at the same time the most difficult,
means of attack. Further a successful stalk usually means a
considerable slaughter . . . The greylag goose is undoubtedly
the most difficult to approach. (Mackie, 338)
By 1930 the entry by J.C.M. Nichols on Wild Geese confirmed
the wildfowler's increased respect for the greylag: 'The first on
our list, the Greylag, is our finest and heaviest wild goose . . .
The great majority of geese obtained in this country are shot on
flight either morning or evening . . . There is no better way of
securing a few geese than by means of a well-planned drive . . .'
(*LL Shooting*, 227).

grey partridge   OED: also called distinctively common or grey
partridge; *Perdix perdix*. ME *partrich*: first attestation in 1290. A
grey-brown game bird with rufous crown of the head and short
rufous tail. Short-winged birds, the chestnut horseshoe on the
breast is usually more marked in the male: the hen has a narrow
wavy crossbar of buff on the wing coverts, while the cock has
dark blotches. The average size is about 12 inches from beak to
tail, and about 13–15 oz in weight. The open season is from 1
September to 1 February. Their habitat is almost anywhere in
the British Isles, except high ground, and their call is a
penetrating 'chissick'. They pair from December to January and
their nests have 10–20 eggs which generally hatch in June.
Partridges form family groups or coveys, and if much shot tend
to form packs, although there is no segregation of the sexes as
with grouse.

One of the earlier references is *c.* 1386 by Chaucer (*The
Prologue*, 349): 'A fat partrich'. One of the earliest behavioural
observations is in 1773 by Gilbert White: 'Thus a partridge will
tumble along before a sportsman in order to draw away the
dogs from her helpless covey.' Daniel also noted 'The Affection
for its young, which the Partridge shows is peculiarly strong
and lively; by her Mate she is greatly aided in the care of rearing
them' (i, 77); 'Mr White in his History of Selborne notes that
after the dry summer in 1740 and 1741, and for some years
after, the Partridges swarmed to such a degree that unreasonable
Sportsmen killed *twenty* and sometimes *thirty* brace in a day'
(ibid.). In 1830 Hawker was more concerned with shooting
them: 'The most partridges I had seen bagged in a day by one
person (when this work was first printed) in a country *not*
preserved, were twenty-three brace, in killing which I remember
. . . he only got three shots before nine o'clock' (*Instructions*,
147). By 1 September 1841, however, he was writing:

Lord Glentworth and I went out from the middle of the day
till a late dinner and so few birds were to be seen and those
few so wild that I got only 6 partridges and Lord Glentworth
1 and 1 hare. I expected vile sport, but not quite so execrable
as this. The farmers, it appears, in addition to mowing all the
wheat stubbles, and destroying for fuel all the turf banks,
where birds could breed free from rain and the scythe, have
been using a solution of 1lb of blue vitriol in a gallon of hot
water to fortify each sack of sowing wheat from becoming
smutty and most people think many birds have been poisoned
by feeding on this corn. Our whole combined bag was only 7
birds and 1 hare. What a miserable first day! (*Diaries*)

In 1856 Walsh noted, 'The Common partridge . . . is the
prevalent species . . . In my opinion the expectation of true
sport in partridge shooting is now for ever defeated in consequence of the improved system of agriculture almost everywhere adopted' (p. 49). By 1884 Speedy was also gloomy about
partridge prospects: 'Since the introduction of reaping
machines, partridge shooting has in a great measure altered for
the worse . . . When flushed, they generally fly to turnips,
potatoes or the best and nearest cover . . . and should they settle
somewhat scattered in alighting, they are more easily bagged,
especially if the old birds be killed in the first rise. Coveys thus
broken yield the best sport . . .' (p. 267). In 1897, however,
John Hall although noting changes, was more cheerful: 'Driving
partridges has become of late years so popular, and has been
found to be practicable in so many parts of the country where
formerly it was unheard of, that it is fast superseding the older
method of shooting over dogs' (*Encyclopedia*, ii, 75). By 1929
Mackie was gloomy once again: 'A new danger seems to have
developed, which some say accounts for the scarcity of partridges in districts where they were once plentiful – that is, the
higher cultivation of the land and the great increase in the use
of artifical manures . . . Another serious factor . . . is the
trapping of rabbits in the open by farmers . . . A large number
of pheasants and partridges are undoubtedly killed in this
way . . .' (p. 224).

Eric Parker expanded on Daniel's observation: 'Partridges are
birds of strongly individual habits. They are affectionate and
faithful . . . You cannot pair off male and female and take it for
granted they will mate, but must leave them to make their own
choice. Once they have paired, the cock becomes a devoted
partner' (*LL Shooting*, 63). Tennyson was forthright: 'The
partridge is the backbone and mainstay of every self-respecting

rough shoot. Without a reasonable partridge stock the shoot loses 2/3 of its interest not to mention its value. There is no life in a shoot without partridges . . . The partridge too, is one of Nature's gentlemen, both in his private habits and his response to correct treatment' (p. 17). In wartime Sedgwick was once again gloomy about their future: 'Most beloved of our game-birds is the native grey partridge . . . Unfortunately modern methods of agriculture tend to have an adverse effect on the well-being of the bird . . .' (*Young Shot*, 147). Yet three years after the 1939–45 war, Drought took a different view: 'The indications are that, despite the general upheaval that war production has occasioned to the countryside, they [partridges] of all game birds, have been least affected . . . with the extension of tillage to every nook and corner . . . they have become more evenly distributed than in pre-war days' (p. 116).

grip   OED: 'that part of the stock which is held by the hand and is roughened to make the grasp firmer': 'Good gun-stocks must be . . . straight in the grain at the grip and head of the gun' (*Greener Gun*, 1881, p. 248).

groan   OED: 'Of the buck; to utter its peculiar cry at rutting time.' The first attestation is in 1486, in *The Boke of St Albans*. The OED states that the usage is now obsolete, but anyone who has heard a fallow buck produce the belching sound made when rutting would disagree. *Groan* is exactly right.

groundgame   hares and rabbits. In 1884 Speedy noted that 'in some parts of England it is a rule that the guns placed in line with the beaters shall shoot ground game only' (p. 288). J.E. Harting declared in 1897:

> One part of the sporting right the occupier cannot resign is the joint right, with the owner of the land, to kill ground game, hares and rabbits. Whatever may be the reservation in the lease to the landlord , or in whatever terms the occupier has parted with his sporting rights to a tenant, the right to kill ground game remains in him, and he cannot divest himself of it . . . a neighbour would probably still be able to maintain an action for any damage caused by keeping an excessive quantity of ground game, the Act not having altered the law in this respect. (*Encyclopedia*, i, 444)

See also *common brown hare*; *coney*; *form*; *hare's birth*; *hare's breath*; *puss*; *rabbit*.

ground scent   scent particles left by the feet of game adhering to the ground, which may be found and followed by a dog with head to the ground following the *foot scent*, as opposed to *air scent*. See *pointer*.

grouse   OED; of unknown origin. In the 16th-century form, *grows*: 'a. In scientific use, any of the gallinaceous birds having feathered feet; b. in popular use restricted almost entirely to the reddish coloured game bird of the British Isles, *Lagopus scoticus*, more particularly called Red grouse, also commonly known as Moor Fowl, Moor Game or Moor Cocks.' It is a plump, short-winged bird with dark rufous-brown plumage, usually darker on wings and tail. The legs are covered with white short feathering. There is a red wattle above the eye. The summer plumage is generally paler than the winter. Their average size is about 15 inches from beak to tail and weight about 1½ lbs. The female is smaller than the male. Their flight is rapid, with alternate periods of gliding and rapid wing-beats. The cry is a distinctive 'Go-back, go-back'. Their habitat is moorland and peat hags, especially with cranberry and blaeberry available. They feed chiefly on young heather shoots, berries and insects. They usually pair in December and nest in March/April, laying 6–12 eggs, depending on feeding and condition. Incubation lasts 24–27 days and the young birds are usually able to fly some distance when about a fortnight old. Late broods are not uncommon if the first nest is subjected to predation by foxes, crows, etc. The weather at the end of May and early June is usually all-important for young grouse's survival. Prolonged rain at this time can result in numerous deaths and late hatches of second broods.

   An early reference is in an Act of James I in 1603: 'Any Phesant, Partridge ... Duck, Teale, Wigeon, Grouse, Heath-cocke, Moregame, etc.' In 1755 Swift ('Receipt to Stella') wrote: 'The squires in scorn will fly the house / For better game and look for grouse.' As late as 1804 Thornton persisted in still terming them moorcocks: 'the pointers had found some game and I killed at two points, an old moor cock and a ptarmigant, which I ordered to be well picked and prepared for dinner' (*A Sporting Tour*, 91); 'August 26: Awakened by the gabbling of moorcocks (and a very extraordinary circumstance) the calling of partridges at four in the morning' (ibid., 129). In 1807, however, Daniel wrote: 'Above the *Black Game* is the *Red Grous* ... higher up the hills are the *barren* Birds and still higher the Ptarmigans inhabit' (iii, 104). Hawker was more specific: 'There are *three* kinds of grouse exclusive of the *wood grouse* or *capercaile* ... Black Grouse, or Black Cock ... Red grouse, Gorcock, or Moorcock (the common muir game) ... White Grouse, or Ptarmigan' (*Instructions*, 203–4). One of the earliest writers clearly intimately acquainted with them was St John who wrote in 1845:

> Grouse generally make their nest in a high tuft of heather . . . In October there is not a more beautiful bird in our island and in January a cock grouse is one of the most superb fellows in the world as he struts about fearlessly with his mate. [. . .] The difference of colour in grouse is very great and on different ranges of hills is quite conspicuous. On some ranges the birds have a good deal of white on their breasts, on others they are nearly black; they also vary very much in size. (p. 28)

In 1856 Walsh also waxed enthusiastic: 'The Red grouse, or Grouse, as they are generally called par excellence is the shooter's delight and affords more sport than all the other birds of Great Britain put together' (p. 38). By 1884 Speedy was advising on moor management for grouse: 'When grouse are plentiful on moors which are carefully burned, and where streams and springlets abound, they may be found anywhere and at any time . . . where the birds are scarce and the ground not so favourable . . . a knowledge of the habits of grouse proves of much advantage to the sportsman' (p. 146). Mackie discussed some of the problems still affecting grouse: 'The migrating of grouse is now pretty well accepted as among the causes of a scarcity of birds on a moor, in addition to grouse disease which used to bear the sole blame' (p. 169). See *grouse management*; *grouse migration*; *grouse moor*.

grouse disease   see *strongylosis*.

grouse management   management of a bird would seem a strange proposition at first sight, but it is now recognised that the careful supervision of a grouse moor, more properly moor management, is essential to maintain a healthy stock of grouse on it. Regular burning of the heather, in stripes to provide cover for breeding on the one side and fresh young heather shoots on the other for feeding, a plentiful supply of grit and water and control of ticks and worms, which cause many deaths in young grouse, as well as regulation of the maximum number of birds the ground will hold consistent with the feeding and shelter available. While a great deal can be done by careful management, any moor may be severely affected by a prolonged spell of bad weather at a critical point in the breeding season, and in this respect grouse moors are always at risk compared with low ground shoots, where birds may be reared artificially and released into the wild to make up for the loss of wild bird broods.

grouse migration   the picture this phrase may give rise to, of grouse contemplating crossing the Atlantic to establish them-selves in the New World, is somewhat wide of the mark, but that grouse do migrate is an established fact. It may only be from one moor to a neighbouring ground, and the reasons may be simple enough, but on occasions grouse undoubtedly migrate considerable distances sometimes for no immediately apparent reason. In 1939 Stephens wrote:

The ordinary view is that grouse are not migratory, except in bad weather, or when the food supply fails, when they will go long distances. Birds have been known to fly thirty five miles across the Pentland Firth and Harvie-Brown mentions a pack seen in the winter of 1878–9 travelling across the Moray Firth, a distance of forty miles, and the dowager Lady Aberdeen records a tame cock grouse given to her uncle and taken by him from Guisachan in Inverness-shire to Henley on Thames. Within a fortnight the bird returned to Guisa-chan. (p. 44)

When moors are *overshot* and driven too frequently, the grouse may form packs and such packs have been seen to move to quieter neighbouring ground where they are less harried. Anyone who has ever studied *grouse management* will agree that some moors in particular are likely to have an influx of grouse after the season has started. This may be due to overshooting elsewhere, but other factors may be responsible, such as the presence of peregrines or other birds of prey harrying the birds, or the presence of too many sheep, or cattle, or even hill-walkers, especially when accompanied by dogs, disturbing them. Another reason for local migration of grouse is the search for better feeding conditions and plentiful attractive food, such as blaeberries. That grouse can move considerable distances, rather than merely from one moor to a neighbouring one, is undoubtedly true, but the reasons for such emigrations are still not clear. Good management and regular heather burning are likely to assist in maintaining good grouse stocks and prevent any migrations to neighbouring moors or further afield.

grouse moor   the grouse has become such an important element in certain areas that moorland with any population of birds is now termed a *grouse moor*. Ground on which grouse breed and feed is generally well covered with heather, which should be regularly burned in narrow strips to provide good feeding on young shoots of green heather alternating with shelter in older heather for the broods. (See *heather burning*.)

Grouse may also be found on land covered with white grass, rushes, crowberry and similar vegetation, admittedly generally near to or between stretches of moorland, and will also sometimes migrate (see *grouse migration*), at least temporarily, to other moors or even to stubble fields and agricultural land adjacent to moorland in times of hard weather when their moor is covered with snow and no feeding is available there.

growth rings   of a deer; the concentric rings often seen in sections of the pedicle and in the teeth.

gun   ME.   OED, originally *hand-gun*, meaning any portable firearm, except a pistol; musket, fowling-piece, rifle, etc. – hence by transference, one who carries a gun, one of a shooting party. In game shooting the term generally refers to the man carrying the gun; the gameshooter. An example of this usage in 1886 is in the Badminton Library volume, *Shooting* (1901, p. 145): 'Where birds are plentiful much delay may be avoided by providing at least as many retrievers as there are "guns".'

gun cabinet   a secure and burglar-proof cabinet, usually of steel, fixed to a wall, in which a gun or guns and rifles may be kept securely. Currently insisted on by most police forces as part of the equipment required to obtain a *shotgun licence* or *firearms certificate*.

gun case   OED: 'a case for holding a gun', usually of mahogany or similar wood, with compartments for the barrels, butt, fore-end, cleaning-rods, jags, oil-bottles, etc. An early usage is in 1877 by 'Mrs Forrester' (*Mignon*): 'The only indication that its owner is a votary of "le sport", is the neat mahogany gun-case fastened to the wall.'

gun cleaning   essential after each day out with a gun or rifle. See *cleaning rod, jag*. Mackie instructed:

1. All guns should be thoroughly wiped immediately after the shooting is over . . .

2. All guns and rifles to be thoroughly cleaned and freed from rust and lead, as soon as possible after they are brought to the gunroom.

3. Wet guns should never be put in a warm place, as this is apt to cause swelling and steaming and rusting of locks.

4. All injuries or inefficient working of any part of guns or rifles should be reported at once to the owners of the same.

5. Great care should be taken that . . . a gun or rifle . . . be not injured by falling or knocking against anything that may damage it . . .

6. If . . . sand or grit gets into the breech or lock, special care must be taken in cleaning.

7. After cleaning a gun, always look through the barrel to
see no obstruction is left in them. (p. 369)

gundog   a dog trained to the gun; may be a crossbreed, or
otherwise one of the four categories of gundogs recognised by
the Kennel Club – retrievers, pointers and setters, spaniels,
German pointers – and those breeds which hunt, point and
retrieve. When the term *gundog* first came into general use is
uncertain, but probably in the late 18th century, as an earlier
version, 'gun-spaniel' is noted in an *Essay on Manning a Fleet* in
1754: 'Every Greyhound, Pointer, Setter and Gun-Spaniel.'
When referring to pointers and setters, or retrievers, it was
customary in Victorian and Edwardian days merely to refer to
dogs; for example Mackie on shooting over dogs stated: 'Dogs
should be given some slight refreshment in the shape of a
sandwich at the luncheon hour. Never give a dog a game- or
chicken-bone' (p. 200). Even more striking is the fact that by
1920 one of the few uses of the term 'gundog' in Sanderson's
book (outside the title, *Gundogs*) is on p. 31, where he mirrors
the attitude of the Victorian gundog trainers, who divided them
rigidly into pointers and retrievers: 'to even mention retrieving
in the work of the Pointer is regarded as overlapping into the
province and work of another type of Gundog altogether.' The
term 'gundogs' is still mainly used to distinguish them from
other types of dogs, e.g. many Show schedules group together
'Gundogs, Hounds and other sporting breeds'.

gunroom   a room maintained solely for the purpose of storing
guns and rifles safely, where they may be cleaned and maintained after a day's shooting. Glass-faced gun-display
cupboards are usually a feature of a good gunroom, but security
is a major consideration. (See *gun cabinet*.) Avoidance of
damp and a steady temperature are also essential in a gunroom.
Mackie advised that: 'Every gunroom should have a card, hung
or pasted up, giving directions for the cleaning and the keeping
of guns and rifles' (p. 369).

gun-shy   of a gundog; to be frightened of the gun. In its worst
manifestations the *gun-shy* dog will try to dig a hole in the
ground at the sight of a gun, and if not on the lead will run
away and hide. Usually caused by an unsuitable introduction to
the gun, especially firing a .22 or rifle near the puppy. A gundog
who is gun nervous, i.e. in the early stages, may be cured by
careful re-introduction to the gun and by encouraging it to
associate cause and effect, i.e. the pleasure of retrieving game
and working, with the report of the gun. This may be done by
shooting game in front of the dog, even at the cost of encour-

aging it to *run-in*, one of the few occasions when this may be condoned. Clapping the hands when attracting puppies to come and even firing blanks to summon youngsters to feed are methods suggested for overcoming any tendency to gun-shyness, but sound breeding and careful introduction to the gun are two basic essentials. First attestation in 1884. An example of the usage is in 1920 by Sanderson: 'The gun-shy puppy is naturally a source of grave concern to the breaker' (p. 7).

gun sleeve   see *sleeve*.

gut shot   of deer stalking, descriptive of a shot which has missed any vital part of the anatomy but has penetrated the stomach wall and entrails. The reaction of a deer shot in this way is to go down, then slowly rise to its feet and set off, unsteadily at first but slowly gaining strength. A second shot should be taken at once, since such a deer may travel long distances and may well be very hard to find. It will probably head for water and, depending on the nature and extent of the wound, will prefer to travel downhill rather than up steep slopes. This is a case where a good tracking dog can be invaluable. If one is not available to hand, it is advisable to go back to base and return with a dog as soon as possible. There is no excuse for leaving a *gut-shot* beast to die a painful and lingering death. The same holds good for a beast when a leg has been broken. In either case it is never advisable to follow the beast immediately.

It is a great mistake which stalkers often commit to run after a stricken beast. Unless the bullet has lodged in a vital part, the wounded animal, discovering its enemies in pursuit, is sustained by the consequent excitement, and will thus strive hard, and often successfully to keep up with the herd for a very considerable distance. When the stalker is positively certain that the shot has taken effect, there will frequently be a loss of blood from the wounded part of the animal. By remaining quiet and watching the wounded deer, he will be able by the aid of the glass to discover its movements. If it sees no one in pursuit it will naturally fall behind, or turn to the right or left, as shall be determined by the incline of the ground. As soon as it finds itself isolated from the rest it will lie down in some spot where it is not likely to be observed. In this position the wounded part will speedily become stiffened, while the probability is a sickening sensation will take possession of the deer. After the lapse of a comparatively short time, by ordinary prudence, the wounded animal may be

approached within a very short distance and speedily despatched. (Speedy, 245)
A good example of the usage is in 1967 by Rex Forrester: 'Tracking Wounded Deer: ... If the blood is dark red the animal is usually gut-shot and if so the blood is often slimy and often mixed with stomach contents' (p. 65).

Half choke   a *choke* of 20 points

Half cock   of a hammer gun, indicating that the hammers were half-raised, off the nipple, or off the steel with *flint-locks*, on the first catch, or notch, in which position they were theoretically safe and unable to be fired, until the hammers were pulled back to full-cock. To be at *half cock* thus implied to be under restraint but ready to explode: in 1837 Benjamin Disraeli in his *Correspondence with his Sister* (21 November) wrote: 'H. Liddell, flushed with his Durham triumph, had been at half-cock all day.' Accidental discharges, however, were quite common, especially if the gun happened to be carried at full cock. In 1814 William Dobson wrote: 'It is in vain to say, that with proper care no accidents can happen . . . there is no man . . . but must confess that he has occasionally found the cock of his gun unwittingly left standing in the position where it wanted only a casual touch of the trigger for a chance of doing the most fatal mischief' (*Kunopaedia, The Art of Shooting Flying*, 179). With the introduction of **breech-loaders** in the 1850s it was necessary to lift the hammers fully to open the gun to reload, and there was then always the danger of an accidental discharge while reloading with the hammers fully cocked and in the firing position. The ability to open the gun at half cock was only introduced in hammer guns after 1875, by which time they were already being swiftly superseded by the hammerless ejector and non-ejector breech-loader. Burrard noted: 'The purpose of this "half-cock" position was to provide . . . a very efficient safety device' (p. 102). A gun could only fire 'at half cock' because of faulty or worn mechanism. The only other explanation could be careless gun handling. In 1897 W.G. Craven remembered 'once being present when an old sportsman . . . just at the luncheon gathering, suddenly fired in the air. We all turned round in amazement . . . in half cocking he had pulled the wrong trigger' (*Encyclopedia*, ii, 328). In the same article on safety he wrote: 'Half cock or put the locks at "safety" the moment a beat is finished' (p. 329). It was a well-worn excuse for a dangerous shot, or for missing, that the gun had gone off at half cock. Hence comes the phrase 'to go off at half cock', implying instability of personality with explosive and ill-directed results.

half curlew   a nickname for the whimbrel, being similar in appearance to but much smaller than the curlew.

half duck   a colloquial term for *teal*.

half snipe   a colloquial name for *jack-snipe*.

hammer gun   a shotgun with an outside hammer operating

the firing pin. It may be single, or double-barrelled. The first *breech-loaders* introduced in the second half of the 19th century were *pinfire* guns where the cumbersome action operated on a cartridge from which a pin projected. In the 1860s these were very quickly superseded by the centre-fire cartridge and the breech-loading *hammer gun* with outside hammers operating on the firing pin. With the introduction of the *hammerless ejector* in the 1870s they in turn became gradually outdated. Although a few are still manufactured on the continent, to all intents and purposes they are obsolete. If the user is accustomed to them they may be amongst the safest of guns, though slow to cock and prepare for firing. If the user is not accustomed to them they can be dangerous, as it is easy to cock them and forget there is no safety catch.

hammerless ejector   with the invention of the *breech-loader* in the latter half of the 19th century, the *pinfire* gun slowly began to supersede the old percussion *muzzle-loaders*, which in turn had superseded the *flint-lock* at the turn of the century. The introduction of the centre-fire cartridge and breech-loading *hammer gun* in the 1860s, however, quickly saw the end of both pinfire guns and muzzle-loaders. By the 1870s the hammerless ejector had been introduced and what was in essence the modern shotgun came into being, although it was after the end of the 19th century before the hammer gun really became obsolete. See *non-ejector.*

hand   OED: 'The part of a gun grasped by the hand.' Or *grip*: the point where the trigger hand grips the stock of a shotgun, generally chequered to improve the grip. The amount of wear here is a pointer to the amount of use the gun has had. 'The circumference of the hand may be obtained by passing a string round it immediately behind the trigger-guard . . . the usual hand is about 5 in in circumference for 12 bores' (*Greener Gun,* 1881, p. 433).

hand reared   of game birds reared by hand, or under a broody hen, or in an incubator, rather than by natural methods in the wild. A common practice with pheasants, less so with *partridges* and mallard, but seldom with other gamebirds. The difficulty with partridges, as with grouse, is that they tend to lose the territorial instinct and form packs on being released.

hard mouth   of a retriever; a very serious fault in a retriever implying the crushing of game, by 'closing the suitcase'. There are, of course, degrees of *hard mouth.* There is the dog with a mouth like a vice which will barely let go of the game and breaks all the ribs. Such a dog may be a brilliant retriever, but since it renders the game uneatable it is worse than useless. Many retrievers will 'take a hold' with struggling game and the game will be dead on delivery, **to hand** with a few ribs broken, but otherwise edible. On dead game they may be perfectly *soft mouthed*. Much depends on any retriever's training and subsequent handling. Too early an introduction to game, or indeed an indifferent introduction to retrieving, may result in an otherwise potentially good retriever becoming hard mouthed. Sanderson warns that: 'in the absence of very definite indications it is incorrect to attach the stigma of hard-mouth to any young dog' (p. 95). See also *retrieve*.

hare   see *common brown hare*.

harem   the OED gives the original Arabic meaning as being 'that which a man defends and fights for,' colloq. 'the following of hinds, or does, acquired by a stag or fallow buck, during the rutting season, which he defends and fights for.'

hare myths   often regarded by countrymen as a somewhat uncanny animal, associated with witchcraft, the hare has always been a source of myth and superstition. In *c.* 1327 William Twici or Twiti (*Venerie*) wrote: 'The Hare . . . she is the most marvellous beast which is on this earth . . . at one time it is male and at another female.' This was repeated verbatim in 1674 by Cox and as late as 1790 by William Osbaldiston in *The British Sportsman*. Although hermaphrodite hares are occasionally found, there is a more probable explanation for this original statement by Twiti. Twiti hunted initially with deep scenting Talbot hounds. Once he found a hare, he then set a pair of gaze-hounds, or greyhounds, on it, hunting by sight. He would often see that he had raised an obvious buck, or doe, and he might subsequently find that his hounds had killed one of the opposite sex. It appears therefore that he, like his hounds, hunting by sight, was confused by the hare's ability to change places with another hare in its *form* at speed.

hare's birth   it is well known that a *leveret* is born fully furred and ready for the outside world. It is also well known that a hare gives birth to up to five leverets at a time. It is, however, argued by various authorities as to whether these are born together, or at various sites. The probability is that if a hare is disturbed while giving birth, it will move its young at the first opportunity and this may well have given rise to the theory that the young are born separately. If the hare is undisturbed, there can be little doubt that the leverets are usually all delivered in the one place and moved afterwards.

it was on April 27th 1955 that my dog came on point ... a
yard or so from a hare lying in its form ... as I watched it
stretched in a typical procreative convulsion ... (in) ... five
minutes ... the process was complete and two slightly damp
but furry and fully developed minute leverets were lying in
the form with their eyes already open ... When I returned in
a matter of two hours the leverets were no longer there ...
On another occasion ... a hare was pointed and moved ...
the dog remained resolutely on point at the form. Investigating it I found five leverets newly born and still wet lying
there. It seems clear, therefore, that normally the mother
gives birth in one place and then transports the leverets to
their separate forms, where she visits them in rotation to give
them their feed. ...' (Brander, *Groundgame*, 24)

hare's breath   a subject of myth and legend through the ages,
and still connected in many minds with witchcraft and necro-
mancy, the *common brown hare* continues to provide
grounds for new beliefs even today. At a Spring Pointing Test
for HPRs, two judges were recently walking together behind a
competitor working his dog up-wind across a field. One, a
suburban executive, remarked that over the years he had often
wondered why a hare in its *form* seemed to have no scent and
had now come to the firm conclusion that it was because it held
its breath whenever a dog or human was nearby. The other, a
country dweller, looked surprised at this assertion.

'Just you think about it,' urged the proponent of this theory,
with the condescending air of one imparting pearls of wisdom.

At that moment, a little in front, they saw a hare lying
clapped in its form, which the dog failed to scent.

'There, you see!' said the oracle, triumphantly.

The countryman remained behind, leaning thoughtfully on
his stick, until the competitor had crossed the field and was
finally returning with the other judge towards him once again.

'Is the hare still there?' called the judge.

'Yes, but it's dead!' replied the countryman.

Almost as he spoke, at the approach of the dog and the
humans, the hare rose from its form and loped off.

'It's not dead,' cried the theorist at once.

'It should be,' was the reply. 'It's been holding its breath for
over nine minutes!'

harl, or harle   v., etymology uncertain. Of groundgame; to
leg. An early example of the usage is in 1787 (*Grose's Provincial
Glossary*): 'Harle; to harle a rabbit, to cut and insinuate one
hind leg of a rabbit into the other, for the purpose of carrying it

on a stick.' In 1878 Jeffries remarked: 'Adept at everything from "harling" a rabbit upwards' (p. 35). See *hock*.

hart   now nearly obsolete term for a red deer stag, e.g. *hart royal*. In 1845 St John wrote: 'All the hinds looked up and following the direction of their heads, we saw an immense hart coming over the brow of the hill three hundred yards from us' (p. 283).

havier   of a fallow buck; one that has been castrated.

head   of deer; the head and antlers; may also be used as referring to the antlers alone; hence a stag, or buck, may be said to have a fine *head*, or a poor head. A very poor head may be referred to as *rubbish*, or it may be a *switch* head. Of game: the total number shot during a certain period. The total is sometimes restricted to one or two species, e.g. pheasants and partridges, but more commonly includes all species, although wildfowl and groundgame may be excluded. The period covered may be merely one *stand* at a *covert shoot*, or the total for the entire day, or for several days, or for the season, or even an entire lifetime: e.g. Lt.-Col. Peter Hawker was credited by Eric Parker with a total *bag* between 1802–53 of 17,582 head of game and wildfowl.

headrig or **endrig**   of a field, the ridge, or the ground near the hedge, or fence, which remains unploughed. This is a favourite shelter for game. In 1884 Speedy noted: 'When shooting over a turnip field has been nearly completed, a gun should be sent to within a few yards of the margin or "head-rig" as it will probably be found that a number of the birds will have made for the end of the rows before they will be induced to rise' (p. 271).

heather burning   although this would appear to have little to do with shooting, heather burning is essential for proper ·management of a moor both for grazing sheep and for grouse. It is usually attempted on a 14–16 year rotation. On 2,000 acres this represents about 125–150 acres annually. It is best for grouse if this can be divided into strips of 2–5 acres, rather than larger patches, but nowadays labour and time available are the problems. There are probably only about 6 weeks throughout the year when the weather is suitable, from the end of the shooting season in December through to the end of March. In effect there may only be some three weeks when burning can be carried out effectively in reasonable conditions, i.e. without a high wind carrying the fires out of control, or with wet conditions hampering the burn. Old rank heather is of no value for feeding. It also harbours ticks, which soon infest and kill young grouse. Young grouse may find it a struggle to move through it, often getting caught up in the thick growth and lost. When burned, the young shoots take longer to grow. In peaty areas care has to be observed that the peat is not set on fire during heather burning, as such peat fires are often hard to extinguish and may smoulder for days on end. All in all heather burning is an extremely tricky operation on which future stocks of grouse and the shooting can depend. See *grouse management*.

hedgehog   OED: 'An insectivorous quadruped of the genus *Erinaceus* armed with innumerable spines and able to roll itself up into a ball with these bristling in every direction. Named from its frequenting hedgerows and from its pig-like snout.' The first attestation is in 1450. A familiar prickly figure of the hedgerow, hibernating in the winter months. Thanks to Beatrix Potter regarded as a 'lovable' creature of the countryside, widely known as 'Mrs Tiggywinkle', but rightly regarded as among the regular predators of ground-nesting birds. It is open to question how much harm hedgehogs do to game, beyond occasionally disturbing and eating the eggs of a sitting bird. They are in any event protected under the Wildlife & Countryside Act and may not be trapped. They can make a surprising amount of noise at times, and are also unexpectedly fast movers. The occasional rogue specimen may be troublesome, sometimes even being known to attack poultry, but though they may not be trapped they may be discouraged. Their most tiresome aspect to the game preserver is probably their propensity for blundering into *tunnel traps*. It is advisable to *stick* any tunnel traps simply to prevent hedgehogs from wandering into them from sheer curiosity, as they will frequently do otherwise.

hedge-pig   one of the many country names for the *hedgehog*. They do in fact make a surprisingly loud grunting noise when rootling amongst soft ground for insects, slugs and similar food. An early attestation of hedge-pig is in Shakespeare (*Macbeth*, IV. i. 2): 'When the Hedge-Pigge whin'd.'

heel   to a gundog; the command to come to the *at heel* position.

heel of the butt   in 1888 W.W. Greener wrote: 'The shape of the heel has much to do with the fit of the gun; too much heel prevents the gun being brought readily to the shoulder and causes it to shoot *lower* than a gun with a full toe' (p. 131). See *butt*.

heel scent   the track leading away from the game, i.e. heading in the wrong direction, towards where the game came from. Often followed by an inexperienced young dog, as Walsh wrote:

'it seldom happens that . . . he can distinguish between a true and a "heel" scent . . .' (p. 59).

herbivorous   of animals which eat plants; includes deer.

herd   of deer; a group, originally of roe, six; of fallow, or red, twenty. See *bunch*; *parcel*.

hide   ME. OED: 'A hiding place.' A small, artificially constructed place of concealment for the gun, usually built when intending to flight pigeon or wildfowl, or shoot the former over decoys. It may be made from straw bales or sacking, camouflage netting or similar materials, including any suitable natural surroundings such as branches, or leafy pieces cut from bushes, which may be to hand. The hide should blend with the natural surroundings and provide room for the gun to stand and swing in comfort. It should also be suitably sited with reference to likely flight lines and also with as wide a range of view as possible. Above all, it should conceal the gun from the view of the approaching birds. Hides may be on three levels: dug into the ground, in the shape of holes, or pits (see *grave*); on ground level concealed in a hedge, or amongst bales; or above ground level in a tree, or on a straw stack or similar site, such as a *high seat*.

The earliest description of the use of hides for shooting seems to be in 1830 by Hawker, describing French hut shooting: 'The common way of making a hut is to dig a hole in the ground by the side of some pool or pond, then roof it over with turf, so that not an opening remains, but one hole, into which you crawl; out of which you fire; and in front of which are fastened . . . two tame ducks and a drake. You cannot, in general, succeed with less than three call birds . . .' (*Instructions*, 387). He also described permanent 'huts' made in the same fashion as in North America today, where they are termed *blinds*, with all creature comforts, including foundations, roofs and windows. It is interesting therefore that the earliest usage quoted in the OED is of American origin in 1864: 'He would go early to his hide and conceal himself with the barrels of his duck-gun loaded with buck shot.' It seems likely that this usage was common in Britain in wildfowling circles in the mid-to-late 19th century, but was not in general shooting usage until probably the 1930s, when pigeon flighting was becoming more widely recognised. An example is in 1938 by Tennyson, on shooting pigeon: 'you must either half bury yourself in a ditch . . . or build yourself a hide as best you may . . .' (p. 175). By 1950 it was in common use, as Sedgwick makes plain: 'During the next half hour I sat in a hide of rushes surrounding a pond halfway up the boundary ditch' (*Wildfowling*, 116). See *platform*.

hie lost   frequently used command to a retriever to seek out dead or wounded game and *fetch* it *to hand*. *Hie* itself probably dates back to the earliest of hunting cries from the OE *higian*, OED 'to exert oneself', hence to hasten, a natural command to a hound. In his erudite work on Hound Language, Hare writes: '*Illoeques; "Here"* (from the Lat. *illo loco*). It has been suggested that the word is the origin of our modern "Yoiks"' (p. 105). It seems logical that 'Hie' meaning 'to hasten' and 'illo loco' meaning 'Here' would be adopted and contracted by the early Norman huntsmen as a cry 'Hie illo', urging hounds into cover, and would have subsequently been used in the 16th and 17th centuries to encourage a 'spaniell' when hawking to 'Hasten here', into a bush or other cover, to push out a bird. (See *retrieve*.) The cry would naturally be further contracted to 'Hie lo,' or 'Hie los,' as it is still sometimes heard today. In the 18th and 19th centuries, as shooting developed into its modern form, the changeover from 'lo' or 'los' to 'lost' would seem logical, since the retriever was being expected to find 'lost' game.

high birds   *high birds* may be taken to mean birds from 30 to 40 yards up, much beyond that and they are starting to be out of range, but as Brander pointed out: 'Few trees are more than 40 feet high and therefore a bird flying over the tree tops is seldom more than 15 to 20 yards up' (*Game*, 90). The object of driven shooting, especially driven pheasant shooting, is to present challenging high birds flying strongly and well. This is achieved by using the ground to the best advantage. Where the ground is suitable and the land has been deliberately laid out with a view to improving the shooting, i.e. with strips of trees running from one covert to another and with copses planted on hillsides, it is comparatively easy to present really high birds when the beaters push them out from *flushing points* at well-chosen intervals to guns at their *stands* marked by numbered *pegs* in the valley bottom below. Where the ground is very flat, however, and there is no natural cover, it is sometimes a problem to produce high birds. Planting strips and patches of kale to provide cover is generally a poor substitute, but if the pheasants can be driven over water, even a quite narrow stream, they will generally rise immediately on seeing it and this can sometimes be used to advantage where the ground is very flat. Where the ground is very hilly, it is sometimes possible to overdo it so that the birds are almost out of shot; see Stanfield's comments on *pricked* birds.

high seat   a straightforward translation of the German 'Hochsitz' meaning *high seat*. First used after the 1939–45 war by sporting servicemen returning from Germany where they had shot deer, mainly roe, in this way. It is basically a platform up a tree for a rifle when waiting for deer, precisely similar to the *machan* widely used in Asia for shooting tiger and other large game. Primarily used for roe-deer, but in certain areas also for red or fallow deer in forested ground. High seats may be specially constructed tubular steel erections, consisting basically of a ladder and a small platform suitable for leaning against a tree, or alternatively capable of free-standing. They may also be constructed of wood, like a wooden tower. They may even be incorporated in the branches of a tree. Since for the purposes of shooting deer it is desirable to have a field of view towards the ground, e.g. down a ride, or rides, or over a likely feeding ground, they are often unsuitable for *pigeon* flighting, but in some cases the two uses can be satisfactorily combined, which is clearly of benefit all round. Holmes makes the further point that: 'A high seat is of particular advantage to the roe photographer' (p. 21).

high tops   see also *tops*. Generally accepted as meaning above the 2,000 foot level. In 1939 Stephens wrote: 'Ptarmigan are found on the higher tops, throughout the Highlands...' (p. 239); and Tegner: 'Up on the high tops it was a world on its own' (p. 40).

hill   stalkers in a *deer forest* may be said to be *on the hill*. In 1897 Augustus Grimble, writing on Deer Stalking, advised: 'In starting out for a day on the hill let the "gentleman" make sure for himself that cartridges, coats, flask, lunch, pipe and tobacco are all with him' (*Encyclopedia*, i, 304).

hind   of deer: the female of red and sika deer.

hind shooting   in deer forests in the Highlands the culling of the hinds takes place during the winter months. It is important for the good of the future stock to select the old, weak and sickly beasts which are unlikely to produce good progeny, not the young, strong and healthy beasts, even if these appear to be without young (see *yeld hinds*).

This question of hind shooting is of primary importance as applied to the improvement of stock. We leave out of account altogether the question of good venison, which ought to be secondary to the desire to assist the general welfare of the forest. In keeping this in view the main thing to be attended to is the destruction of old hinds, whose calves are in 90 per cent of cases feeble and unhealthy, and – in the opinion of many authorities – chiefly females. The stalking-gillie is too apt to lose sight of the primary object of his work, and to select well-conditioned hinds, instead of the decrepit females before-mentioned. (Mackie, 267)

hob   OED: 'a male ferret'. An early example of the usage is in 1688 by Randle Holmes: 'The male Ferret . . . [is] the Hob' (*Academy of Armoury*, ii, 136). See *ferret*.

hock   to nick the hind tendon of groundgame after *harling* or *legging*, to prevent the legs slipping apart. From the noun *hock*, OED: 'the joint in the hinder leg of a quadruped'. Sometimes used to describe the entire operation of legging/harling. See *couple*.

hog dressed   of a deer; the weight of the carcase minus head, feet and entrails, but unskinned.

hold game   of gundogs; to *hold game* fixed by staunch pointing. Any pointer or setter worthy of the name should be a staunch pointer, freezing solidly on point at the first scent of game. The dog which fails to point staunchly and tends to move forward and flush game out of shot is better discarded, or else only worked within shot.

holding cover   ground, or covert, suitably planted with trees and bushes, or other cover attractive to game, including ground-game, and providing both feed and protection from the elements. Ground may thus be described as good or bad *holding cover*. Certain bushes such as bramble, wild snowberry, privet and Lonicera can provide good natural holding cover inside a wood. On the edges and at intervals, taller shrubs such as laurel, rhododendrons and cotoneaster, and smaller trees such as hazel and sweet chestnut, or rowans, might be included, providing feeding and cover. Where the cover is old and thin, or overgrown and tangled, draughty and open to the wind or rain, it is unlikely to attract much game.

home range   of deer; the area where a deer spends most of its time. This may be forestry, or on the hill, but in most cases there are distinct areas in which a deer, of any kind, will spend most of the year. During the rut, however, male deer especially will be found to move sometimes quite considerable distances (see *wanderer*). Most deer tend to mark their territory. See also *scent glands*; *scrape*.

honour   of a pointing dog; to *acknowledge* the point of another dog by *backing*, i.e. also freezing in a point, although unable to scent the game. Also to acknowledge the *flush* of

game by dropping, or standing or sitting and watching the game
depart. 'As soon as one dog comes on point, however, the other
must honour that point by backing' (Brander, *Dog*, 92). These
usages are not included in the OED.

hooded crow or **hoodie**   *Corvus cornix.* Readily distinguished
from the *carrion crow* and the rook by its grey back and grey
underparts. A rapacious egg-eater and enemy of young game
chicks, as well as the young of most birds. Its habits are similar
to those of the carrion crow, with which it interbreeds. It is a
voracious feeder and among its more unpleasant habits is that
of pecking out the eyes of any sheep too weak, at lambing time,
to resist it. Many sheep have been blinded in this way and
lambs too weak to resist have died. It should be shot by the
game preserver or trapped in cage traps or *Larsen traps*,
whenever possible. *Hoodies* will quarter the ground in search of
nests, and the emptied eggshells in their feeding areas will bear
testimony to their abilities. The first attestation is *c.* 1500:
William Dunbar: 'The hudit crawis his hair furth ruggit'
(*Poems*). 'The Hoodie-crow and the carrion-crow may be
bracketed . . . as enemies of game . . . I have seen a pair of
hoodies endeavouring to get at young grouse which were pretty
well grown and had got their tail feathers . . . Setting the game
preserver aside, the destruction of these birds is a necessity in
the interest of the stock-farmer' (Mackie, 147).

hoop headed   of a stag; with antlers curving upwards, but
tending to come together.

horns   often used, incorrectly, to describe antlers. Goats,
sheep or antelopes may have *horns*, but deer have antlers.

hound work   of a gundog; to scent like a hound. 'To see the
dog using the wind, to watch it scenting with head held high
one moment and low the next, to watch it race on a scent
breast-high, or work out a ticklish scent at a nearly comparable
speed, that is all hound work' (Brander, *Dog*, 89).

hummel   of Scottish and Northern dialect origin related to the
Low German *hummel* = hornless beast. Of cattle, hornless; of
red deer, a male which grows no antlers. Such deer may grow
to very considerable size and *hummels*, like *switches*, are best
culled whenever possible since they may pass on their genes.
Although extremely rare, roe hummels have been known.

hunt   OED: 'to search, seek (after or for anything) esp. with
eagerness and exertion.' Of a gundog, to search for the scent of
game. A gundog should *hunt* naturally with keenness and
interest. It may sometimes be described as a natural hunter, a
merry hunter, a good hunter, or alternatively a lazy/bad hunter.

Sanderson specifies the 'duties of the Spaniel' as 'to hunt ground of prescribed dimensions in front of a gun and display systematic ranging with the maintenance of pace, which at all times must be accompanied by the fullest use of nose' (p. 117).

hunting   OED: 'to pursue (wild animals or game) for the purpose of catching or killing.' Almost everywhere in the world, apart from Britain, this definition of hunting first attested in 1000 also applies to shooting. To go *hunting* in the USA is generally interpreted as meaning to go shooting with a dog or dogs. The advent of specialised forms of hounds, specifically for hunting either fox or hare, in the late 17th and 18th centuries started the change in this country. In the 19th century the Victorians, keenly conscious of class and other shibboleths, differentiated firmly between hunting and shooting. As late as 1788 William Blane wrote: 'The hunting the wild buffaloe is also performed by shooting him from elephants' (*Hunting Excursions*, 16). In 1957 Brander wrote: 'To use the wind correctly, to interpret the signs the dog makes, invisible to the unknowledgeable, as correctly as the handler's signs must be interpreted by the dog, that is all hunting' (*Dog*, 89).

hup   this would appear to be an interesting survival, a corruption of the old command 'Up Muskets', in muzzle-loading musket drill the command for downing the musket butt after firing, preparatory to re-loading. The first part of the drill command 'Up Muskets' was prefaced in the drill-square by the typical drill-sergeant's command 'Hup', probably then frequently followed by 'Wait for it.' Subsequently used by ex-army gamekeepers after a shot had been fired at game; hence also utilised as the command for spaniels or other hunting gundogs to drop. Still used, unwittingly repeating the words of command of bygone army sergeants to their recruits, by modern generations of gundog trainers, who learned it from previous generations, as a command to their gundogs to drop, when what they clearly mean is 'Sit.' There seems no other logical reason for this archaic survival, which merely illustrates the remarkable strength and innate conservatism of oral tradition in certain gundog training circles, notably those of spaniel owners.

I **mperial** of red deer; a term sometimes used, without any justification, to refer to a stag with fourteen *points*.

mproved cylinder very slight *choke*, from 3 to 5 points. Usually in the right barrel.

in season of a gundog bitch; to be receptive to the male. It is thoroughly undesirable to bring a gundog bitch in this condition into the shooting field where male dogs may be present, since they will become completely unmanageable and lose any interest in their work. It will also probably be the case that the bitch when in season will not work nearly as well as usual, often being deliberately disobedient and very flighty.

in tatters of deer; the *velvet* is said to be *in tatters* when pieces are hanging from the antlers. This usage does not appear in the OED.

in velvet of male deer, both bucks and stags; when growing antlers are still covered with a soft and tender outer skin they are said to be *in-velvet*. 'In the north-easterly distribution areas frostbite of antlers in velvet . . . occurs not infrequently during severe winters' (Holmes, 67). See *velvet*.

inner see *target shooting*.

inside span of antlers; the widest measurement between the beams.

interdigital gland of deer; the scent gland to be found above the cleaves.

intergrade of deer; a hybrid of two species; e.g a wapiti and a red deer, at one time a deliberate introduction with a view to improving heads. More common today, see *red deer* and *sika*.

into the wind a pointer or setter for preference will normally be expected to *quarter* its ground *into the wind*, i.e. the game will all be *up wind* and will not be prematurely flushed by scenting the dog and handler's approach. Pointers and setters may sometimes have to work with a *cheek wind*, or even *down wind*.

Irish setter or **red setter** a breed of gundog established in Ireland during the early 19th century. It has never acquired any great degree of popularity in this country as a shooting dog, due to a largely undeserved reputation for unsteadiness, although it became very popular in showing circles. It is, however, still popular in Ireland and the USA. Fast and stylish, as well as handsome, it looks a thoroughbred with typical setter feather and flagged tail in dark chestnut. The average height of the dogs at the shoulder is 26–28 inches and of bitches 24–26 inches. In 1938 J.A. Carberry wrote: 'Since pace is one of the leading essentials in an Irish Setter, the dog must be built on

119

galloping lines. He should have well-laid back shoulders, straight forelegs and strong pasterns, deep chest, well sprung ribs, strong loin, well bent stifles and well-let-down hocks . . . The colour should be a rich golden chestnut with no trace whatever of black . . .' (Sanderson).

Irish water spaniel   this breed of gundog is clearly closely related, like the *poodle*, to the Portuguese cao d'agua, or water dog, used by the fishermen to retrieve their nets from the sea. Although it is claimed that the breed has been established in Ireland for centuries, there is no possibility of denying this close relationship between the breeds. It is an excellent water dog, liver coloured, with a close curly coat, very thick and naturally oily. Although it has never been greatly popular in Britain, where it has tended to have a reputation for strong headedness, it is highly regarded in the USA. The height of the dogs at the shoulder averages 25–27 inches and of bitches 23–24 inches.

Jack   ME *jacce*. OED: a male hare. An early usage is to be found in Fielding's *Adventures of Joseph Andrews*, 1742: 'Swearing it was the largest Jack hare he ever saw' (ii, vi).

ack-snipe   *Lymnocryptes minimus.* OED: a small species of snipe, *scolopax gallinula*; also called *half snipe*; a small migratory gamebird breeding on the continent. It is about 7½ inches long and weighs 3½ oz., by which it is easily distinguished from the *common snipe*, as well as having a more straightforward flight, although it is liable to drop suddenly as though shot and will then rise unharmed. It makes a drumming sound similar to the common snipe. Its food and habitat are also similar. In 1768 Pennant noted: 'The Jacksnipe . . . Its weight is less than two ounces inferior by half to that of the snipe' (ii, 359).

jag   OED: 'a jagged piece of metal fitted to the ramrod of a rifle and used with a piece of tow or a rag fastened to it to clean the barrel; now superseded by the pull-through.' First attested in 1844.

This is a very important item as it carries the principal cleaning material. The form of jag depends on the cleaning material used. Gunmakers invariably use tow and this is well suited for the purpose as it is cheap and absorbent. It is however by no means easy to twist the right amount of tow onto the jag. If there is too little the gun is not cleaned and if there is too much there is the risk of damaging the barrel. I fancy most shooters have seen some keeper cleaning a gun with tow and banging the end of the cleaning rod on the ground in order to push a lump of tow through the barrel that is really too big for the purpose. A shotgun barrel is a thin tube and this is one of the easiest ways of bulging a barrel and thus spoiling its shooting that exists. Consequently I would never advise the use of tow outside a gunmakers shop. Flannel patches similar to those used for cleaning rifles are better for the actual cleaning and much easier to manipulate. (Burrard, *Shotgun*, iii, 281)

jill   of ferrets, the female.

John McNab   named after John Buchan's book following the exploits of three bored sportsmen, who each agree for a wager to emulate the feats of a legendary laird-turned-poacher of that name, by poaching stags, or salmon, on their neighbour's ground. The concept was based on the original feat of Captain James Brander-Dunbar of Pitgaveny, who sent his neighbour a letter wagering £20 that he could poach a stag from his ground between certain dates without being caught, and duly did so. By a rather strange metamorphosis a *John MacNab* is now

121

accepted as one individual's feat of shooting a brace of grouse, and a deer, and catching a salmon on the same day.

jouk, jug, juk   OF. OED: 'roosting: to lie asleep or at rest.' First attestation 1400. OED claims it is obsolete, but it is still commonly used of partridges – to go to rest for the night, after a last short flight. Habitually, in pairs, the birds rest nose to tail for all-round observation, or in a *covey* in a circle facing outwards; the droppings may be clearly seen the following day. In 1672 Stephen Skinner (*Etymologicon Linguae Anglicanae*) wrote: 'To juke or jug as birds doe.' Hence *jouking*: the act of resting. It was while jouking that partridges were at risk of netting, when this was practised; the poachers would mark their final flight to their jouking spot and then draw the net over the resting covey. See *bush*.

jumps   of deer; places where deer jump over obstacles, rather than go under them, which in most cases is the deer's favoured method. They usually only leap an obstacle when the way under is blocked, or if in a hurry, e.g when alarmed.

K**id** ME. OED: of roe deer; the young in the first year. Earliest attestation in *The Boke of St Albans*, 1486: 'Iff ye of the Roobucke will knaw . . . the first yere he is a kyde souking on his dame.'

kindle OED: of a female animal; to bring forth, give birth to (young). Of a rabbit doe; to give birth, usually in the dead-end of a *burrow* or *stop*. The young are born blind and naked, but are able to venture forth in about a fortnight or so. A good example of the usage is in Shakespeare's *As You Like It*: 'As the Conie that you see dwell where she is kindled'. (III.ii.)

kite hawk OE. OED: *kite* v: 'to terrify grouse or partridges by flying a paper kite shaped like a hawk over their haunts to make them lie close till the guns come near.' Seldom used today, but flown sometimes when partridges or grouse are very wild and will not sit to a pointing dog. Its use may be counter-productive, driving the birds off the ground. By 1897 it was noted: 'Partridge shooting with the kite, which, twenty or thirty years ago, was not uncommonly practised by sportsmen, is now largely a thing of the past' (*Encyclopedia*, ii, 336).

knobber OED: 'a male deer in its second year,' also sometimes spelled <knobbler>, derived from *knob*. The OED states that it is obsolete, but the term is still sometimes used.

knuckle of action Burrard defined it thus: 'The Knuckle of the Action is the rounded end of the bar on to which the fore-end fits' (*Shotgun*, i, 39). See *fore-end*.

Labrador retriever a well-known breed of gundog evolved during the latter half of the 19th century from a cross with Newfoundland dogs, mistakenly thought to have come from the coast of Labrador, hence the name. Some were probably crossed with black pointers and other breeds. In about 1878 the Earl of Malmesbury, who had long had the breed and called them Newfoundlands, started calling them labradors, and these he gave to the Duke of Buccleuch in 1822. The breed became extremely popular in the early 20th century. Then the *yellow labrador* was introduced as a separate variety and has now become almost as common as the blacks. Dogs stand between 23–25 inches at the shoulder and bitches from 17–19 inches.

lagomorpha the collective classification for rabbits and hares.

lair of deer, mainly fallow; sometimes used to denote the impression left behind where a beast has been lying. Originally a hunting term. In 1626 Nicholas Breton wrote: 'The stately Harte is at layre in the high wood' (*Fantasticks*).

lap, lapping OED 'of obscure etymology; perhaps the original tool may have been a "lap", or wrapping of cloth or leather': a rotating disk of soft metal or wood used to hold polishing powder in cutting or polishing gems or metal. In shot guns, the act of boring out the barrels when they develop pitting, i.e. small pits caused by corrosion of the metal, through lack of care or cleaning, or through rust. *Lapping* is only possible if the barrels are thick enough to stand losing the necessary amount of metal. After lapping the barrels must be re-proved. (See *proof*.) 'The lap is fixed into a head revolving 650 times to the minute' (*The Greener Gun*, 238).

Larsen trap a small type of reasonably portable and extremely effective *cage trap* for *corvids*, named after its Swedish inventor. It consists of two parts divided from each other down the middle. In one is a live decoy bird, equipped with perch and food. In the other is the bait, set to trip the entrance door on being touched.

lay-up see *lie-up*.

leak of pheasants during a *drive*. Especially in the course of a long drive, it often happens that pheasants find a dry ditch or similar unguarded exit, down which they run or *leak*. If *stops* are not placed at every such possible leak, the drive may well be a failure. Avoiding any leaks and placing stops correctly are essential factors in pheasant driving. See *sewel*.

leash OF from Latin *laxus*. OED: 'A set of three; Orig. in sporting language used of hounds, hawks, foxes, hares, deer,

etc.' Hence gen. 'three of a species'. The usage originated from
the leash, or thong, on which coursing dogs, or hounds, were
held, three at a time. An early example is George Turberville's
Book of Faulconrie, 1575: 'They cast off a cast or a lease of
Sacres, which follow the peregrine falcon.'

leather polisher   literally, leather disks fitted on a *jag* for the
purpose of cleaning the barrels. 'It is a most excellent device
. . . consisting of a number of circular leather discs fixed one
in front of the other on a common stem' (Burrard, *Shotgun*, iii,
281).

left   as a noun: implying *left* barrel, commonly employed in
'left and right', meaning a successful shot using each barrel with
the butt not removed from the shoulder. N.B. since the left
barrel is usually slightly **choked** and the right more open it is
correct to refer to a **right and left** at going away shots and a
left and right at approaching shots. Pulling the incorrect trigger
and hence firing the wrong barrel can be the cause of missing.
First attestation in 1958, Brander: 'When a covey of grouse was
flushed, 1 only managed to bring down one bird. The others,
however, performed more than adequately, each bringing down
a right and left' (*Sport*, 217).

leg   v. Of groundgame: to slit one hind leg above the *hock*,
between the tendon and muscle, and slip the other leg through
it for convenience in carrying on a stick. The leg slipped
through should then be hocked, i.e. the tendon over the hock
cut, to prevent the leg slipping back. It is customary once one
beast is *legged* and hocked to *couple* it to another, so that the
coupled pairs may be thrown over a pole and balanced evenly
for ease of carriage and of counting. Also known as 'harling',
see *harl*; sometimes also termed 'hocking'. This usage does not
appear in the OED.

lek   OED: possibly from the Swedish *leka*, to play. Said of
grouse; to congregate; also a gathering. In 1871 Charles Darwin
wrote: 'as many as forty or fifty or even more birds congregated
on the leks. The lek of the capercailzie lasts from the end of
March . . . to the end of May' (*The Descent of Man*, xiv, 405).
In 1884 John Dixon wrote: 'Some particular spot is chosen in
their haunts, where they [black grouse] congregate, or lek, as
it is sometimes called' (Henry Seebohm's *History of British
Birds*, ii, 436). Of blackgame in particular; the elaborate
mating dance of the black game, when the cocks display in front
of the hens, hence *lekking ground*: the ground where it is
performed, usually the same ground year after year. See also
black grouse.

length   of antler: measured on the outside edge from the base of the coronet to the tip of the longest top tine.

lever of action   'The Lever is the arm which brings into operation the mechanism for opening and closing the gun. This lever is usually sited on top of the action . . . in which case it is called a Top Lever. It can, however, be placed at one side of the action, or under the trigger-guard, when it is known as a Side, or Bottom Lever' (Burrard, *Shotgun*, i, 37). See *action*.

leveret   OED: 'A young hare, strictly one in its first year.' The word originates from the diminutive form *levrette* of OF *levre*, a hare. In 1607 Topsell wrote: 'In ancient time, if the Hunters had taken a young Leverit, they let her go again in the honour of Diana' (*Four-Footed Beasts*, 211). See *common brown hare, blue hare, hare's birth*.

licence   see *Game Licence*.

lie   v. of game birds: to remain sitting tight at the approach of gun, or dog. They may be said to *lie well*, or *lie tight*, or 'tightly'. (The OED also gives 'lie dead', but this usage is now unusual.) They may thus be said to 'lie well to the dogs'. 'If grouse lie well to dogs . . . they give easy marks to the gunner.' (*Shooting*, The Badminton Library, 1885)

lie-up, lay-up   n. the term used to describe the situation when a *ferret* remains down a rabbit hole and cannot be enticed to the surface when for instance it has killed and gorged itself on a rabbit, or for some other reason is unable to return. '[a wounded rabbit may] fall an easy victim to a ferret and so cause a lay-up' (Sedgwick, *Young Shot*, 101); 'A line ferret is . . . attached to a line. The object is to send him down to find where the lie-up is' (Brander, *Groundgame*, 72).

line   of *guns*; may be static, waiting for *driven game* at a covert or on a moor, or mobile, when *walking-up* game. When placed outside a covert awaiting driven game, although sometimes in the shape of an L or a half-circle they are still said to be a *line of guns*; similarly when in butts waiting for grouse. When walking *in-line* it is important to *keep the line* and not to lag behind or press forward too fast, also to maintain the distance between each gun and his neighbours. The pace of the line should be taken from the centre except when turning, when the wing on which the turn is being made should stand still and allow the line to turn on them, but still controlled by the centre. *Breaking line*, either by stopping for any reason, or continually walking too fast, a common fault, and not keeping a constant distance from your neighbours, are forms of behaviour which merit a severe public reprimand from the organiser or host.

Where *beaters* are incorporated in a line of guns, usually one or two beaters between guns, it is especially important to maintain a straight line at all times and only birds in front of the line or behind the line should be shot. Whether static or walking, for obvious safety reasons no gun should ever swing *through the line*. A bird which flies well in front of the line from one end to the other is said to have flown *down the line* and a fast, high bird flying in this way can often prove an object lesson to the guns, being 'saluted' by several and perhaps escaping unscathed or being shot by the last gun of all. This is sometimes wrongly termed a *gallery shot*. *Stops* are often placed to the side of a line of guns around a covert and *pickers-up* may be standing behind. It is advisable to check beforehand where such helpers are standing so as to avoid any possibility of a dangerous shot. Nor should any gun ever leave his appointed stand in a line, even where he thinks there may be a *leak* of birds near him. Such behaviour is just as dangerous and stupid as forging ahead or lagging behind when *walking-up*.

line ferret   a ferret attached to a nylon cord knotted at set intervals which is used to locate the scene of a *lie-up*, so that the first ferret may be dug up. By counting the knots on the cord, it is sometimes possible to calculate where the lie up is and dig down to it. Alternatively, it is possible when following up the cord to tell when the digger is approaching the ferret and thus avoid injuring it with the spade. With modern electronic collars and tracking devices, a *line ferret* is now less commonly used.

load   see *charge*.

loader   OED: 'An attendant whose business it is to load guns for a man who is shooting game.' In the *Pall Mall Gazette* (1 September 1869) it was noted: 'A quick man with a good loader at his back will not unfrequently get at least three barrels into a rise of birds.' One who loads for a game shot when two or more guns are being used at driven shooting. *Loader* and shot should be practised in exchanging guns after each shot in complete safety and accord. Without practice beforehand there is a danger of barrels being dented, or worse still, an accidental discharge. With practice, the changeover of loaded for empty gun should be natural and easy. A loader is only required when game is likely to come over in such quantities that a single gun would be inadequate. A good loader may also mark the birds which his gun shoots, but normally in shoots requiring a loader there will also be a *picker-up* behind each gun. In the days of *muzzle-loaders* it was quite common to have one or even two loaders in attendance so that time was not wasted, especially, if the terms allowed it, when shooting a wager; for example in the early 1830s Lord Kennedy shot forty brace of grouse and rode 160 miles in a day to win a wager of 1,000 guineas. He used relays of horses for the ride and loaders to speed his shooting. With **breech-loaders** and **battue shooting** in the 1860s and 1870s, loaders became necessary for driven days.

Shooting with a Pair of Guns; For choice the loader should stand just behind the right-hand shoulder facing the same direction as the "gun." He should be well prepared with a stock of cartridges conveniently carried in a bag, an assistant having a further supply for replenishing the bag between drives.

The gun he is holding should be in his right hand with muzzles up and slightly sloped to the left. After his "gun" has fired either one or both barrels, the loader should take the discharged gun with the left hand, passing the second gun, which he has loaded in readiness, with the right hand holding the small of the stock only, and taking the fired gun with the left hand by the barrels, and the "gun" should take the loaded gun from the loader also with his left hand. The drill is practically that each shall 'take with the left hand.'

The "gun" should at all times, before handing the gun to the loader, pull the safety slide back, so that the word "Safe" is exposed, the loader having nothing to do with it. Should the "gun" not do this, I would suggest that the loader be instructed to warn him that he has not done so; otherwise should only one barrel be fired, he would be passing back to the loader a gun loaded in one barrel, and ready to fire, a *very* dangerous proceeding. (Lancaster, 103)

lock   OED: 'In fire-arms the piece of mechanism by which the charge is exploded.' First used in the sense *fire-lock*, i.e. 'A gun-lock in which sparks were produced (either by friction or percussion) to ignite the priming.' The term fire-lock was at first extended to the **wheel-lock** in the 17th century and later to the *flint-lock* before being shortened simply to *lock*. Today it is taken to mean the mechanism of a shotgun for firing the cartridges; it may be:

1. box-lock: most commonly made in Britain on the Anson and Deeley system. The simplest, most easily adjusted and best known, which fits into a solid action body;

2. side-lock: mounted on removable plates in the side of the action. More complex than the box-lock and more expensive to make, it is, unless of cheap quality, preferable to the box-lock;

3. Dickson's round action: to all intents and purposes a side-lock, except that the locks are mounted on one central plate and by virtue of the design the action is particularly strong and suitable for a lightweight gun.

lodge   specially of fallow deer: to lie down in the lair. Hence when 'roused' it is 'dislodged'. The OED gives: 'to discover the "lodge" of a buck' and quotes Turberville, 1576: 'We harbor and unharbor a hart, we lodge and rouse a buck' (*Venerie*, 239).

lofted decoy   a decoy bird, specially a pigeon, raised to tree-top level, to attract others of the species: '. . . one or more lofted decoys are often useful when flighting pigeons' (Brander, *Pigeon*, 99).

long drop   of a gundog; to drop at a distance to a signal of the handler, or to whistle, or command. One of the vital basic obedience commands, which should be taught while still a pup.

long-net   a net some three feet or so in width and anything from thirty to a hundred yards in length, set up on stakes at intervals of several feet. Used for trapping rabbits or sometimes hares. Several long-nets may be set together and entire areas driven into them. See *Caldra system*.

lumps   'The "lumps" or "irons" are the two large projections which protrude from underneath the breech end of a pair of barrels and are utilised for holding the barrels to the action, or stock portion, of the gun. They are frequently differentiated by the terms "forward lump" and "rear lump"' (Burrard, *Shotgun*, i, 19). See *action; barrels*.

Magnum   not in this sense in the OED. A term somewhat loosely applied to any bore of shotgun of any
type which is chambered for a heavier load than is
customary, i.e with the larger *chamber* goes a heavier load.
The advantages are lightness of weight, since a smaller bore
fires a similar load to a heavier gun, although of course it is
bound to be heavier than a normal gun of its own bore; and
flexibility, since a light shot may be fired when less range is
required, but the punch is there if needed. The disadvantages
are undoubtedly a heavier recoil and the squeezing of the shot
in a narrower bore, resulting in *stringing* of the shot pattern.

magpie   the OED notes: 'A common European bird . . . of the
family Corvidae, having a long pointed tail and black and white
plumage . . . its habits of pilfering and hoarding are proverbial
and it is popularly regarded as a bird of ill-omen.' *Pica pica* is a
well-known *corvid*, with its distinctive contrasting black and
white plumage and long tail. It is also a rapacious feeder in the
eggs of nesting birds, regardless of species. The game preserver
will do his best to trap or shoot magpies whenever possible.

The magpie feeds much in the same manner as the hoodie,
though it searches amongst underwood more, in order to get
at the nests of small birds. The nests of the pheasant and
partridge are very frequently discovered by the magpie's
sharp piercing eyes, after which shells will be found minus
the contents. The vigilance of the keeper should never relax
so long as his ground is infested by any of the corvidae
species. Though he should manage to shoot the hen bird off
her nest, he must not imagine that he has destroyed the brood
for that year. Another mate will soon be found and hatching
will go on. I have repeatedly shot a magpie off her nest and
in a few days a second one shared the same fate. (Mackie,
148) See also *target shooting*.

Magyar Vyszla   or Hungarian pointer. Imported to this
country since 1945; of reddish colouring, with a docked tail.
They are another of the pointer-retriever breeds common on
the continent. They are attractive-looking and work well in the
HPR role. Height at the shoulder, dogs 23–25 inches, bitches
21–23 inches.

male deer   of red deer; the term for a yearling *stag* which has
not yet grown antlers.

mallard   of obscure origin. The term first appears in the 12th
century, as *mawdelarde*, but the form *maslart*, traceable possibly
to OF *masle*, or *male*, came later, and it has even been suggested

it could originate from OHG proper name *Madelhart*, stemming possibly from a figure in some lost 'Beast-epic'. *Arthur & Merlyn*, *c.* 1330: 'De cherl bent his bowe sone & smote a doke mididone & with a bolt afterward Anon he hitt a maulard.' OED: '1. the male of the wild duck . . . 2. Used for either sex: A wild drake or duck: Formerly also applied to the domestic variety.' *Anas platyrhinchos*, well-known wildfowl. The drake has a green, glossy head, white collar and purplish brown breast, yellowish green bill and pale grey underparts. The duck is mottled brown with a greenish bill and orange legs. The average size is 23 inches from bill to tail, and the weight about 2½ lbs. The mallard pairs in January/February. Its nest may have 8–10 eggs which hatch in March/April. They are surface feeders and their call is the well-known 'Quack'. Season as for other wildfowl.

perhaps the most charming sight is the anxious mallard duck shepherding her young brood to water's edge. She will usually nest quite a distance from the water itself and, once the eggs are hatched, in the sometimes quite difficult cross-country journey to the water she may lose some of her brood in spite of her efforts. Once on the water too the little black balls of fluff are prey to a number of enemies, but their mother still does her best. In the spring months if an apparently wounded mallard is seen flapping his way across the water it is always a safe bet, as it is when almost any adult bird indulges in these manouevres, that the young are somewhere close at hand. A quick search round will probably reveal the mother hiding with her brood. Once discovered she will probably move off at speed and it is surprising to see how fast the little ducklings can follow, running on the surface of the water for a short distance. (Brander, *Sport*, 88) See *flighting*, *wildfowling*.

march OE *mearc*. OED: boundary, border: the boundary between estates. Used especially in the Highlands of deer forests. An example of the usage in the Highlands is in an Act of 1886: 'Any questions relating to the boundaries or marches between crofters' holdings.' Such boundaries usually follow some clearly defined line, such as the crest of a hill, a burn, or similar landmark, although increasingly some estates are erecting deer fencing. In the normal course of events deer are likely to cross *marches* for one reason or another, e.g. for feeding, or for the *rut*, or for shelter because of changes in the weather, and such fencing is generally neither effective, nor desirable. It can result in over-stocking, and sometimes in deaths in hard weather when deer are unable to follow their natural instinct to range widely in search of food or shelter from heavy snow. See also *stalker's law*.

mark   of game; the OED gives: 'to note and keep in mind the spot to which (the game) has retired after being "put up".' This, however, appears to be in relation to falconry; in shooting it is rather to note where game lands after flight, or where it falls when shot, or sometimes in the case of groundgame, where it took cover. An early example is to be found in Hawker's Diary for 26 January 1803: 'The moment we arrived at the river 5 ducks and 1 wigeon flew up; we marked the former down . . .' Careful assessment of distance and line is all important in *marking* well. A point behind where the marker is standing and a point beyond the fall of the game should be noted and checked before moving, so that the line is exactly clear. Any special landmarks on the ground, trees, bushes or tufts of coloured herbage near the point of fall should also be noted to assess distance as closely as possible. *Towered* birds are a particular problem and notoriously difficult to mark. 'To mark a towering bird effectively it is a good plan to go down on one knee . . . to watch its fall. . . . This will give you a false horizon and a second angle of view, helping you to fix both direction and distance . . .' (Brander *Shooting*, 143).

master buck   of fallow deer, *buck* holding a rutting territory; of roe deer, the buck who controls a given area.

master eye   when one eye is stronger than the other it is said to be the *master eye*. This can lead to inaccurate shooting, especially missing behind at crossing-shots. There are several solutions to the problem of a master eye, see *cast* and *crossover stock*.

melanistic   OED: 'Characterised by melanism . . . darkness of colour resulting from an abnormal . . . development of black pigment in the epidermis or other external appendages (hair, feathers, etc.) of animals': 'I took no specimens in the melanistic state of plumage' (Elliott Coues, *Birds of the North West*, 1874, p. 357). Of pheasants; a dark mutant strain, notable for the pale soles of the feet. Both cocks and hens have notably dark plumage, the hen being similar at times to a grouse in colour. *Melanistic* pheasants are considered by some to have wandering propensities, but are now common in many game farms, pheasant coverts and rearing fields.

menil, menild   of fallow deer, a colour variant which remains obviously spotted throughout the year. The OED gives *Menald*: 'Of a deer: of a dappled chestnut colour'; '*Grivele*, peckled, speckled; meneld, mayled. (black and white)' (Randle Cotgrave, *Dictionarie*, 1611).

metacarpal   of deer, or horse; the cannon bone of the foreleg.

metatarsal   of deer, or horse; the cannon bone of the hind leg. This is the bone most frequently broken when the hind leg of a deer is caught in the top wire of a fence. Although weak deer almost invariably die when thus caught, strong young males are sometimes to be seen minus the lower part of a hindleg and functioning almost normally.

meuse, muse   OF. OED: 'An opening or gap in a fence or hedge through which game, especially hares, habitually pass and through which they run when hunted for "relief".' Now largely obsolete in general usage. An early example is in Turberville's *Venerie*, 1576: 'She . . . will all the daye long holde the same wayes . . . and passe through the same muses untill hir death or escape.'

mewing   echoic; of fallow deer, the submissive sound made by does and by fawns; the latter's sound is also termed *peeping*.

mink   from the Swedish *menk*. There is no special word for it in Finnish; in Finland it is simply known as 'a stinking animal', which is a very apt description. While the skins were first mentioned in 1462, the animal itself was not attested until 1604. A comparatively new predator, now common throughout the country as the result of accumulative escapes from game farms and deliberate releases by misguided, self-styled humanitarians. It is now widely established and, as it has no enemies apart from man, it tends to thrive at the expense of most other animals and birds. It is a natural killer, death in poultry runs or fish farms, where it will kill large numbers. It will also attack and kill cats and small dogs. It should be trapped and shot whenever possible. It has nothing to recommend it. Rivers without breeding stocks of familiar birds such as moorhens and coots, as well as areas without any songbirds, are typical of mink depredations over wide areas. The water vole is another animal which is now barely to be found in places where it was always to be found, purely as a result of mink depredation. *Cage traps* are particularly effective on mink at certain seasons of the year.

misfire   uncommon with modern cartridges, but may happen occasionally, although generally because of a defective *striker*. After a *misfire*, examine the cartridge and if the cap is slightly dented that is an indication that the striker is defective. Try the cartridge in the other barrel. If it then fires there is no doubt that the striker needs attention. In many cases, however, the gun will still be usable that day at least, with merely an occasional repetition of the trouble. It may be that there is a build-up of oil or dirt, preventing the striker from functioning properly, but in general after a misfire the sooner the gun is taken to a gunsmith for an overhaul the better. There are few things more disconcerting than uncertainty as to whether a barrel is going to fire or not. The first attestation is in 1859.

mixed woodland   of woodland containing both softwood and hardwood trees, i.e. coniferous and deciduous.

modified choke   see *quarter choke*, i.e. 10 points. *Modified choke* is a vague and meaningless term, as some gunmakers bore improved cylinders to as much as 8 points.

Mongolian pheasant   *Phasianus mongolicus*. Introduced during the 19th century, the Mongolian pheasant has an even wider neck ring than the *Chinese pheasant* and also distinctive white wing coverts. This too has been perpetuated in pheasant plumage throughout the country.

monocle   OF. OED: 'A single eye-glass.' Sometimes used to overcome the problem of a strong *master eye*.

monorchid   of male animals, including deer and dogs, with only one testicle dropped into the scrotum; frequently with the sexual urge, but not usually fertile. First attestation 1822–34. See *cryptorchid, havier, rig*.

mouth   v. of a gundog; this may take various forms: to play with game in the mouth; to open and close the jaws when picking or carrying game; to 'close the suitcase'; to squeeze or damage game. What may start as puppy playfulness, tossing the dummy, or the game, in the air through sheer high spirits or over-eagerness, or pouncing on the dummy or the game and then playing with it, can very easily develop into *hard mouth*. Where the puppy starts *mouthing* the dummy in training it is a sign that the youngster is being pushed too hard, and it is usually advisable to lay off for a while and go back to basic obedience. There are occasions when an experienced gundog may find it necessary to stop and in exceptional circumstances may even have to put the game down simply to re-adjust its hold, but in general any form of mouthing must always be suspect. See also *soft mouth, to hand*.

moving   of deer; persuading deer to move gently in a desired direction by letting them scent one's wind, rather than driving them. The difference is one of pace. Deer *moving* while not unduly alarmed may only be walking or trotting. Driven deer tend to be moving at a trot or a gallop.

muntjac   OED: 'A small Asiatic deer of the genus *Cervulus*.' The name is adapted from the Malaysian word *minchek*. Of two kinds in Britain, Chinese or Reeve's muntjac, *Muntiacus reevesi*, and Indian muntjac, *Muntiacus muntjac*. Originally escapees from Woburn, they have now populated a large diamond-shaped area of countryside, from around Sheffield in the north to Southampton in the south, reaching into Wales on the west and the Norfolk coast in the east. These deer are noticeably short in the leg and their bodies tend to have a hunched appearance, but their most noticeable feature is their ribbed face, giving them a Roman-nosed appearance. The two varieties and hybrids are similar, but the Indian is larger, 22–23 inches, the Reeve's only 17–18 inches and hybrids 19–20 inches. The Indian has a deep chestnut body, dark back and paler belly. The Reeve's is a deeper chestnut. Both have a six-inch-long tail and when running this is raised, showing a white underside. Both male and female have noticeable canine teeth, about 1½ inches long in the male. The males have short antlers growing from noticeable *pedicles* extending down the forehead in pronounced ribs, hence the nick-name 'Rib face'. Fawns are dropped at about seven-month intervals and copulation follows within three days. There is no set season for the rut and fawns, normally only one, may be born at any time. Their normal method of movement is a steady trot, but when alarmed they usually move extremely fast for the nearest cover, holding their heads low. They can jump five feet with ease.

mute   ME *muet, mewet*. Interestingly, the term *mute* in the 14th century originally referred to the cry of hounds, working: 'Hit was ye myriest mute that euer men herde' (*(Sir Gawaine & the Green Knight, c.* 1350). By transference the term also appears to have been used to describe someone unable to produce articulate sound, hence a dumb person: 'She..stod forth mewet, mylde and mansuete' (Chaucer, *Troylus, c.* 1374: v, 174). By the 17th century this meaning so predominated that the sporting sense had become exactly reversed, referring to hounds running without *giving tongue*: 'When Hounds, or Beagles, run long without opening, or making any cry, we say they run Mute' (Nicolas Cox, *The Gentleman's Recreation,* 1667). Of a gundog: to hunt without giving tongue; generally regarded as a highly desirable characteristic, although some gundogs, such as the *Clumber spaniel,* were at one time trained to give tongue in covert when *flushing* woodcock. The latter trait is now uncommon except in excitable young puppies. To whine, yap, or bark excitably is referred to as *noisy* and is regarded as an undesirable trait in a gundog, especially in a retriever waiting at the covert-side. It is thus generally penalised at Field Trials.

muzzle-loader   a gun which was loaded from the muzzle with powder and shot charges, using a ramrod to push them down the barrel with wads between them holding them in place. Initially muzzle-loaders were equipped with *flint-locks*, which were replaced by *percussion caps* in the early years of the 19th century. With the introduction of the *breech-loader* and the *hammer-gun* in the 1850s, the muzzle-loader became obsolete. They are now collectors' pieces, used only by enthusiasts.

myxomatosis   a disease caused by the myxoma virus affecting rabbits, first reported in 1898 in South America, then developed in the laboratory in the late 1930s. It was introduced to Europe in 1952 by a M. Armand Delille, a retired French physician, who obtained a sample of the myxoma virus from a friend in Switzerland. He innoculated two rabbits with the virus and released them on his rabbit-infested estate near Paris. The disease spread rapidly and by early 1953, in spite of attempts to stop it, had spread to the south of France. In the same year it spread to Britain. By 1954 it had begun its rapid spread throughout the country, and was already known by the familiar diminutive *mixy*, a name which belied its deadly effect. The clinical description is that it has an incubation period of five–six days when there is a watery discharge from the eyes. This thickens to a pus within a day or two and the eyelids swell and stick together, rendering the animal blind. Further swellings at the base of the ears, on the nose, under the chin, around the anus and genitals, as well as possibly on the body and feet, may also be visible. Death usually occurs from 11 to 18 days after infection and the mortality rate in the laboratory is in the unusually high region of 99.5 per cent. This does not take into account that successive infections of rabbit colonies leave progressively more survivors, who pass on immunity to the disease in their genes, so that successive waves of the disease, which tend to occur annually, have less and less effect. Rare cases have been reported of hares having been affected. It has also been claimed that humans and gundogs much in contact with infected specimens have been seriously ill.

Near side   OED: 'with reference to animals, left, as opposed to *far*, *off*, right.' This use is based on the fact that horses and cattle are commonly mounted, led or approached from the left side, which is consequently the one *near* to the person dealing with them. Hence of a deer, as of a horse; the left hand side.

Nitro proof   in 1930 Burrard defined it thus:

Nitro Proof: This test was introduced in 1896 and was an *optional* Proof in that it was not legally compulsory. This Proof put a somewhat greater breech strain on the gun than did the Definitive Proof and its purpose was to test guns which were intended to be used with the then new nitro powders.... By 1906 however the use of nitro powders had become quite general, and consequently the majority of guns were declared for use with nitro powders as the Rules of Proof laid down that they should be when submitted for Proof. So after this date almost all high-grade guns received Nitro Proof in addition to Definitive Proof and their barrels were impressed with special Marks to indicate that this test had been carried out successfully. (*Shotgun*, iii, 307)

noisy   of a gundog, to *give tongue*, to whine or bark. Usually used in a pejorative sense, since it is widely regarded as an undesirable trait, see *mute*. In 1774 Goldsmith wrote: 'It is more noisy in its pursuits even than the dog' (*Natural History*). Of beaters; to make too much noise instead of relying on the tapping of their sticks to move the birds. Speedy deprecated the use of boys as beaters, stating firmly: 'Boys are also apt to get unnecessarily noisy, which is most objectionable. Nothing is more annoying than to hear beaters shouting and yelling ...' (p. 281).

non-ejector   a shotgun having the extractors in one piece for both barrels, so that they merely withdraw the cartridge slightly without ejecting it. 'It should be noted that when certain alterations or conversions are made in guns they call for the gun to be submitted to re-proof ... The most usual of such conversions is the converting of non-ejectors to ejectors ... a very essential precaution, since there is usually less spare metal left at the breech end of a non-ejector gun than there is in an ejector' (Burrard, *Shotgun*, iii, 329). See *ejector*; *hammerless-ejector*.

nose   OED: 'The sense of smell; a (good, bad, etc.) faculty of smell, or power of tracking by scent.' First attested *c.* 1350. In 1611 Cotgrave's *Dictionarie* gave: '*Nez*: a dog of deep nose, or good sent.' Of a gundog: the ability to detect *scent*. Hence to 'use' its nose, the major factor in the success or otherwise of a gundog in the field. 'What is usually referred to simply as "nose", is the pup's reaction to scent. The greater its "nose" the greater its ability' (Brander, *Pointer-Retriever*, 101). See *air scent*; *foot scent*.

noose trap   OF. OED: 'A loop, formed with a running knot, which tightens as the string, or rope, is pulled.' As in a *snare*. A trap set in the form of a running noose, so placed, usually on a well-defined *run*, or track, as to be calculated to let the desired quarry run into it. May be of brass wire for rabbits and hares, but for larger quarry, e.g. foxes, usually galvanised. An early example is from William Camden's *Britannia*, 1610: 'To lay gins for birds, to set snares for birds to allure them with noose or pipe' (i, 293). See *stop*.

nott   OE. of obscure origin; of sheep or cattle, hornless; hence also of deer. Also a west country term for a *hummel*.

nye   OF *ni*, modern Fr *nid* – a nest; L *nidus*. OED: 'A brood of pheasants.' An early example of the usage is in *The Boke of St Albans* 1486: 'A Nye of Fesaunttys'. In 1818 Henry Todd's *Dictionary of the English Language* stated misleadingly: 'A Nye of Pheasants; a brood of pheasants. So an eye is sometimes called.' In 1830 Hawker gave another version: 'In a small covert of my own I had one *nide* of twelve . . . pheasants' (*Instructions*, 213). The OED also gives *eye*, 'Obs; used erroneously for nye.' In this sense it is used in *The Boke of Hawkyng*, c. 1430: 'I have founde a covey of pertrich . . . and an eye of fesaunt.' As may have been the case with Hawker, this could have been a local variant at the time, both now obsolete.

O **estrus** of animals, the rut, resulting in conception; of *lagomorpha*, one may be followed by another, resulting in a delayed second conception.

off side OED: 'of horses; right as opposed to left, or near side where the driver walks, the rider mounts.' Of a deer, as of a horse, the right-hand side, hence *off-antler, off-fore leg*, etc.

off-the-face of a shotgun when so worn by use that light can be seen between the barrels and the *face of the action*.

ossification of antlers; conversion to bone, as while *in velvet*.

outer of target-shooting with rifle. A shot on the outer edge of the target.

outside curve of antlers; the measurement of an antler from the base to the tip on the outside of the curve, for the purposes of trophy measurement.

over-and-under one of the common categories of shotgun, generally side-*lock* and *ejector* with the barrels fitted one under the other; a favourite gun for the clay-pigeon shooter, largely because of the single sighting plane. It tends to be heavier than the side-by-side. Originally they appear to have been commonly referred to as 'Under-and-over' guns, but as they became more commonly used in the 1930s, and especially since the 1950s, when they became popular for clay-pigeon shooting, the wording has been reversed. In 1889 Charles Lancaster stated: 'The "under-and-over" principle is probably as old as the use of two barrels in a gun' (*Shooting*, 120). By 1930 Burrard was discussing 'The fit of Over and Under guns' (*Gunroom*, 30). The latter is now common usage.

over shoot OED: 'To shoot too much over (a moor etc.) so as to deplete it of game.' The likely result of *yuppy shooting* or *greedy shooting*. Only those with no interest in conserving game for the future would over shoot their ground, e.g ignorant shooting tenants or those with no security of tenure. The *Manchester Examiner* of 1 August 1884 noted: 'Disease together with over shooting by greedy lessees had played such havoc with the moors.'

overshot OED: 'having the upper jaw projecting beyond the lower,' first attested 1885. In a gundog: a fault in a show-specimen, but of little importance in a working gundog unless very pronounced and affecting the *pick up*. Also of a pointing dog, when nearly missing game. 'Sometimes all four feet will be firmly on the ground and the head crooked at an odd angle backwards when game has been almost overshot' (Brander, *Dog*, 63).

Pace   OED: any one of the various gaits or manners of stepping of a horse, or mule; hence also of deer; the gait, which can be measured by the *track*. May be a walk, trot, or gallop, or in some cases such as *muntjac*, a run.

pack   OED: 'A number of birds (e.g. grouse) naturally congregating together.' Grouse start to form *packs* quite early in the season if much driven, although much depends on the locality and the circumstances, quite apart from the numbers of grouse available. They do not necessarily form packs at all if only *dogged* and if there are not a great number in the first instance. Packs in some areas may be of as many as a hundred, or even two hundred, birds. Even then there are usually single old birds and pairs which do not join the packs scattered about the moor. Grouse tend to form segregated groups of cocks or hens. Partridges if much driven may also form packs, but these are not segregated by sexes. The only time partridges are likely to form segregated packs is when they have been introduced to the ground straight from the incubator and have lost their territorial instinct. See also *grey partridge*. An early example of the usage is in 1688, when Randle Holme noted 'A Pack of Grous, or Heath-cocks' (*Armoury*, ii, 311).

paint   OED: 'to colour or stain', hence colloquially used in the New Forest and North America for the trail of blood staining the ground left by a badly wounded deer.

pair   OF. OED: as a verb: 'to unite with one of the opposite sex.' Of birds, especially grouse and partridges, to mate. In 1897 it was noted, 'A kite should never be used after the birds have paired, which in average seasons may be taken as January 10th' (*Encyclopedia*, ii, 337). *Partridge* coveys in some years may be found to break up and pair as early as December, and may re-form coveys if the weather becomes severe, finally pairing in January or February. T.S.D. & J.A. Purdey advised: 'Once birds have paired, they should, of course, never be shot at – and one finds it a general rule that Christmas sees the end of partridge shooting' (p. 73).

palm   OED: 'the flat expanded part of the horn in some deer from which finger-like points project.' Especially of *fallow buck*; the flat tops of the antlers. Such antlers are technically termed *palmated*, as with reindeer, etc. First attested in the 12th century. Sir Thomas Cockaine wrote in his *Treatise on Hunting* (1590): 'Divers Buckes have sundrie slots in their palmes.'

parcel   Fr. OED: 'of animals, a small party, or herd.' An obsolete usage was 'a small party, company, selection or assemblage (of persons, animals or things' but this is a survival, still in use in the Highlands. William Scrope in *Days of Deer Stalking* (1839), wrote: 'Peter now pressed his master's arm and pointed; "Did you no see yon parcel of hinds – those towards the shank of our hill?"' See *bunch*; *herd*.

park   OF *parc*, preserve for beasts of the chase. OED: '1. Law; An enclosed tract of land held by royal grant or prescription for keeping beasts of the chase, (Distinguished from a *forest* or *chase* also by having no special laws or officers) 2. Hence extended to a large ornamental piece of ground usually comprising woodland and pasture . . . used for recreation and often for keeping deer, cattle and sheep.' See *deer park*. Daniel, quoting from the Forest Laws, stated that: 'A Park is an enclosed territory which has a privilege for Beasts of Chase, by Prescription or by the King's Grant . . . To a Park, three things are required: 1. a Grant thereof. 2. Inclosures, by pale, wall, or hedge. 3, Beasts of a Park, such as the Buck, Doe &c. . . .' (i, 261).

partnership shoot   a shoot shared by two or more people as equal or unequal partners; often an arrangement by the owner of a shoot who does not wish to syndicate his shooting, with another, or others, who see to the bulk of the work, such as rearing, preserving game, trapping and shooting predators, etc. and share the shooting. Or it may just be a mutually amicable arrangement to share a shoot between two or three, but seldom many more, individuals. The difference between a *partnership shoot* and a *syndicate shoot* is basically that in a partnership matters are managed by mutual agreement, whereas in a syndicate a shoot manager makes the arrangements. A partnership shoot is not, however, necessarily a *roughshoot*, since a partnership may, like a syndicate, pay for the costs of a keeper and regular driven days. On the other hand, a partnership is usually a happier arrangement for running a roughshoot than a syndicate, depending always on the size of the shoot and other circumstances involved, on the basis that too many cooks clutter the kitchen.

pass   ME. OED: 'A way . . . through . . . or over a mountain range, also (less usually) through a forest, marsh, bog or other impassable ground.' Of deer; the place deer are known to use regularly to cross a hill, river or any obstacle. A good example of the usage is by Speedy: '. . . very soon all the groups concentrated into one large herd of at least 1500 deer and began to ascend the "pass"' (p. 244).

patches   flannel or linen squares made to fit the *jag*, or the *cleaning rod*, of a shotgun and used to clean the barrels.

pattern   OED: 'Gunmaking: the marks made by the shot from a gun on a target in respect of their closeness together and evenness of distribution within a certain radius from the central point.' Hence a *declared pattern* became a selling point for gunsmiths, guaranteeing a certain number of pellets within a given radius in specified conditions. Of a shotgun: the density of shot at the target. The pattern is measured by *plating* the shotgun, i.e. measuring the number of pellets in a 30-inch circle at 40 yards when the shotgun as been fired at a whitewashed steel plate. W.W. Greener defined a declared pattern in 1892: 'When a gun is said to make a pattern of 200 it means that 200 is the average number put within a circle of 30 inch in diameter on the target, the butt of the gun being 40 yards from the target, the load being 3 drams of black powder, or equivalent in nitro powder and 1½ oz of No. 6 shot' (*The Breech-loader*, 124).

paunch   ME. OED: 'to cut open the paunch (of an animal) and take out the viscera.' Of rabbits: to remove the stomach and entrails. First attested in 1570. In 1776 Mrs Elizabeth Raffald instructed: 'When you have paunched and cased your Hare . . .' (i.e. gutted and skinned it) (*English Housekeeper*, 135). *Paunching* should be done soon after shooting, or trapping. Insert a knife under the apex of the ribs, making a sizeable slit in the skin towards the tail, then hook a finger round the stomach and turn out the entrails with a twist of the wrist. Hares are not customarily paunched in the UK, being treated like other game and hung for a period to improve the flavour. It is customary to hang hares by the head and only to skin and gut them prior to cooking. It is however desirable to empty the bladder of any *groundgame* by holding the head and pressing a hand slowly down the body to squeeze the bladder dry as soon after trapping or shooting as possible, otherwise there is a danger of the flesh being tainted by the urine.

pearl, pearling   OED: 'one of the bony tubercles encircling the bur, or base, of a deer's antler; the rough formation on the beam and burr sometimes termed the pearls.' An early usage is in 1576 by Turberville: 'That which is about the crust of the beame is termed pearles . . .'

pedal gland   see *inter-digital gland*.

pedicle   OED: 'Zoology; the process of bone supporting the horn of a deer or any animal of the family Cervidae.' The bone of the skull from which the antlers grow each year.

peep   OED: 'to utter the weak shrill sound common to young birds, mice and some kinds of frogs.' First attested c. 1403. In

1601 Holland wrote: 'By the 29 day . . . ye shall heare the chick to peepe within the verie shell' (*Pliny*, i, 298). Hence *peeping*, *piping* and sometimes *pheeping*; of a fawn, see *feep*; *mewing*.

peg of uncertain etymology. Of a gundog, OED: 'to point at, set (a game bird)'; 'Then Satin found birds and directly after pegged a single bird that Crab had passed' (*The Field*, 7 May 1892). This usage is obsolete and it now means a gundog picking game, usually **groundgame**, but possibly also game-birds, unshot. This is a not-infrequent occurrence with dogs much used for beating and is often encountered with hunting dogs, such as spaniels, when game sits *tight*. 'It must be taught not to try to peg (or seize) the game' (Brander, *Pointer-Retriever*, 101).

pegs on a driven day's covert shooting, the numbered sticks, sometimes termed pins, or *pegs*, set out for the guns to mark their stands at each drive. At the start of the day the guns usually draw for numbers and move up two numbers each drive to provide, theoretically, even chances of good sport. In some cases the host, however, will deliberately place his guns, usually so that any poor shots have good guns on either side of them in order to ensure there are no obvious gaps in the *line* which might be caused if two or three poor shots happened to draw neighbouring guns. In 1884 Davenport wrote on *covert shooting*: 'Hazel slips stuck in the ground about eighty or a hundred yards from the covert, with a small piece of paper in a cleft at the top, mark the several positions of the four forward guns' (p. 133). On some well-organised shoots a post with a number on it may be driven into the ground with a nail near the top to provide a *peg* for the gun on which to hang his *cartridge bag*. In 1939 T.D.S. & J.A. Purdey wrote: 'The first stand after lunch is near the house and my peg is on a small round of lawn just in front of . . . the house' (p. 100).

pelage Fr. OED: 'the hair, wool or fur of an animal in reference to its kind or colour.' The earliest attestation appears in 1828–32, in Noah Webster's *Dictionary*: '*Pelage*: the vesture, or covering, of wild beasts, consisting of hair, fur or wool.' Of deer; the hair, e.g. the summer *pelage* of the *fallow* has white or grey spots.

percussion cap OED: 'a small copper cap or cylinder containing fulminating powder, exploded by the percussion of a hammer so as to fire the charge of a firearm.' This definition is, however, somewhat obsolete. It is now generally recognised as the cap in the centre of the base of the *cartridge*, which contains the detonator compound. One of the earliest references is in 1810: 'He used one of Forsyth's gunlocks, which flintless, goes off by percussion' (*The Sporting Magazine*, XXXIV, 273). In 1892 W.W. Greener stated: 'The percussion cap gun was a great improvement on the flint-lock, and although its day was short, it may be regarded as the most durable gun ever made' (*The Breech-loader*, 2).

perruque, peruke   of antlers; a malformation, generally due to damage to the testicles, causing the growth of a grotesque mass, usually remaining in velvet, and often quite closely resembling the 18th-century wig after which it is named. It is sometimes also termed a *wig-antler*. In normal bucks the antler growth-hormone rises with the increasing light levels from late December onwards and is only inhibited by the rising testosterone levels in the spring. Dr Frank Holmes explained it thus: 'In castrated bucks antler growth hormone is not inhibited at all, because no testosterone is secreted, and therefore growth continues unchecked . . . a so-called peruke head' (p. 79).

pheasant   see *common pheasant*.

pheasant driving   see *covert shooting*.

pheasant pen   a pen used for keeping a cock and a number of hens, or a hen and chicks, for breeding purposes, similar to a poultry pen. 'The two plans of construction which find most favour with pheassant rearers are; the one, a series of small pens, in each of which one cock and five or six hens are confined, and the other, the large pen enclosing a considerable area of ground, where any quantity of birds proportioned to the size of the pens may be kept' (*Encyclopedia*, ii, 82). Ninety years later, Ian McCall, the Scottish Director of the Game Conservancy, stated that

> There are three basic systems of penning pheasants for egg productions: The simplest is to place six to eight hens and one cock in a standard, covered moveable pen. This is a little smaller than the ideal for the number of birds and a pen made up from rearing sections to 3 m (10 ft) square is still light enough for one person to shift but will enclose nearly double the area. At the other end of the scale open-topped communal pens should use less man hours per day to manage – providing the eggs can be found without difficulty. . . .'
> (p. 21)

pheep   see *feep, mewing, peep*.

pick-up   of a retriever; there should be no *mouthing* when the retriever finds its game; the head should go down and the game should be picked up cleanly. At Field Trials the judges are likely to mark down any dog which fails to make a clean *pick-up*, however brilliant the rest of its work. Also after a *drive*: the act of picking up the dead birds and *runners* by those appointed to do so; hence *pickers-up*, the pick-up, or picking-up. In 1920 Sanderson remarked: 'The bulk of the picking up was done by one or two dogs' (p. 100).

piece   colloquial Scots term for sandwiches, in this context sandwiches taken out on the hill, or midday food for beaters or guns. An example of this usage is by Mackie: 'as the boys may have a long wait, see that they have a "piece" with them' (p. 315).

pigeon   see *wood pigeon*.

pigeon decoy   see *decoys*.

pigeon platform   a platform *hide* in the tree-tops to which access is gained by ladder; such platforms can provide excellent flight shooting, with birds coming from all angles over the tree-tops. They can also sometimes be used for roe shooting, if sighted conveniently for the purpose. They seem to have been introduced on any scale after the Second World War. See also *high seat*.

pin feather   the small inside feather at the base of the primary, to be found in *woodcock*, snipe and curlew, at one time much sought after by artists and now often worn in hatbands by sporting gentlemen. In 1936 Eric Parker wrote of curlew: 'Woodcock and snipe are not the only birds with that strange stiff little quill, and the pin feathers in the old days might have furnished miniature painters with three brushes of different sizes' (*LL Shooting*, 117).

piner   OED: 'One who, or that which, pines; spec. an animal suffering from a wasting disease.' The *Pall Mall Gazette* (26 July 1882) noted: 'A large proportion of the grouse have the appearance of having died from starvation . . . the keepers . . . call the emaciated birds "piners".' Still used of gamebirds and of deer; i.e. in poor condition. This may be the result of disease, a bad winter and lack of feeding, or old age, but in general such beasts are better culled whenever possible. Also known as a *waster*.

pinfire guns   the earliest *breech-loaders* were equipped with a cumbersome action and the charge was fired by a pin projecting from the cartridge itself. During the 1850s these pinfire breech-loaders were still vieing with the old *muzzle-loaders*. It was not until the 1860s with the invention of the centre-fire cartridge and the *hammer gun* that the pinfire gun and the muzzle-loader both became obsolete.

pink-footed goose   *Anser brachyrynchus*, a small goose with pink legs and feet like the *greylag*. It has a short pink and black beak, by which, as well as by its smaller size, it may be recognised. Weighing 5–8 lbs and 24–30 inches long, it is often found in arable fields and may be shot inland from 1 September to 31 January and on the foreshore from 1 September to 20 February.

pins   etymology uncertain. Of deer; hairs and small spots of blood (pin-spots?) left behind, showing that a bullet has hit the body, see *paint*. The type of blood and hair may have considerable importance, e.g. light-coloured blood and dark hair indicating a lung shot.

pintail   *Anas acuta*. The male has a chocolate-coloured neck and head, and both duck and drake are notable for their long slender neck and pointed tail, hence the name. In the female especially it is the distinguishing feature between the pintail and the mallard duck. The length from beak to tail is about 22 inches and the weight is about 2½ lbs. The season is as for other wildfowl.

pits, pitting   OED: 'The formation of small pits by corrosion.' Of shotgun barrels: corrosion caused by lack of care, or rust. It can sometimes be improved by *lapping*.

plane   v. OED: 'of a bird: to soar on outstretched motionless wings', but this is as used in falconry and has not the same sense in shooting. Then it is generally used of driven *pheasants*, although sometimes also applicable to other driven birds in similar circumstances and more rarely to *walked-up* birds. It means to glide downwards with set wings, usually after being *pricked*. Such flights may last several hundred yards in favourable conditions, even if the bird has been extremely hard hit. When there is any doubt the *gun*, or *picker-up* standing behind the guns, should follow the flight until the bird alights, or falls dead. After such a flight a bird may often be seen to perch and then fall dead a few moments later. When walked-up birds *plane* they are more usually only wing-tipped and the planing flight is much shorter. The word itself does not seem to have been used until aircraft and flying had become commonplace sights in the 1930s. One of the earlier usages is in 1942 by Lynn-Allen: '*Behaviour of Hit Birds*: A partridge or pheasant which planes to earth is probably hit in the wing and is fairly sure to be a runner' (p. 155). A good early description of this reaction by a shot bird is in 1845 by St John regarding geese: 'I was about two hundred yards from the birds . . . they . . . flew directly towards me . . . I killed a brace, one dropping perfectly dead and the other extending her wings and gradually sinking till she fell on the top of a furze-bush three or four hundred yards off, where I found her lying quite dead' (p. 174).

plantation   of trees; an area all planted at the same time.

plate   v. 'To fire a shotgun barrel at a whitewashed steel plate (hence the verb) at 40 yards to check the *pattern* of shot. Also termed *plating* a gun.

platform hide   a hide in the tree-tops for shooting pigeons, 'Excellent sport at pigeons can be had from platforms constructed in suitable treetops' Brander (*Sport*, 195).

pneumatic wad   an expanding card wad used instead of felt or compound.

poach   the etymology stems from OF *pocher*, to thrust or dig out with the fingers, a collateral form of *poke*, and hence to put in a bag; the connection between 'poke', 'pocket' and 'bag' is still close in many dialect forms in the north of England and in Scotland, e.g a 'poke of sweets' = a bag of sweets. OED: 'to encroach or trespass (on the lands or rights of another) in order to possess oneself unlawfully or unfairly of something, especially in order to steal game', hence to take game, or fish, illegally or by unsportsmanlike devices; to kill or take game on another person's ground, or where the sporting rights belong to someone else, without permission, by means of a gun, net, trap, or dog or any other manner; to kill game illegally on another's ground. 'He poach'd the wood and on the warren snared' – George Crabbe, *The Parish Register* (1810).

poacher   OED: 'also potcher: One who poaches or trespasses in pursuit of game: one who takes or kills game unlawfully.' One who takes game with gun, traps, nets, dog, or by other means, on ground where he has no sporting rights. In 1666 John Evelyn described 'The young potcher with his dog and kite, breaking his neighbour's fences or trampling o'er his corn for a bird not worth sixpence' (*Public Employment*). Thomas Otway in *The Orphan* (1680) used the more modern spelling: 'So Poachers basely picked up tir'd Game Whilst the fair hunter's cheated of his Prey.' The term may also be applied to a *greedy shot*, or *poaching shot*.

poacher's pocket   a capacious game pocket inside the lining of a shooting coat, so termed from the old poacher's habit of slitting the lining of a coat in order to carry game hidden from view. If game is carried in a poacher's pocket it is advisable to have a removable lining, or a plastic bag inside it, to avoid the coat's becoming extremely smelly.

poaching shot   one who poaches his neighbouring gun's shots on a driven day and takes birds which are really theirs. (See

greedy shot.) Alternatively, one who poaches his neighbour's boundaries and shoots those birds which stray over onto his side.

point   the OED states rather uncertainly 'of a hound; To indicate the presence and position (of game) by standing rigidly looking towards it.' Also 'of a pointer or setter; The act of pointing: the rigid attitude assumed on finding game, with the head and gaze directed towards it. Usually in phrases *to make*, *to come to* (a point).' More accurately today would be: of gundogs, particularly ***pointers/setters/pointer-retrievers***: to indicate the presence of game by a rigid stance with the muzzle generally, but by no means always, pointing towards the game itself. Hence to come *on point*. In 1742 William Somerville wrote: 'My setter ranges in the new-shorn fields . . . there he stops . . . And points with his instructive nose upon The trembling prey' ('Field Sports', line 257). Surtees described a *point* well:

> Ponto, whose energetic exertions had been gradually relaxing, until he had settled down to a leisurely hunting-dog, suddenly stood transfixed, with the right foot up and his gaze settled on a rushy tuft.
>
> "P-o-n-t-o!" ejaculated Jog, expecting every minute to see him dash at it. "P-o-n-t-o!" repeated he, raising his hand. (p. 330).

Brander remarks: 'The point itself is literally an arresting spectacle. The handler's attention is attracted willy-nilly by the rigid pose' (*Dog*, 63). See also *false point*.

pointer   OED: 'A dog of a breed nearly allied to the true hounds, used by sportsmen to point at or indicate the presence of game, especially birds; on scenting which the dog stands rigidly with muzzle stretched towards the game and usually one foot raised.' Today the Kennel Club lists pointers and setters together, including ***English pointers***, English setters, English, Irish and Gordon setters in the same category. They are not expected to retrieve. This was not the case before the introduction of the ***breech-loader*** in the 1850s. Hawker noted in his Diary for 26 February 1820:

> 5 snipes: This evening poor old Nero died . . . He was the best dog I ever had, ever saw, or ever heard of . . . I almost always used him single-handed for every purpose as he would of his own accord "down charge" and bring the game when told; at a hedge he would stand till I came, and then, if ordered, go all the way round and drive the game to my side. For a river, for a boat, for everything, he was the perfect

wildfowl dog, although a high bred pointer with a cross of foxhound. The game that I calculate has been killed to this dog . . . I estimate at about 5,000 head.

In 1832 *The Sporting Magazine* noted: 'A Pointer or Setter to deserve the name should hunt high but steadily; quarter his ground with truth and judgement; turn to hand, or whistle; drop to hand, bird and shot; back at all distances; be steady from a hare, yet follow a wounded one, if necessary; and recover a dead or wounded bird well.' One of the earliest references to pointers is by Pennant in 1768 where he noted 'The Pointer, which is a dog of foreign extraction, was unknown to our ancestors' (i, 54). See *false point*.

pointer–retrievers   the HPR breeds are classified by the Kennel Club as 'German Shorthaired Pointers and those breeds which hunt, point and retrieve' (e.g. *Magyar Viszlas*, or Hungarian pointers, Munsterlanders, Weimaraners and Brittany spaniels). They are expected to work precisely as indicated in *The Sporting Magazine* of 1832 for a *pointer* or setter. See also *English pointer*.

points   OED: 'tines of a deer's horn'. Of antlers; alternative term to *tines*. In 1884 Richard Jeffries wrote: 'An antler is judged by the number of points or tines which spring from the beam. The beam is the main stem and the points are the branches' (*Red Deer*, 84).

poke   with a shotgun. Not included in this sense in the OED: to take aim and fail to swing, a beginner's fault, almost certain to result in a miss. Once starting to aim and hence to slow the swing and to *poke*, this can become a serious fault. Even experienced shots can be afflicted by this fault at times. It can often be caused, especially when shooting in company, by becoming too eager and tense, and the best solution is to relax. Unfortunately the more he misses, the tenser the gun becomes and the worse the problem. In 1930 Leslie Sprake advised: 'The novice . . . should endeavour to pass the stage of *conscious poking* . . . it is better to swing and miss than poke and hit' (*LL Shooting*, 35). A good example of the usage is by T.H. White: 'the last pheasant day of the season . . . I only got four birds all day . . . I don't know what I was doing wrong. I was probably poking and pulling to the right . . . It was a humiliation' (p. 302). The final word on the subject is probably best left to Purdey: 'The great secret of shooting rabbits well is to keep the gun moving – swing will make you a good shot and poking will make you a bad one' (p. 106).

poodle   the name originates from German *Pudel hund*, or

water dog, and the dog is in fact a true water dog. Although not
generally recognised as a gundog breed, they were at one time
undoubtedly a sound working breed, closely related to the
Portuguese water dog, or cao d'agua, used by the coastal
fishermen to retrieve their nets. It is reasonably certain that the
Irish water spaniel and curly-coated *retrievers* also owe their
origins, in part at least, to the same source as the poodle. In
1845 St John recorded that he used a poodle as his working
gundog. See *retrieve* and Gervase Markham's description of
training the Water Dog. There is little doubt that, properly
trained, the poodle can make an excellent gundog although
seldom seen in the shooting field.

poult   ME *poullet* allied to the Fr *poulet*, a diminutive of *poule*,
a hen. OED: 'The young of the ... pheasant ... and various
game birds.' First attested in 1425. In 1863 Sabine Baring
Gould wrote of 'Ptarmigan poults, barely fledged' (*Iceland*,
162).

pre-orbital gland   of deer; the scent gland situated near the
corner of the eye. See also *sub-orbital gland*.

prick   v. To wound game with a few pellets by only catching
it in the edge of the pattern, or by firing inaccurately, or firing
at too great a range, so that it flies on, or runs off, *winged* or
wounded, possibly to die later and unlikely to breed if it does
recover. In this sense not in the OED and it only seems to have
come into use in the post-1945 period (Brander defines it in
Sporting Terms, 1968). See *plane, pricked bird*.
   OED: 'of a hare; to make a track in running.' Now virtually
obsolete. An example of this usage is to be found in 1632 by
John Guillim: 'For when she (a hare) ... Beateth the plaine
high-waie where you may yet perceive her footing, it is said she
... Pricketh' (*Heraldry*, 176). Also OED, to trace or track a hare
by its footprints. An early example is in 1756 (*The Connoisseur*,
No. 105): 'We were often delayed by trying if we could prick a
hare.' This may not be entirely obsolete, since as late as 1886
Frederick T. Elworthy noted the usage: 'To examine the mud
in a gateway, or road, to see if a hare has passed is "to prick the
hare"' (*The West Somerset Word Book*).

pricked bird   a bird which has received one or more shotgun
pellets in the body but has not been killed. A great deal depends
on the circumstances. An indifferently shot bird may be
obviously *winged* and a *runner* or merely *wing-tipped* and a
runner, or it may drop one or both legs, or it may be lightly hit
as described without apparent immediate effect. A *pricked bird*
will probably be clearly seen to flinch, or stagger, in its flight

when the shot is fired. Its flight should thereafter be watched
carefully either by the gun, if he is able to, or by the picker-up,
whose task it is to note such birds, and it should be marked
down and followed up if it is possible to do so. If a driven bird,
it may set its wings and *plane* downwards. If a going-away bird,
it may sometimes be seen to *tower* some distance away. It is
always regrettable to prick a bird and usually means the bird
was for some reason not caught fully in the *pattern*, or was
fired at at too great a range. It is generally a sign of faulty
shooting, but if it occurs frequently and the reason is not
obvious it may pay to examine the cartridges and/or pattern the
gun. Badly pricked birds will almost certainly die, although
some lightly pricked birds do recover. The meaning as noted
does not appear to have been commonly used until after the
1939–45 war, although an early example is in 1939 by Purdey:
'Don't shoot at a bird . . . too far out . . . one or two pellets may
strike the bird. A pricked hen often doesn't lay again' (p. 76).
In 1950 Sedgwick wrote: 'On his rounds next day he finds
pricked birds which may eventually recover – or may not'
(p. 152). F.G. Standfield makes the valid point: 'there is
nothing sporting in birds being pricked instead of killed' (p. 62).

pricket   from the English *prike* with the Roman suffix *ettus*
Anglo-Latin, *prikettus*. OED: 'a buck in its second year having
straight unbranched horns.' Of fallow deer: a male in the second
year: but in the New Forest used to describe a yearling with its
first spike antlers; also, obsolete, a red deer in the third year.
First attested in the late 13th century in a Latin text. In 1486
The Boke of St Albans noted: 'The secunde yere a preket.'

proof   OED: 'The testing of . . . small fire-arms by firing a
heavy charge.' A gun which has passed through the Proof
House, is said to be *in Proof*. Hence *proof marks,* the records of
proving, stamped on the barrels of a shotgun by the Proof
House testing the gun. It is illegal to sell a gun without modern
proof marks and it is highly dangerous to use such a gun with
modern powders.

pronk, pronking   not included in the OED; possibly a dialect
derivation of 'pronging', from the stabbing action of a fork, up
and down, which it resembles. Used particularly of *fallow
deer's* gait when bouncing away stiff-legged if disturbed. This
gait, with all four legs stiff and moving as if on springs, is in fact
characteristic at times of almost any deer and antelope, or most
ruminants on occasions, especially when young and at play.
Even sheep may be seen to *pronk* at times, viz. lambs in the
spring. In 1983 Charles Coles wrote: '. . . fallow under tension

or excitement indulge in a very characteristic "pronking" gait –
a high bouncing canter with all four limbs held rigid' (*Stalking*,
142).

ptarmigan   *Lagopus mutus*: a game bird, cousin to the *red
grouse*, found only above the 2,000-foot level in Scotland. The
cock is white-chested and white-winged with a grey to black
body, and the hen is grey to buff. Both cock and hen turn white
in winter. Both have feathered legs. Slightly smaller than the
grouse, about 1¼ lbs. The open season is from 12 August to 10
December. Their food is varied – mosses, blaeberries, etc. They
pair as early as the grouse, but nest later, generally hatching
5–9 eggs. They are amazingly well-camouflaged to suit their
rocky habitat on the high tops of the mountains. Generally shot
over dogs, or walking-up, their call is a croaking sound, but
they are notably silent, especially in flight. The Gaelic *tarma-
chan* was also Lowland Scots usage before 1600. In 1618 John
Taylor the Water-Poet in his *Pennyless Pilgrimage* around
Scotland wrote of 'Capons, Chickins, Partridge, Moorecoots,
Heathcocks, Caperkellies and Termagants'. In 1684, however
Sir Robert Sibbald in *Scotia Illustrata* introduced a pseudo-
Greek etymological <p> before the <t>: 'Lagopus Avis. . . .
Nostratibus the Ptarmigan.' This was unfortunately taken up in
1766 by Pennant when he wrote: 'The tail of the Ptarmigan
consists of sixteen feathers' (i, 206). Since then the OED states
rather sadly: 'it has passed into ornithological and general
English use.' The spelling was not always quite the same, for in
1804 Thornton wrote:

> After five hours absence they came up, quite exhausted, and
> found me looking for some ptarmigants I had killed . . . and
> had now anxiously sought . . . near two hours without
> success. At length, by the assistance of Dargo they were
> found. Captain Waller had begged me to leave him to himself
> till he recovered, he was so much fatigued.
>
> A thought struck me. I placed a ptarmigant in such a
> position that it appeared to be alive and then mentioning to
> the captain that I had seen one, which he never had,
> immediately on discovering it, he fired and shot it; this
> revived him more than anything I could have given him. The
> having shot a ptarmigant was now the only topic of conver-
> sation, and it would have been cruel to have undeceived him.
> (*Sporting Tour*, 93)

Hawker, although he had never seen one, perpetuated Sibbald's
spelling: 'White Grouse, or Ptarmigan: These birds, instead of
becoming wild in the winter, like the two others, may at any

time be easily shot, if we can but reach the inaccessible parts of
the northern mountains, which they frequent' (*Instructions*, 20).
In 1845 St John knew more about their habits:

Being visited by the sportsman but rarely these birds are
seldom at all shy or wild, but if the day is fine will come out
from among the scattered stones, uttering their peculiar
croaking cry and, running in flocks near the intruder on their
lonely domain, offer, even to the worst shot, an easy chance
of filling his bag. When the weather is windy and rainy, the
ptarmigan are frequently shy and wild; and when disturbed,
instead of running about like tame chickens they fly rapidly
off to some distance, either round some shoulder of the
mountain, or by crossing some precipitous and rocky ravine
get quite out of reach. The shooting these birds should only
be attempted on fine calm days. The labour of reaching the
ground they inhabit is great and it often requires a firm foot
and steady head to keep the sportsman out of danger . . .
(p. 37).

Speedy gave explicit instructions about the birds:

To know their haunts and search for them on the lee side of
the hill, to single out the old birds at the first rise, to mark the
covey and follow it, is about the whole secret of ptarmigan
shooting. As they – especially in hot weather – sometimes sit
very close, an old dog, if he is free from hare, is a valuable
attendant. Even when shot, if falling among grey and white
stones, usually in abundance in ptarmigan haunts, there is a
difficulty in picking them up without a dog, so closely do
they resemble the stones in colour. As the hills become white
with snow, so the ptarmigan also change their plumage,
which vies with the snow in whiteness. (p. 217)

In 1897 John G. Millais was more concerned with the naturalist's viewpoint:

Ptarmigan are monogamous like grouse, but they do not split
up into pairs at once after the males have had loose fights
with others, but the whole covey holds a sort of day-break
tournament in which the males fight somewhat after the
manner of blackcocks. The same spot is resorted to every
morning at daybreak, but it is not maintained from year to
year like the blackcocks' playing ground . . . Ptarmigan are
very much affected by the weather and are as unapproachable
in rain and storms as they are tame on a still sunny day. They
possess the power of ventriloquising to quite as great an
extent as the corncrakes . . . They nearly always all rise at

once, keeping close together and straight shooting is essential to make any sort of bag. (*Encyclopedia*, ii, 139)

Since even by 1929 most gamekeepers, like Colonel Peter Hawker, had never seen a ptarmigan, let alone shot one, and a good many would have been unable to spell the name any better than Thornton, Mackie was unwise to suggest: 'Every gamekeeper is aware of the fact that ptarmigan are like woodcock in one respect. They always lie in accordance with the wind. They are therefore to be found on the lee-side of hills' (p. 219).

pull through   a weighted cord used to pull cleaning materials through a rifle, or, less commonly, shotgun barrels. Care should be taken to pull straight to avoid wear on the ends of the barrels from an indirect pull. In 1930 Burrard opined: 'A pull-through . . . is not nearly so effective a means for cleaning a (shotgun) barrel as a rod because no backwards and forwards motion can be obtained' (*Gunroom*, 90). See *cleaning rod*; *jag*.

pump action shotgun   a type of *repeater* shotgun in which the fore-end slides back by hand action and ejects the cartridge. On being returned to position, the gun is automatically reloaded and the breech closed. Also known as a *pump gun* and a *slide-action gun*.

pump gun   see *pump action shotgun*.

punt gun   a gun of very large bore fitted to a wildfowling punt and generally held in place by *breeching*. It may be a 4 bore or greater and may be muzzle-loading or breech-loading. In either case it is generally fired by a toggle lanyard operated by the *punt gunner*, who is lying in the bows and aiming the gun, while the punt is propelled by his companion with paddles in the stern. 'A Hampshire punt is made so light and narrow as just to hold one person, with a gun of about seventy pounds weight' (Hawker, *Instructions*, 311).

punt gunner   one who goes after wildfowl equipped with a large bore gun fitted to the punt. Now barred by bye-laws as illegal in most areas of the British Isles, because of the disturbance to wildfowl at rest.

purse net   OED: 'a bag-shaped net, the mouth of which can be drawn together with cords', used especially for catching rabbits. A net designed to fit over rabbit holes, formed like an old-fashioned draw-string purse. Pegged securely in position with one or more pegs, when the rabbit bolts from its burrow the strings draw tight and the rabbit is firmly caught. The earliest use of the term appears in *The Master of Game*, *c.* 1400: 'Men taketh hem with houndes, with grehoundes, with heyes and with pursnettes.' It is clear from Turberville in 1576 that little has changed except the spelling since then: 'Set purse-nettes upon al the holes, or as many of them as you can finde' (*Venerie*, 179).

puss   OED: 'A word common to several Teutonic languages usually as a call-name for the cat (rarely becoming as in English a synonym of "cat").' Also applied to a hare. Often used of a hare by sportsmen and countrymen, because of the feline movements and likeness to a cat frequently discernible. In 1668 Sir George Etheredge was one the earliest to use the term: 'If a leveret be better meat than an old Puss' (*She Would If She Could*). In 1858 R.S. Surtees wrote descriptively: 'After scudding up the hill puss stopped to listen and ascertain the quality of her pursuers' (*Ask Mamma*, XXXVIII). Tom Speedy used the term admiringly and again with the feminine bias: 'the hare, as a general rule, doubles back on her own track . . . Those who may have the curiosity to track a hare in the snow will find how invariably this practice is adopted and how well adapted it is to aid "puss" in effecting her escape' (p. 284). Julian Tennyson considered it male: 'The signs of a snared hare are easy to find. Fur is freely scattered round a patch where the grass has been trampled and thrashed by poor puss in his dying struggles' (p. 59). Brander indicated why the word could be used for either sex: 'Hares are always fascinating to watch, especially when they are not aware that they are being observed. It is easy to see from their almost feline movements at times why they are called "Puss." The way their body arches and the fluidity of certain of their movements are in strange contrast to the apparent clumsiness of their slow lollop along, when their long hind legs are not extended' (*Sport*, 84). See *blue hare*; *common brown hare*.

Q **uarry** from OF *curee*, itself derived from the Latin *corium*, skin. The OED states first 'Certain parts of the deer placed on the hide and given to the hounds as a reward.' Derived from the word *Quyrreye*, or entrails, originally fed to the hounds after a successful hunt. First attested *c.* 1300. By transference, secondly taken to mean 'the animal pursued or taken by hounds or hunters', then 'any object of chase, aim, or attack; an intended prey', hence any animal stalked or hunted over dogs or driven to guns, for example 'The Game which it was their interest to preserve, both for their Sport and the Quarry' (Sir William Temple, *History of England*, 1695, p. 180).

quarter OED: 'to range or traverse (ground etc.) in every direction; said especially of dogs in search of game.' Not attested in this sense until 1700, but this is not surprising since pointers *quartering* the ground were not common until the 18th century. In 1768 Pennant wrote: 'Who pass over the fields and quarter the ground as a setting dog' (ii, 235). Of a gundog, especially a *pointer* or *setter*, but of any hunting dog, to hunt the ground in a regular manner usually in a zig-zag pattern and using the wind correctly to find all the game on the ground. See *cheek wind; down wind; into the wind; up wind*.

quarter choke 20 points of choke; but see *modified choke*.

quartz grit grit derived from quartz required by grouse in order to digest their diet of young heather shoots. A plentiful supply of *quartz grit* is essential to the well-being of grouse stocks.

Rabbit ME. OED states 'A common burrowing rodent of the hare-family *Leporidae*, especially the common European species *Lepus Cuniculus*, which is naturally of a brownish-grey colour, but in domestication also white, black or pied.' *Oryctolagus cuniculus cuniculus* of the *Leporidae* family: a four-legged short-furred animal with a short white tail, or *scut* and long ears, familiar throughout Britain. Although predominantly brown in colour, the possible variations are considerable. Pure black, and pure white, or black and white are common colour variations. Less commonly encountered, but very striking, is a yellowish, sometimes lemon-yellow, sometimes orange-yellow, colouration, particularly in sandy soils. It breeds throughout the year and generally lives in holes, or *burrows*, and sometimes in *warrens*. Its weight and size are governed by the feeding available, but it is generally from about 2–3lbs. in weight. Since there is no closed season and it is regarded as a pest, it may be shot, trapped, netted, bolted by *ferrets*, gassed, or poisoned throughout the year. Litters may vary from 2 to 11 born blind and helpless in holes where the doe *kindles*. Her gestation period is six weeks and the young are unable to look after themselves for a further three weeks. However the rabbit has a remarkable ability to survive, despite diseases deliberately introduced from the laboratory such as *myxomatosis*.

Surprisingly, the rabbit is not indigenous. It seems rabbits were introduced to Britain by the Normans, since there is no mention of them in the Domesday Book (1086). The OED notes of the word rabbit: 'Originally applied only to the young animal the full grown one being called a Cony.' *Coney* continued in use until slang sexual connotations brought it into disrepute in the 17th century. In 1386 John de Trevisa (*Bartholomeus*) mentions that: 'Conynges . . . bring forth many rabettes and multiplieth ful swythe.' Turberville still uses the terms in 1576: 'The Conie beareth her Rabettes XXX days and then kindeleth.' By 1768, however, Pennant notes: 'Rabbets will breed seven times a year' (i, 91). In 1807 Daniel wrote of:

Rabbits: The shooting Rabbits in covers or hedge-rows is a pleasant diversion. Three or four Dogs, that will thread the thick parts of either are necessary, and which, when the Rabbit is started, will drive it smartly. The cry of the dogs will point to the Sportsman how to place himself, to catch sight of the object, and his aim must be *quick*; the course of the Rabbit is more rapid and twisting than that of the Hare; it rather glides than runs, and the proper moment of firing is

not easily seized; the Rabbit flies like lightning, when she sees
the Sportsman, or in crossing a road or path cut through the
wood, or if the Dog has struck at but missed her. The best
time for this shooting, is when there is *Snow* upon the ground,
the animal being *then* better seen. Some (*Poachers*) watch,
upon a tree, the appearance of the Rabbits from their earth
... to shoot them; but so barbarous a practice ought to be
restrained by all possible means. (i, 493) And he quotes
(Supplement, 699):

> For *Rabbits* hot, for *Rabbits* cold,
> For *Rabbits* young, for *Rabbits* old,
> For *Rabbits* tender, *Rabbits* tough.
> We thank Thee Lord, *we've had Enough!*

Speedy was appreciative of the sport they provided:

Rabbits also greatly enhance a day's covert shooting when
they are fairly numerous. It is customary in some places for
the keepers to stop up the burrows, in order that outlying
rabbits may be driven to the guns. This method adds
materially to the bag, more especially if ferrets have been
used some days previously, and pieces of white paper stuck
between two split sticks in front of the holes. The object of
this is obvious, as rabbits very naturally object to go into a
hole with such a suspicious-looking thing as a piece of white
paper stuck between two sticks or fluttering in the breeze.
This method is now very generally in use and practised with
much success. Indeed a day's shooting in open cover where
rabbits are numerous and where they have been ferreted and
the paper placed as described, partakes very much of the
character of a day's pheasant shooting in one of the best
Norfolk preserves. Having frequently been engaged rabbit-
shooting in such places, we have found it no unusual thing
for considerably over a thousand to be brought to book.
Having been hunted out of the holes with ferrets for a week
previously, and the burrows stopped up, they utilised every
tuft of grass or bit of cover for a hiding place, and of course
great numbers came to grief.

Their habits resemble very much those of the hare, only
they will more frequently pass the guns at full speed. In such
circumstances the sportsman must, as a matter of course, aim
well forward, otherwise they will frequently be so little injured
by the shot as to be able to run some distance, and thus
occupy time – specially valuable in cover-shooting – in
picking them up. (p. 286)

In 1889 Lancaster took a different view:

Shooting Rabbits. This is always good fun and splendid practice for the beginner, because it teaches him to keep a good look-out and handle or mount a gun quickly. Rabbits as a rule only give time for a short sight of them. When bolting across a ride, always bear in mind to shoot where they are running to, and not where they are when you first see them.

Rabbit shooting in rough grass land, or in bracken or furze is excellent sport, if with the assistance of beaters. A perfect line with the guns must be kept, so as to allow of shooting either forward or at rabbits that may break back and run through the line.

A good hedgerow will sometimes hold a great number of rabbits; and a spaniel or terrier working them, with a gun on other side of the hedge, is good sport at certain seasons – December and January for choice. Great care must be exercised in this sport, so as to avoid wounding the dog or your friend. Remember, as a golden rule, never to shoot at a rabbit on the top of a hedge bank and on no account be led into shooting into or through the hedge, but let the rabbit be clear and going forward or back along the outer edge of the ditch, well out in the field. Keep whistling to the "gun" with you, so that you may be opposite to each other; and never shoot at a pheasant or any other bird that may be put up if it is crossing to your friend's side of the hedge, but let him shoot when it has got over and clear; simply call to him that something is crossing to his side, so that he may be ready for it.

Rabbits are generally found lying out in tufts of grass in fine weather, and when started are certain to make for the hedge or covert. To make sure of killing them get well ahead and shoot at the first chance because a second is seldom given. (p.55)

rack   OED: 'The track made by an animal, especially that of a deer as marked by gaps in hedges, etc.' Also paths worn in woodland which deer are in the habit of following. In 1611 Cotgrave's *Dictionarie* gives: 'Les passees d'un Cerf: His racke or passages, the places he has gone through or by.' In 1817 John Mayer wrote: 'Rabbits are taken in various ways . . . If they lie in hedge-rows . . . plant one or two guns ate the end where the racks meet' (*Sportsman's Directory*, 23). The usage is now rare. Also, colloquial and descriptive usage in North America meaning the *antlers* of deer.

range   of a shotgun; generally accepted to mean the effective killing range, e.g. of a 12 bore accepted as 50 yards maximum. No shots should be taken at game beyond that range. On the other hand, shot may carry considerably further and thus safety is always a point to consider when firing a shotgun. If fired at an angle of thirty degrees, shot might travel as far as three hundred yards. Burrard stated categorically: 'If it is assumed that the extreme range for any ordinary shot size is just under 250 yards the error will not be material' (*Shotgun*, iii, 446).

rat   the OED states 'The ultimate origin of the word is uncertain, but it seems probable that it was adopted first in the Teutonic languages when the animal came to be known in western Europe and thence passed into the Romance tongues.' It is defined as: 'A rodent of some of the larger species of the genus *Mus*, esp. *M. rattus*, the black rat (now almost extinct) and *M. decumanus*, the common, grey, brown, or Norway rat.' Present in any quantity they can prove an unwelcome presence on a shoot, but fortunately they are usually comparatively easily dealt with by using *Warfarin* laid out in drainpipes where dogs and cats, or other animals cannot get at it. First attested around 1000; in 1377 William Langland wrote: 'Had ze rattes zoure wille ze couthe nouzt reule zourselue' (*Piers Plowman*, Prol., 200).

recess choke   formed by boring out a portion of the barrel to give a choke constriction. The effects are limited and it is usually inserted as a regulating device by the barrel regulator when test-firing the barrels to perfect the final pattern.

red grouse   see *grouse*.

red-legged partridge   *Alectoris rufa*: a game bird which has a red bill and legs, a grey crown to its head, a white eye stripe and throat patch and is larger than the *grey partridge*, but is similar in habits. About 13½ inches from beak to tail and 16–18 oz., it has a harsher call than the grey partridge, a deliberate 'Chuk-chuk'. Nesting habits are similar but they are possibly hardier birds. They do not fly so readily and will frequently run long distances, especially in front of dogs, so are not popular for shooting over *pointers*. In heavy wet land, such as parts of East Anglia, when driven they often collect balls of mud on their feet and are unable to fly, and are unpopular on these grounds. It is also claimed that they tend to drive grey partridges off the ground. They are not native, but a successful, if often contro-versial, introduction from the continent from the 17th century onwards, hence possibly the nickname 'Frenchman' (see below), which, although probably sometimes used during the 19th century, especially in East Anglia, does not seem to have come into general usage until after the 1914–18 War, when many of the country people had been abroad to France to fight. The season is as for the grey partridge. It is largely a matter of taste and the expertise of the cook, but it is also held by some that they are not as good to eat as the grey partridge. In 1807 Daniel noted:

So far back as the time of Charles II several pair of these Red legged Partridges were turned out about Windsor to obtain a stock; but they are supposed to have mostly perished . . . The late Duke of Northumberland preserved many . . . but the late Earl of Rochford and the Marquis of Hertford have been at the most expence and trouble to establish them in this Country . . . The Compiler in 1777 found within two miles of Colchester a Covey of *fourteen* . . . from that time until November 1799 he never shot one; he was then out at Sudbourn with a Gentleman who was particularly anxious to kill some of these *red Partridges* and hunted with a brace of capital Pointers for them only; the instant the Dogs stood, the red birds ran, and always took wing . . . out of the range of the shot from any fowling piece. Upon the same Grounds and on the same Day, they laid until the *Springing Spaniels* (with which the Compiler was shooting) almost touched them before they arose and in a short time he killed two brace and a half. . . . they have one peculiarity, that when wounded, they will go to ground in the Rabbit burrows. (iii, 94)

One of the earlier usages of the term Frenchman is to be found in Purdey's *The Shotgun* (1939), given in parenthesis along with a possible explanation of the origin: 'They run faster and more frequently than the English bird, and sometimes you hear people say that because they have red legs and run fast they are like the French Infantry Soldier of many years ago, hence the name "Frenchman"' (p. 74). In 1942 Lynn-Allen was writing familiarly, but still in parenthesis, 'it may be admitted at once that the "Frenchman" does prefer to use his legs rather than his wings' (p. 70). Two years later, the Editor of *The Shooting Times*, Sedgwick also wrote in parenthesis: 'the "Frenchman," as the red-legged partridge is often called' (*Young Shot*, 153). By 1948, however, Drought is writing with unqualified enthusiasm: 'Once a Frenchman gets on the wing he is not only quicker off the mark . . . he makes a bee-line for his objective and nothing will turn him' (p. 114).

redshank   OED: 'A wading bird (*Totanus calidris*) of the snipe family (*Scolopacidae*) so-called from the colour of its legs.' First attested in 1525. A wader found on foreshore and inland meres;

as well as the red legs distinguished by a typical flash of white in flight and a warning liquid call, well known to most sportsmen. Now much less common inland than a few decades back and a protected species.

repeater   one of the single-barrelled group of shotguns. Of two kinds, the pump gun, or *slide-action*, and the *bolt action* type.

retrieve   the OED states that the word is from the OF *retrouver*, to find, and the ME usage was *retreve*, but in the 16th and 17th centuries was retrive, with the changeover to the modern spelling *retrieve* from around 1650. The OED first gives the usages as applied to hunting and falconry before shooting became a recognised sport, i.e to find or discover again game (which has been temporarily lost); especially to flush or set up (partridges) a second time (for the hawks). For example in 1658 Andrew Topsell: 'These are taught by Falconers to retrive and raise Partridges' (*Four Footed Beasts*, 122). Secondly the OED gives: 'To find and bring in (a bird etc.) that has been wounded or killed' and quotes Walsh in 1856 writing of 'a little rough terrier': 'He . . . will retrieve any game from the snipe to the pheasant' (p. 36). Of a gundog; to fetch game once it has been shot.

A gundog should *retrieve* well **to hand**, without mouthing, after a **clean pickup**. A retrieve may be after flush and shot or to driven game. A retrieve may be marked and in the open, probably the simplest of all, or marked and in cover, or else unmarked and in the open or in cover. It may be a retrieve on dead game, on wounded game, or on a *runner*, and may thus be classified as easy or difficult. When a dog has marked and can retrieve by eye it is probably the simplest of all, but when it is unseen, on a runner, at a distance, the dog has to use all its experience and instinct to find the fall of the game and once the scent has been *struck*, to follow it up and retrieve the game tenderly to hand. Retrieving training may start as a puppy, but too much training or bad handling, or an unsuitable introduction to wounded game, can result in **hard mouth**. The ideal retrieve should be fast, with a clean pick-up of live or wounded game, and brought to hand with a **soft mouth**.

retriever   OED: 'A dog used for the purpose of retrieving.' It gives: 'a. One employed to set up game again.' It quotes *The Boke of St Albans* in 1486 on dogs used in falconry and only then: 'b. One of a breed specially adapted for finding and bringing in wounded game.' The first attestation for this usage given is in 1841 by Frederick Marryat (*The Poacher*): 'Tell them to come down with their retrievers.' It also quotes George Jesse, historian of the *British Dog* (1866), writing: 'He sent his retriever after it, who ... caught and killed the hare and returned with it in his mouth.' This behaviour is scarcely conducive to *soft mouth*, but in practice any type of dog may be used for retrieving game. The Kennel Club list of retrievers includes in Group I Black and Yellow Labradors, Golden Retrievers, Flat and Curly-coated Retrievers. Spaniels in Group III and the HPR breeds in Group IV are also expected to retrieve.

rib-face nick-name for the *muntjac* deer, because of the noticeable ribs running up their faces giving them a Roman-nosed effect.

ribs the steel strips between the two barrels of a side-by-side shotgun, known as the top rib and bottom rib.

ride OED: 'A road or way made for riding on horseback, especially through a wood.' In 1856 Walsh, writing of woodcock, noted 'in flying, even from one covert to another, they may always be seen to take the same ride, or break in the woods' (p. 61). In forestry terms, *ride* means the division between blocks of trees in woodland. Strategically placed guns in rides may often have good shooting, although, depending on the width of the ride, *snap shooting* may be the order of the day.

rifle OED: the origins of the verb from which the noun is derived are somewhat obscure, possibly Fr, *rifler* 'to scratch'; Ger *riefeln*, Danish *rifle*, or Swedish *reffla* 'to groove'. The OED gives 'Rifle v. To shoot with a rifle', but this form is now obsolete. It also gives interestingly: '1. One of a set of spiral grooves cut on the interior surface of a gun barrel with the object of giving the projectile a rotatory movement on its own axis.' This is first attested in 1751. This original sense of 'rifling' was almost at once qualified by the addition of combinations such as 'rifle-barrel, -carbine, -musket, -piece'; an early attestation is in 1788: 'Wolfe ... was marked out by a miscreant who was provided with a rifle-piece' (*New London Magazine*, 520). The OED continues: '2. A firearm, especially a musket or carbine, having a specially grooved bore.' To this it adds 'A breech-loading rifle is now one of the most usual types of firearm.' By transference, when stalking, the person shooting the deer is referred to as the *rifle*. 'I have known a "rifle" go out and ... bring in five, or even six, stags in a day ...' (Mackie, 264).

rifle range the OED states, somewhat archaically: '1. The distance that a rifle-ball will carry.' Modern rifles fire bullets, but the meaning remains the same. OED also gives: '2. A place for practising rifle shooting.' An Act of 1885 stated: 'Title; Land held by . . . a Volunteer Corps for an Artillery or Rifle Range.'

rig   the etymology is interesting and can be traced thus: the OED gives: 'Ridge: 1. The back or spine in man or animals *Obs*: . . . b. Of the back or other parts of the body.' An entry by Henry Best in his *Yorkshire Farming Accounts* (1641) reads: 'Close tuppes are such as have both the stones in the ridge of the back.' The OED under 'Ridgel' gives: 'An animal which has been imperfectly castrated . . . or whose genital organs are not properly developed: esp. a male animal (ram, bull or horse) with only one testicle.' First attested in 1597. Variants given include: *rigg, ridgel, riggald*: of a male animal imperfectly castrated, the testicle being supposed to have lodged near the back (i.e. ridge) hence also *rig*. The earliest attestation for this appears to be *c.* 1430 and the term also includes deer. A note in 1881 (*Greener Gun*, 509) reads: 'Ox-deer, or "heaviers," and rigs are in season with the yeld-hinds until the end of January.' See *cryptorchid; havier.*

right and left   two birds killed by firing the *right and left* barrels without the gun leaving the shoulder; i.e. the gun is swung from one target to the next without appreciable pause. Since the right barrel is usually improved cylinder, whereas the left may be choked to a greater degree, it may be assumed that a right and left correctly taken are at birds flushed in front of the gun and flying away. Thus the nearer bird is shot without any choke and the further away bird is shot with some degree of choke. Birds being driven towards the gun should be taken *left and right*. Walsh wrote: 'in many cases very wild birds will allow him to come up and get a "right and left"' (p. 52).

rights   of sporting, or shooting. Shooting *rights* should be specifically laid down in a shooting lease. They may include the right to shoot only certain types of quarry; e.g. pheasants and partridges, wildfowl or hares and rabbits, with **groundgame** being expressly excluded, or vice-versa. Anyone shooting on ground without invitation or without having the shooting rights is *poaching*. Of antlers, obsolete a stag was said to 'have its rights' when it had **bays, brows** and *trays*.

rim-fire   not in the OED: of a .22 rifle cartridge, one in which the explosive cap composition covers the entire base of the cartridge not merely the centre, so that the striker need not strike the centre to explode it. In 1972 Geoffrey Boothroyd wrote: 'A study of the rim-fire rifle scene is made very much easier by the fact that we are dealing with but one type of ammunition, the .22 rim-fire. Today there are four different varieties of .22 rim-fire ammunition, the .22 short, the .22 long, the .22 long rifle and the .22 rim-fire magnum' (Brander & Zern, 101).

road   OED: 'of doubtful origin: v. of a dog to follow up (a game bird) by the foot scent.' It quotes Walsh: 'As retrievers do all their work by "roading" or "footing" they require that peculiar kind of nose and not the high winding nose which the pointer and setter display' (p. 47). This was based on a misconception of a dog's scenting and retrieving powers, as were the later comments by Speedy: 'It is almost impossible to pick up runners in rank turnips without the assistance of a retriever; for although a pointer may "road" them up (and point at them) they often slip off again and escape' (p. 269). Of a pointing dog; *to road* means to *work out* a scent after a point to ensure that all the game has gone after a covey has been flushed. Individual birds, especially grouse, may often be found sitting tight and may be flushed subsequently after the main covey has flown. Various prepositions may be added, as *road-out, road-down* a furrow, or ditch, or *road-up*.

roar   of red deer stag; descriptive of the sound made during the *rut*. In 1845 St John wrote:
He instantly halted and looking in that direction roared repeatedly, while we could see in the evening air, which had become cold and frosty, his breath coming out his nostrils like smoke. Presently he was answered by another and another stag and the whole distance seemed alive with them. A more unearthly noise, I never heard as it echoed and re-echoed through the rocky glens that surrounded us. (p. 283)

rocketer   OED: 'A game-bird that "rockets"'. A quote from 1883 reads 'The "rocketer" which I may at once define as a bird flying fast and high towards the shooter.' A *rocketer* is the accepted term for a fast climbing and accelerating bird, usually a driven pheasant, but sometimes also grouse or other game-birds, coming high and fast over the guns. In 1884 Davenport wrote: 'So should the "rocketer" fall; as straight to earth as the velocity of his previous flight, or the force of the wind will allow, and, falling, never move so much as a feather' (p. 135). In the same year Speedy noted: 'in some parts of England it is a rule that the guns placed in line with the beaters shall shoot ground game only, in order that those stationed at the end of the wood may get "rocketing" shots at the pheasants' (p. 288).

rock dove   *Columba livia*. It has similar glossy green neck markings as the *stock dove*, but the throat and breast are grey. Found on cliffs and quarries near the coast it is a protected bird under the 1981 Wildlife & Countryside Act.

rode, roding, also **road**   the OED states origins obscure, but gives: 'v. 1. Of wildfowl; to fly landward in the evening' and quotes Pennant, 1768: 'As soon as the evening sets in, the decoy rises (as they term it) . . . This rising of the decoy in the evening is in Somersetshire called the rodding' (ii, 464). Also: 'Gunners wait in the marshes in the Bristol Channel in the evening to shoot wildfowl "roding-in" half an hour after sunset' (*N & Q*, 1885). Also see *roading*: 'The practice on the part of certain birds of flying in the evening.' Under this OED quotes the 1888 *Encyclopedia Britannica*: 'During this season the Woodcock performs at twilight flights of a remarkable kind . . . This characteristic flight is in some parts of England called "roading"' (xxiv, 651). The OED also adds 'Rode: 2. To perform a regular evening flight during the breeding season.' In 1907 Bensusan noted: 'When a woodcock is roding he must not vary his pace, his flight, or his song' (*Wildlife Stories*, 208). From these quotations it would seem that *rode, road,* or *rodd,* and *roding, roading* and *rodding,* may all have West Country connections and similar meanings, implying regular flighting in the evenings. Since woodcock were and still are common in the West Country, this is perhaps not surprising.

The regular flight of *woodcock* through the woods in spring evenings is widely known as *roding*. These flights, mainly by the cocks during the mating season and while the eggs are incubating, take place over set areas and the birds follow a strict flight pattern repeated evening after evening, uttering their strange croaking call as they fly along the *rides,* or pathways through the trees. They were thus often netted or shot by poachers out of season. In 1845 St John wrote of these flights:

I rather astonished an English friend of mine who was staying with me in Inverness-shire during the month of June, by asking him to come out woodcock shooting one evening. And his surprise was not diminished by my preparations for our shoot, which consisted of ordering out chairs and cigars into the garden at the back of the house, which happened to be just in the line of the birds' flight from the woods to the swamps. After he had killed three or four from his chair we stopped murdering the poor birds, which were quite unfit to eat, having probably young ones, or eggs to provide for at home in the quiet recesses of the woods. (p. 253)

In 1938 Tennyson observed:

This "roding" is a strange performance. During courtship and while his mate is sitting, the cock bird rises each evening at dusk, skims slowly down the glade on a definite and unchanging line of flight and, once out in the open rises to a very great height, tumbling and diving about in a manner quite foreign to his normal dignity, uttering all the while loud grunts and croaks and shrill squeals known as "whisps". Normally the woodcock is a very quiet and solitary fellow, but now, if a number of birds are nesting in the wood, the cocks will join together for this curious "roding," 20 or 30 of them chasing each other high up in the air, swooping, rushing and falling at great speed, until the game comes to an end and each bird flits slowly and soberly home along his chosen path. The "roding" flight is often repeated in the early dawn. (p. 68)

roe deer   etymology uncertain. OE *raha, raa*; MDu *Ree*; ON *ra*; OS *reho*; OHG *reho*. After 1300 the a forms are only northern and Scots. The OED gives: 'A small species of deer *Capreolus Capraea*, inhabiting various parts of Europe and Asia.' The quotes given date from the 8th century and among the earlier ones in English is *c*. 1386 from Chaucer: 'is ful wight, god waat, as is a raa' (*The Reeve's Tale*). In 1576 George Turberville wrote: 'They never part until the Row-doe have fawned' (*Venerie*, 142).

Capreolus capreolus: the male is known as a buck, the female as a doe and the young as kids or fawns. The smaller of the two indigenous British deer: they measure about 25–30 inches at the shoulder and some 44 inches from muzzle to rump, weighing between 45 and 65 lbs. In summer their coat is bright red with pale underbelly, changing to a greyer colour around October, and the caudal disc below the rump develops a distinctive white flaring effect known as the *target*, when alarmed and retreating at speed. They have all the gaits of a horse, but generally move in a gentle bounding canter. They may sometimes *pronk*. They can jump six feet with ease. The buck sheds his antlers annually from mid-October and starts re-growing them at once. By March/April they are generally free of *velvet*. Bucks and does are not strictly monogamous, but are frequently seen together and small family groups are not uncommon. The birth of twins is normal and triplets are not unknown. They are usually born towards the end of May or early June. In late June the roe doe often runs circles and figures of eight while playing with her fawns, forming very visible *roe rings*. The rut takes place between July and August and preliminaries may take some days, with the doe again running rings this time with the buck in close attendance. Roe deer are to be found throughout most of Scotland and most of northern England down to a line from east to west about level with the Tees. They are also to be found throughout East Anglia and most of the southern counties, with their range extending. With the steady development of foxhunting in the late 17th and throughout the 18th and 19th centuries, they were nearly exterminated in many popular hunting areas in England and have only begun to recover ground during the latter part of this century.

roe rings   of roe buck and roe does; the circles and sometimes figures of eight made by the buck and doe during the *rut*, when the buck is chasing the doe. Also formed by the does when playing with their kids, prior to the rut.

rogue   OED: 'An elephant driven away or living apart from the herd, and of a savage or destructive disposition', also, 'Any large wild animal of a similar character.' In 1872 R.F. Burton wrote: 'The "rogue" is found amongst hippopotami, elk, deer and other gramnivors, as well as elephants, lions, tigers and the larger carnivores' (*Zanzibar*, ii, 244). Also used of a deer which is causing serious damage to forestry or crops. Such deer usually have to be *culled*.

roller   this usage is not in the OED. Used of a deer, when falling from a height after being shot, as when shot on a steep hillside, rolling over and over, breaking numerous bones, probably the antlers as well, and spoiling the venison (Brander, *Sporting Terms*, 102). Care should always be taken when taking a shot that the deer is not likely to become a *roller*. In 1884 Speedy wrote: 'his bullet . . . struck the third one, which brought it rolling down the declivity' (p. 233).

rook   OE. OED: 'A black, raucous-voiced European and Asiatic bird, *Corvus frugilegus* nesting in colonies; one of the commonest of the crow-tribe; and in the north of Britain generally called a *crow*.' Distinguishable from crows by the bare whitish face and a more pointed greyish-black bill. Much more gregarious and usually seen in company with many others. 'One rook is a crow and several crows are rooks' as the saying goes. They are still undesirable company for the game-preserver, but nothing like as deadly as the *hooded crow* or the *magpie*. Mentioned from the 8th century onwards, they are used in characteristic simile *c*. 1386 by Chaucer in his *House of Fame*: 'The halle was al ful y-wys of hem . . . as ben on trees rokes nests.' In 1486 there is a note in *The Boke of St Albans* concerning 'That hawke that will slee a Roke or a Crow or a Revyn.'

roughshoot   it appears to have been chiefly in the post-war period of the 1920s and 1930s that the concept of the rough-shoot became really popular for the first time. Shooting had been chiefly a matter of driven shooting, or sometimes walking-up, while *dogging* or shooting over pointers had almost ceased save for some diehard enthusiasts. Almost anyone who could afford to rent a shoot could also, before the First World War, and even into the 1920s, afford the then minimal cost of a keeper. Only with the introduction of a Minimum Agricultural Wage embracing keepers was this situation finally changed. The actual concept of the roughshoot, however, seems to have originated in the late Victorian period, as an advertisement in *The Field*, 29 September 1900, makes clear: 'Wanted; a good rough-shoot, commencing season 1901–1902; on Lease; plenty of rabbits essential; 2000 to 5000 acres.' In 1930, however, Richard Clapham wrote rather vaguely:

> We may define a roughshoot as an area of ground which the owner or lessee can look after by himself, or with the help of a keeper, or general factotum. In the North, grouse and blackgame will probably help to swell the bag, whereas on a southern shoot, wild pheasants and partridges will take their place. Rabbits may be the mainstay of such a shoot, with the addition of a hare or two, and the "various" will include wood-pigeons, wild duck and plover, according to the local-ity. (*LL Shooting*, 252)

In 1938 Julian Tennyson wrote even less definitely:

> It is a vague term, embracing everything from thousands of acres of barren moorland on the fringes of the country to the neat little plot of grass and arable which is typical of the tenant farmer. A 'Rough Shoot' may be a marsh a heath, a moor; it may, or may not, have a wood; it may be literally rough, or not rough at all; it may in fact consist of any type of land imaginable. But the distinction of a rough shoot is that it has no fully qualified and recognised keeper and that no large scale rearing of birds is done within its grounds. (p. 3)

Captain Drought maintained that:

> Roughshoots are not measurable in acreage. They may as easily comprise small plots of good mixed ground as larger areas of neglected bog and moorland. One cannot admit that the designation "rough" fits any shoot that demands the full time services of keepers. It is essentially an affair of two or

three guns, any sort of clothes and bye days. And the sport shown depends almost entirely on those guns' own activities in the close, and their fieldcraft in the open, season. (p. 41) In 1958 Brander defined it as: 'any shoot which is not regularly keepered, where game is not reared artificially on any scale and is not generally driven by beaters systematically over organised parties of guns' (*Sport*, 18).

rouse   AF. OED: v. 'to cause (game) or rise or issue from cover or lair.' 'The huntesman ... shall then go before them and rowze the Deare.' (Turberville, 106). Now generally obsolete, except possibly of fallow deer; to disturb with hounds when *lodged*.

rubbing   of deer; damage caused to trees by deer rubbing their antlers to get rid of the *velvet*; hence *rubs*, places where they have rubbed velvet off their antlers.

rubbish   of deer; colloq., poor heads on weakly beasts which are better *culled*, since they will not do any good if left and may in fact actively harm the breeding stock if they do succeed in covering a female.

ruggle   of obscure origin. OED: 1: 'a plaything, toy' 2: 'a species of shell.' Also, the small bells once commonly fastened to the collars of ferrets, and sometimes to the jesses of hawks, or on the baby harness of a child; these were also used at one time on *sewin*.

run   OED: 'A regular track made by certain animals.' Of groundgame; the track they habitually follow, often visible in grass and corn as a distinct worn track. A *snare* may be set successfully in the *run*. An early example of the usage is in 1878 by Jeffries: 'Hares have their regular highways or "runs"' (*Gamekeeper*, p. 149). Also, of a stag: when condition has been lost as a result of the rut it is said to be *run*. In a similar condition a human might be said to be 'run down'.

run in   of a gundog; to run forwards without orders after game which has been flushed, or shot. A common fault when groundgame is flushed. It is a bad fault at any time, but particularly irritating when the guns are *walking-up* game. It is not conducive to good sport. Hawker noted in his Diary for 10 September 1842:

> It blew a gale of wind and I crawled over to Bullington, where I found a good show of birds; but old Don ruined my sport by running in to every covey; and such vile retrievers were he and the old bitch that at one time I killed 2 birds with the first and 2 more with the second barrel and lost 3 out of the 4! . . . All I got was 5 partridges a hare and a landrail . . . Had I been

well, and in luck, with good dogs . . . I should have killed 20 brace.

'Running in to shot; Of all errors in the training of a dog this is the most common and probably the worst' (Mackie, 102).

runner a bird which has been shot and wounded, generally in the wing, but is still capable of running, often considerable distances and at considerable speed. Speedy explained:

> When shooting either in a turnip or potato field, care should be taken not to fire at too long range. When this is disregarded many of the birds which have been winged become "runners," and in the absence of suitable and experienced dogs will very often be lost. . . . We have ever laid it down as a rule that we would rather, even at the loss of a little time, bag a bird of this description than a brace which might subsequently be obtained during the time spent in recovering the "runner." It is almost impossible to pick up "runners" in rank turnips without the assistance of a retriever. (p. 269)

Although partridges, pheasants and occasionally grouse are the birds most likely to be *runners*, any bird which has been only slightly *winged* may prove a runner, even snipe and woodcock. In 1930 Iain Ramsay writing on woodcock noted their surprising powers when 'runners': 'It is as well when a 'cock that is wounded is marked down to try to get on to it as soon as possible, as, in spite of what we have read in some books to the contrary, we have found that a woodcock, whose legs were sound, would at times run nearly as well as a cock pheasant' (*LL Shooting*, 195).

rut OF *rut*, from the Latin *rugire*, to roar. OED: the annually recurring sexual excitement of male deer. The *rut* differs with differing types of deer, as do their actions when rutting. In 1576 Turberville wrote truly enough: 'During the time of their rut they (harts) lyve with small sustenance.'

Saddle the stag   to load the stag on the special deer-saddle of a *garron*, after the stag has been *gralloched*, to take it off the hill. Also *saddle up*; of the garron, when the stag has been loaded on the special saddle to take it off the hill.

safety catch   a slide, generally mounted on top of the *stock*, which merely acts as a check on the *triggers*. In 1889 Lancaster warned:

> Whatever the specification of a gun, the safety mechanisms must be satisfactory. The thumb-piece on top must be bold enough to allow of easy use when the hands are cold, yet it should not be so large as to be in the way at other times. When it is in the back position with the word "SAFE" showing the triggers are bolted so that they cannot be pulled. See that in any gun you ever use this position is taken up automatically every time the lever is moved to open the gun. A gun with a "non-automatic" safety may be safe in the hands of a man accustomed to it, but otherwise may be highly dangerous. (p. 120)

safety first   the most important aspect of shooting, whenever carrying a loaded gun. The sportsman should always be conscious that he is holding a lethal weapon. As early as 1830 Hawker wrote: 'Let everyone, who begins shooting . . . start with *the determination of never suffering a gun, at any time, to be held for a moment, or even carried, . . . so as to come in the direction of either man or beast*' (*Instructions*, 125). In 1884 Speedy wrote: It is the duty of every sportsman to be as mindful of the safety of his companions as himself' (p. 65). Lancaster began *The Art of Shooting* (1889) with: 'The first lesson to be learnt by the beginner and one to be remembered all his life, is "Safety."'' He was echoed by Purdey in 1936: 'Until you are really experienced it is just as well to proceed on these lines – safety first – later it becomes second nature' (p. 67). From these beginnings, the concept of 'Safety-first' seems to have spread into the vernacular. See also *swing*; *walk up*.

saltings   OED: 'Lands regularly covered by the tide as distinguished from salt marshes.' In 1712 William Derham wrote of 'These Lands they call Saltings when covered with Grass' (*Philosophical Transactions*). Salt water marsh, or meadows flooded by sea water, beloved of wildfowl and wildfowlers.

sanctuary   that part of the deer forest generally left undisturbed as a holding ground. This may apply to any ground with a deer population primarily reserved for stalking deer. First

172

attested in this sense in 1603, an interesting example is to be found in 1892: 'Application was made to the Chief Ranger ... for her [the hind's] recapture; but he promptly refused on the grounds that the Forest was a "sanctuary"' (*Daily News*, 19 April).

scaly leg   a disease affecting poultry and both pheasants and partridges, caused by a mite *Sarcoptes mutans*, which burrows into the feet and legs and sets up an irritation causing scaly crusts on the legs. The bird becomes lame and may lose a joint. The disease, generally due to contact with poultry, or rearing game on ground where poultry has been, is curable in young pheasants by carbolic solution or paraffin poured over the legs.

scaup   possibly derived from *scalp*. *Arythya marila:* in the drake the head and foreparts are black, the back and underparts pale grey and white. The stern end is also black, so that the drake is clearly distinguished by being black at both ends and white in the middle. The duck has a browner appearance, with a bold white patch at the base of the bill. Generally found in bays and estuaries, seldom inland, its size is about 19 inches from beak to tail and the season is as for other wildfowl.

scent   ME. The OED notes 'Originally a term of hunting it is possible there may have been an Ancient French word *sent*, a verbal noun from *sentir* to scent; the spelling "scent" does not occur until the 17th century.' The OED gives '1. The faculty or sense of smell ... exclusively with reference to animals (especially dogs) which find their prey or recognise objects by this sense': 'The perfect Hound, in Scent and Speed Unrivall'd' – William Somerville, *The Chase* (l.94), 1735. The OED then gives '2: the odour of an animal or man as a means of pursuit by a hound: hence a track or trail as indicated by this odour' (it also notes cold scent and hot scent): 'When they have well beaten and founde the tracke or sent of the Harte' – Turberville.

As a verb, the OED gives '1. transitive: of a hound or other animal; to find, or track (Game or prey etc.) by the smell': 'By the time he has gone xx or xxx paces, the slot is better and the houndes shall sent him much better' – Turberville; '2; intr. of a hound or other animal; to hunt by the sense of smell; also ... sniff the air for a scent': 'And he shall kepe hym ... always in ye myddell of the water for cause that the houndes shall not sent of hym' – *The Master of Game* (ii, 11), *c.* 1400.

In the modern sense, the *scent* left by game which is detected by a gundog; may be *air scent* or **ground scent**. A scent that is fresh may be termed 'hot' and a scent that is old may be termed 'cold'. Clearly any gundog, however experienced, may

find it more difficult to follow the latter, hence the importance
of setting a dog on a scent when as fresh as possible and not
obscured, or fouled, by other scent, such as that of other
gundogs, or human scent. A good gundog can at once detect
the difference between the scent of wounded and unwounded
game and follow the former on command. In deer, the scent
may be produced by the traces of body oils from the feet. In
1807 Daniel was amongst the many to find the matter a difficult
one.

The reasons of good and bad scent is a puzzling theme to the
Sportsman. Scent cannot be ascertained by the air only, it
depends also on the soil, doubtless the scent most favourable
to the Hound is when the effluvia constantly perspiring from
the Game as it runs, is kept by the gravity of the air to the
height of his breast, for then it is neither above his reach, nor
need he stoop for it; this is what is meant when scent is said
to lie *breast high*. Experience tells us that difference of soil
alters the scent. When the leaves begin to fall, and before
they are rotted, scent lies ill in Cover, a sufficient proof that
it does not depend on the air only. Scent also varies by the
difference of motion, the faster an animal goes, the less scent
he leaves. (i, 85)
In 1957 Brander summed it up thus: 'The ground, the wind
and the weather, quite apart from the game and the dogs
themselves, are the ever variable factors affecting scent and
scenting' (*Dog*, 61).

scent glands   areas of skin producing strong smelling body
oils; in deer, *scent glands* are found in the feet and around the
eyes.

scoring   of deer; the marks left by the antlers on the bark of
growing trees. Serious damage can be caused in this way and it
may be desirable to cull a beast where the damage is considerable, especially if the head is a poor specimen in any event.

scrape   OED: 'A place where the soil has been scraped up.' In
1862 it was noted: 'The deer which . . . were addicted, at certain
seasons, to dig up the land with their fore feet to the depth of
. . . half a yard, contributed a new word to our language. These
were called "scrapes"' (*The Athenaeum*, 27 September). *The
Scotsman* recorded: 'Rabbit holes and scrapes at once appeared
in shoals to the terror of the old golfers' (9 April 1901). Of a
hare; the seat, or *form*, where it lies: see *common brown
hare*. Also, of deer; the marks left by a deer's feet on a patch of
ground, as a means of marking its territory, frequently seen
during the *rut*, especially of fallow deer, but a reaction common

to most deer. In 1973 Holmes described and explained the actions noted in the *Athenaeum* article: 'This is the only form of territorial marking performed in a ferocious manner and for this reason I suspect it is the result of immediate threat to the territory. It can be heard at some distance and debris can be seen flying as the buck scrapes the ground with a forehoof' (p. 43).

scrub rabbit   a rabbit which lies out in the open in a *scrape*, like a hare, rather than in a *burrow*. Such rabbits are less liable to catch *myxomatosis*, which is transmitted by the rabbit fleas, mostly passed between rabbits living underground.

scut   of obscure origin. Possibly derived from ON *skut-r*, the stern of a boat, and the Norwegian *skut*, either end of a high prowed boat. OED: 'a short erect tail, especially that of a hare, rabbit or deer.' It is more prominent perhaps on the rabbit than on the hare, largely because of the difference in size, and the fact that it is often the only part of the animal seen as it bobs away at speed. It is important when shooting not to be attracted by the sight of the white *scut*, but to swing well ahead and beyond the running beast. The scut of the roe can seem very prominent, but this of course is because it is only part of the distinctive white rump patch or *target.*

season   OED: '5. The time of year when an animal is in heat, pairs, breeds, migrates, is killed for food, hunted, etc.' *In season:* OED: '15. Of game, etc. At the time for hunting ... *To be in season*; (of an animal) to be in heat: of female animals; the period of oestrus, or heat, when they are said to be "in season" ready for the male.'

seat   OED: 'The form of a hare; ?obsolete.' In 1735 William Somerville (*The Chase*) wrote: 'So the wise Hares Oft quit their Seats, lest some more Curious Eyes shou'd marke their Haunts.' In 1856 Walsh mentioned 'The Form of the Hare, or as it is sometimes called, her seat' (p. 139). The term is still occasionally used and embraces also the scrape where a rabbit lies in the open.

self-hunting   of a gundog; to go off on its own, hunting for game along the hedgerows and over the fields; one of the most difficult of vices to cure once started and one which can lead to sheep worrying. Only likely to arise in a dog that has insufficient work and interest. In 1936 Dugald Macintyre wrote very rightly: 'The Crime of Self-Hunting; This is a common fault of young setters and is a most annoying one to the trainer' (*LL Shooting*, 320).

setter   a dog used to *set* – or indicate the presence of – game, originally for falconry and for netting game. For the latter they were taught to crouch to allow the net to be drawn over them, a reaction still inherent in some breeds. The Kennel Club now lists pointers and *setters* in one classification as dogs which *point* game. The classification includes English pointers, English setters and Irish and Gordon setters.

sewelling or **sewin**   from ME *shewel*. The OED spells it <shewel>: obs: a scarecrow. OED: 'hunting: something hung up, or set up, to keep a deer from entering a particular place, or from going in a particular direction: hence shewelling: hanging up shewels.' First attested in the 13th century. In 1576 Turberville wrote: 'When they hang yppe any paper, clout, or other marke, then it is to be called sewelling' (p. 242). In 1897 J.F. Hall preferred the word *sewin*:

> The sewin . . . is not a modern invention, although . . . much modified and improved in recent years . . . Moreover owing to the difficulty experienced in obtaining the requisite numbers of boys as stops, the practical use of the sewin is likely to be extended . . . The sewin itself consists simply of a white cord in 300 or 600 yard lengths to which is attached, at intervals of twelve inches, white feathers and scarlet tape. Brass ferret bells or 'ruggles' are also fastened at intervals of 5 yards. The cord thus prepared is wound round a large reel . . . Prior to the placing of the sewin in position hazel or ash sticks 2½ feet high and split at the top should be inserted in the ground at suitable intervals to carry the sewin. Directly the sewin is set up a boy is left at the reel end whose duty is to keep jerking the cord. The sewin is used not only inside the covers, but also at varying distances outside . . . generally supplemented by red and white flags . . . placed in position first thing in the morning. (*Encyclopedia*, ii, 335)

The Gamekeeper (December 1902) used the word *sewelling*: 'Sewelling is a piece of cord with rags and feathers fixed at every six inches . . . at a reasonable distance in front of the guns will ensure good flying birds.' Mackie chose *sewin*; 'Sewin may be used as an excellent form of stop both for hares and pheasants' (p. 315). Leslie Sprake wrote: 'Sewelling is . . . better than the use of any netting . . . and will also make the pheasants fly better – but to be effective the attendance of a keeper is necessary to keep the sewelling in motion; and it is absolutely essential that such an individual should be experienced and careful, or he may do more harm than good' (*LL Shooting*, 161). Today sewin, or sewelling, is made from nylon cord with white and red strips of plastic attached at foot-wide intervals wound round a plastic reel, but principles similar to those noted above apply to its use.

shed   OED: 'to cast off by natural process'. Of antlers; to cast. In 1721 Richard Bradley wrote: 'The Stag and some other sorts of Deer are subject to shedding and renewing their Horns annually' (*Philosophical Account of the Works of Nature*, 21). Both sexes are known to chew antlers which have been *shed*, probably as a source of vitamins. Antlers will often be found with teeth marks apparent on them.

Many are slow to believe that the deer themselves eat their shed antlers, on account of their extreme hardness. Several instances, however, have been recorded of their being seen in the act; and if not sought for at the shedding-time, pieces of them only will be found three or four inches long, with the burr end intact, while the marks of chewing are quite visible. A general notion persists that the cast horns of stags are eaten by hinds only; but from observations in such places as the sanctuary of Strathconan forest, which is almost exclusively the habitat of stags, they are found eaten till within a few inches of the base, in the same manner as in places chiefly frequented by hinds. That both hinds and stags make a practice of chewing cast antlers will not be disputed by any intelligent forester who has given attention to the subject. (Speedy, 237)

sheep tick   the OED indicates that the word *tick* is possibly derived from the Old English *ticca*. It gives it as 'The common name for several kinds of mites or acarids which infest the hair or fur of various animals ... and attach themselves to the skin as temporary parasites.' The *sheep tick* is given as 'a similar parasitic dipterous insect of the family *Hippoboscidae*'. One of the earliest references appears in John Rowland's *Theatre of Insects* (1658), where there is a note on 'The Tick, or sheep fly'. In 1688 R. Holme was more vague, recording that: 'The Tike is another kind of Louse ... a Companion for Dogs, Sheep and Cattle' (*Armoury*). Where prevalent, sheep ticks climb grass or similar vegetation and wait for a prospective host – sheep, grouse, dog, or man – to pass and then transfer to them. They multiply excessively if no effort is made to get rid of them. They can be a very serious pest affecting young grouse.

As many as 140 ticks have been found on the head and neck of young grouse and the cause of death of many birds sent for pathological examination appears to be attributable to tick infestation. Older birds do not appear to be killed by tick infestation, but it is inevitable that they must be weakened

178 sheep tick - shootable beast

and this, of course, lays them more open to attacks of grouse disease. (Stephens, 198)

shoot   OE. OED: '1. a game shooting expedition.' 'The Prince is much pleased with his shoot this year. One day he killed five stags' (Viscountess Canning, *Two Noble Lives*, 1852, p. 360). This usage is acceptable but uncommon. '2: the right to shoot game in a given area; and the area itself.' 'The sportsman whose shoot is small and the game . . . scarce and wild will be unable to practise driving to any advantage' (W.W. Greener, *The Breech-loader*, 1892, p. 221). A *shoot* may vary vastly in size and the nature of the ground, e.g. a small low-ground shoot, or a large Highland moor. It may be keepered or unkeepered. It may have a lot of varied wild game, or only reared game, or, if it has been *overshot* virtually none. A great deal depends on the *shoot management*.

Also 'v. to fire a gun': 'The gun is now stocked and screwed and then in the rough state is sent to the ground to be shot and regulated.' – Lord Walsingham and Sir Ralph Payne Galloway (*Shooting*, 71), 1886. 'A high-class gunmaker will spend days in shooting a gun in order to get its pattern and force up to the mark he considers requisite to make it a perfect weapon.' (ibid., 75). An example of the noun and verb used together is by T.W. White in 1938: 'there is Watson . . . with . . . a shoot in Norfolk . . . And there is Tilly, who doesn't shoot' (p. 196).

Also, 'to shoot flying': 'It is now the Mode to shoot flying as being by Experience found the best and surest Way.' – Richard Blome, *The Gentleman's Recreation*, 1686. As late as 1830 Hawker remarked that 'little more than half a century ago one who *shot flying* was viewed with *wonder.*' (*Instructions*, 125), and a further example of this now obsolete usage is to be found in Thackeray's *Esmond* (1852): 'He had learned to ride, and to drink, and to shoot flying.'

Also 'to shoot over, or to a dog. To shoot over a tract of country.' On 4 July 1868 *The Field*, using the now obsolete form of 'shoot to' advertised: 'For Sale. A Brace of Spaniels . . . They have been thoroughly broken and shot to by an experienced breaker.' The *Century Magazine* for March 1888 recorded the now accepted usage: 'This holiday he was about to spend shooting over his two handsome young setters.' In *The Times* weekly edition (19 January 1894) it was noted: 'During his stay the Belvoir covers were shot over' (p. 58).

shootable beast   a deer, generally a stag or buck, considered by the stalker to be worth shooting from its age and general condition. Also conversely, an unshootable beast: i.e. one that because of its size, age and weight should not be shot. Mackie advised firmly: 'on no account should you be bloodthirsty – it is much better, to my mind, to have a blank day than to bring in an unshootable stag; it spoils the average weight of the year, and, if many of that sort are shot, it spoils the reputation of a forest' (p. 264).

shooting partner   see *partnership shoot.*

shooting stick   a walking stick with a folding seat and a round flat guard above the pointed tip to prevent it sinking too deeply into muddy or soft ground when used as a seat. Although perhaps more commonly seen at point-to-points, they can be useful when covert shooting to sit upon while waiting for a drive to begin. There are many varieties on the market. The best are telescopic, since they can be adjusted to any height and can be folded down to the size of a guncase and strapped to it for convenient carriage. A large folding seat is advisable, for maximum comfort and a folding guard on the tip is useful. Three-legged varieties are also available. They seem to have first become popular in the 1920s and 1930s.

shooting syndicate   see *syndicate shoot.*

shoot management   the control and efficient management of a *shoot,* including game preservation and rearing. This should be the task of the owner of the land, but may often be delegated to the manager of a syndicate, and, where neither are sufficiently keen, sometimes devolves on the shoulders of the Headkeeper. Some keepers relish this state of affairs, but it is not desirable to let them have complete control in this way. The landowner, or shoot manager, should, at the very least, consult with the keeper at frequent intervals and discuss all matters concerning rearing of game, siting of release pens, the management of each day's shooting and similar matters. To leave it all to the keeper is likely to result in even the best of men feeling he is not fully appreciated, and either becoming slack and inefficient or else leaving for a better post. A great deal depends on the size and nature of the shoot, whether low ground or moorland or a mixture of the two, and the amount of shooting involved. Even a small *roughshoot* requires management and the more management time put into any shoot the better the results are likely to be. See *grouse management.*

shot   OED: 'Lead in small pellets, of which a quantity is used for a single charge of a sporting gun.' This appears to refer to muzzle-loaders, which is confirmed by the example in 1770 (*Philosophical Transactions*): 'I would not recommend shooting them . . . with shot smaller than common partridge shot, or

No.5.' This should be defined as: 'Lead in small pellets, of which, dependant on their size, a certain number are used in a shotgun cartridge.' The pellets used in the cartridge of a shotgun are generally of chilled lead *shot*, but this may soon be banned. They are of varying sizes, see *shot size*.

shot column   the shot after it has left the muzzle of a shotgun. It forms a strung-out length, visible in certain lights as a distinct bar, or column, of shot. See *shot stringing*.

shotgun licence   introduced under the Firearms Act 1968; issued by the police to all wishing to possess and use any shotgun after they have satisfied themselves as to the applicant's background and suitability. Full details and serial numbers of all shotguns possessed must be included. See *gun cabinet*.

shot size   the size of shot, or pellet, used in the *cartridge* may vary with the size of the quarry being shot. The sizes in the UK vary from BB, often used for geese, then No. 1 to No. 8. *Shot sizes* vary from country to country and are not standardised.

shot stringing   the formation of the *shot column* after the shot has left the barrels is known as *shot stringing*. At forty yards the stringing may be as much as 8 feet. This makes little or no difference in practice, except in the case of *magnums*, where there may be excessive shot stringing because of the greater quantity of shot being crammed through narrower barrels. Burrard declared that: 'The whole question of the Stringing of Shot was dealt with exhaustively in *The Field* of March 18, 1926' (*Gunroom*, 74).

shoveller   OED: 'From the latter half of the 17th century applied to the *Spoonbill Duck. Spatula elypeata*: a bird with a broad shovel-like beak.' 'Shoveller, or Broadbilled Duck; Birds of this kind are more common in the fens of Norfolk than in those other marshy parts of England which lie further from Holland . . . The flappers of this species are easier found and show more sport than those of the common wild duck. Their flesh, too, I think, is of a superior flavour' – Hawker (*Instructions*, 196). Brander writes: 'These ducks are easily distinguished by the very obvious spatulate bill. The drake has a black and white back with a green head and a chestnut belly and flanks. The duck is mottled brownish with blue shoulders and is quite unmistakeable. Its length is about 20 inches and the season is as for other wildfowl' (*Sporting Terms*, 105).

side-by-side   one of the main categories of shotgun, it includes hammerless box lock ejectors, or non-ejectors, hammerless sidelock ejectors, or non-ejectors, the sliding breech, or

Darne action gun, and the hammer non-ejectors, now generally obsolete.

side lever   see *lever of the action.*

side lock   see *lock.*

sight-aligner   not in the OED. An extremely useful device for checking the accuracy of the telescopic sights, which is inserted in the barrel by means of a steel rod, changeable to suit any calibre. (See Brander, *Deer*, 1986, p. 84.) By avoiding the need to fire shots to *sight-in* the rifle, this device not only saves considerable outlay in ammunition, but also means the rifle can be checked at any time after it has been dropped in case the sights have become unaligned. If only as a confidence booster, the *sight-aligner* is well worth the money paid for it. It was first introduced after the Second World War. See *bore-sight, zero.*

sight-in   to adjust the sights of a rifle to ensure that the bullet fired hits the target where it is desired to place it. 'Sighting-in a rifle fitted with a telescope is very similar in principle' (*Forrester*, 1967, p. 116). This usage is not in the OED.

sign, signs   OED: 'Sign: USA; the trail or trace of wild animals.' In 1847 George F. Ruxton wrote: 'On the banks of the river I saw some fresh beaver "sign"' (*Adventures in Mexico and the Rocky Mountains*, 170). The plural *signs* may also be used of deer tracks, by which the species, size, sex and age may be judged. Not common usage in the UK. See *shot; trail.*

sika   Japanese sika deer, *Cervus nippon.* As with red deer, the male is known as a stag, the female as a hind and the young as calves. Since several sub-species appear to have been introduced at different times the *sika* deer in various areas vary considerably in size, appearance, habits and behaviour. The stag may stand from 32 to 34 inches, the hind 30 to 32 inches; the stag may weigh 8 to 10 stone and the hind 6 to 7 stone. The body colour is reddish brown with not very prominent yellowish spots on the flanks in summer, but darker brown above and greyish brown below in winter. The head is generally paler than the body and there is a light coloured U-shaped stripe above the eyes. At all times the caudal patch is noticeably white and outlined in black. The metatarsal *scent glands* are light coloured and very noticeable throughout the year. As with *fallow* deer, gestation is about seven and a half months. Their general treatment of calves is also similar to fallow. The growth is very rapid and the hind calf will be full grown at two years, although the male will take longer to reach maturity. As with *red deer*, the rut takes place towards the end of September. The stags tend to fight hard for their *harems*. In place of a *roar* the stags have a particular call, very like someone blowing a whistle. Their gaits are similar to the red deer, but the sika has a furtive walk and the stags move at a heavy gallop. They are widely spread throughout the country. In Scotland they are found in Angus, Argyll, Caithness, Fife, Inverness, Perth, Ross and Cromarty. They are also found in widely separated pockets in Devon, Dorset, Hampshire, Kent, Lancashire, Oxfordshire, Somerset, Surrey, Sussex, Wiltshire and Yorkshire.

single   of red deer; the tail. In 1576 Turberville stated: 'The tayle of Harte, Bucke, Rowe or any other Deare is to be called the Syngle' (p. 241). Rarely used today.

single barrel   one of the commoner categories of shotgun. There are three main types of single barrel; the single barrel drop down, the hammer, or hammerless ejector and the non-ejector. Generally a cheap gun for rough work, the classification covers repeaters, either pump guns, or bolt action, and automatics.

single trigger   a feature common in certain makes and types of double-barrelled game gun. One trigger fires both barrels. It may be a simple single trigger, firing first the right and then the left barrel, or a selective trigger pushed forward to fire the left barrel first, or some similar arrangement.

skeet   not included in the OED. Derived from ON *skjota*, related to OE *sceotan*, to shoot. By transference now used for a form of *clay-pigeon* shooting using two traps opposite each other, one firing clays from at least ten feet up and the other from under three feet. The gun shoots at a clay from each tower in turn from seven positions equally spaced on the circumference of a semi-circle whose diameter is a line drawn between the two towers. The traps are fixed so that the clays are thrown directly over the other trap. The guns are not allowed to raise their gun to their shoulder until the 'bird' is in the air. They may choose to take a 'bird' from either trap first and then one from the other, but must continue to take them in this order thereafter. Only one gun shoots at a time, but any number may compete and each gun takes it in turn to shoot two birds from each position. The angles are thus constantly changing and one bird may be approaching when another is going away, or each may be crossing in different directions, so that it can become very competitive. After the initial round of single birds from each tower in turn, the guns return to the initial stations and shoot double birds from the two outside positions on each side. Each gun thus has sixteen single shots and four double shots. This is followed by an optional shot, which may be taken from any

position, making up twenty-five shots in all. It is very different
from **down-the-line** clay shooting.

sleeve or **gunsleeve**   a suitably shaped container for the gun
made of canvas reinforced with leather, or of soft leather,
sometimes with a fleece lining, and zip or strap fastening,
usually fitted with a sling and/or carrying handle. It is useful for
carrying the gun between drives and if padded helps to avoid
accidental damage to the barrels when carried in a car. A zip
fastener which opens up the full length is preferable to a strap
opening at one end, since, if the gun has got wet during the
day, the inside of the sleeve may then be readily dried out at the
end of the day before it is used again.

slide action gun   see *pump action shotgun.*

sliding breech gun   see *Darne action gun.*

slot   OED states 'OF *esclot*, "hoofprint of a horse," or more
probably ON *slod* "track".' '1. the track or trail of an animal,
especially a deer, as shown by the marks of the foot; sometimes
misapplied to the scent of an animal; hence generally track,
trace, or trail.' In 1576 Turberville instructed: 'Take your
Bloodhoundes and with them finde the view or slotte of the
Harte or Bucke' (p. 36). In 1735 Edward Somerville wrote:
'See here his Slot; up yon green Hill he climbs' (*The Chase*, line
372). Of deer: it is regarded as the track of the feet. From the
depth and size of the *slot* its size, sex and age, as well as the
pace at which it was moving may be estimated; a young doe
moving at a trot would be readily distinguishable from a well-
grown roebuck moving at a gallop from the difference in the
slots. OED '2. A deer's foot.' In 1876 it was stated: 'As to what is
the correct name for a deer's foot . . . I never heard it called
anything but "slot"' (*World*, i:121, 15).

snag   probably of Scandinavian origin; developed from the
idea of a short projection sticking out from a tree stump. OED:
'a tine, or branch, of a deer's horn, which is short or imperfectly
developed.' In 1673 John Ray wrote: 'The horns have no Brow
Antlers but only a broad palm with several snags upon it'
(*Observations made in the Low Countries*, 27).

snapcaps   dummy cartridges, used to prevent the strikers
being damaged if the triggers of a shotgun are pulled.

snap shot   OED: 'A quick or hurried shot taken without deliberate aim, especially one at a rising bird or quickly moving
animal.' In 1808 Hawker recorded: 'Almost every pheasant I
fired at was a snap shot among the high cover' (*Diaries*), and
later in *Instructions* wrote: 'In killing *snap shots* fix your eyes and
immediately pitch your gun and fire, as it were, along, or rather

over the *backs* of the birds' (p. 137). Lancaster advised: 'Snap shots have frequently to be taken at snipe, woodcock and ground game; and to be able to kill well it is essential that the gun should fit well and mount at once to the shoulder. A snap shot is more easily taken by leaning well forward . . .' (p. 54). Hence by obvious transference the *snap shot* with a camera came into common usage. Hence *snap* = photograph.

snare   ON. OED: 'A device for capturing small wild animals or birds, usually consisting of a string with a running noose in which a foot, or the head, may be caught.' Originally made of horse-hair, the noose is nowadays generally of brass or galvanised wire; usually of brass wire when used on rabbit runs. It should be set a hand's breadth high for a rabbit and a hand and a half for a hare, according to the old saying; may also be used for foxes, when usually of galvanised wire. See *noose trap*, also *stop*.

soar   obsolete; of fallow deer; in the fourth year.

soft mouth   of a *retriever*; to retrieve gently without damaging game, breaking ribs, or rendering it uneatable as in the case of the converse, *hard mouth*. A retriever with a soft mouth, however, may not necessarily retrieve *to hand*. In 1964 P.R.A. Moxon (*Gundogs*, The Shooting Times Library, 64) wrote: 'A Question of Mouth; The all-important question of mouth, hard or soft, causes the gundog trainer many anxious moments.'

soil   OED: 'a pool or stretch of water used as a refuge by a hunted deer; frequently in the phrase *to go to, to come to, to take*.' In 1576 Turberville wrote: 'When an Hart or any Deare is forced into the Water, we say he goeth to the Soile' (p. 241). Also, 'of a deer; to roll or wallow in mud or water.' See *wallow*. In 1884 Richard Jeffries wrote: 'A stag generally drinks before entering cover, and afterwards "soils"; that is lies down and rolls in the water' (*Red Deer*, 102). Both usages are now somewhat archaic, as the parenthesis in the Jeffries example indicates.

sord or **sute**   OF. OED states this may originally have been the act of taking wing, but subsequently came to be recorded only in the 'proper terms'. Now virtually obsolete: 'A flight or flock of mallards.' In 1856 Walsh wrote: 'The following Terms are in Use among Wildfowl-shooters; A flock of wigeon is termed "a company" . . . of mallards, "a sord"' (p. 78). The term is repeated in 1939 by C.E. Hare who noted: 'Sorde, Soute, etc., derived from the Latin *surgere* – to rise' (*The Language of Sport*, 142). The term has been misspelt by several authorities, but its original meaning is quite clear, i.e. the uprising of 'duck' when 'flushed'.

span   OE. Of antlers; the widest distance inside the beams, as opposed to the spread. 'The three first (antlers) are termed the *rights* . . . the horn itself the *beam*; the width, the *span*' (Walsh, 82).

spaniel   OF. OED: 'from *Espaignol*, "Spanish dog."' A variety of dog characterised by large drooping ears, long silky hair, keen scent and affectionate nature, some breeds of which are used for sporting purposes, especially for starting and retrieving game.' Chaucer: 'For as a spaynel, she wol on hym lepe' (*Wife of Bath*, c. 1386). In Blaine's *Encyclopedia of Rural Sports* (1840, p. 2550) it was noted: 'The varieties of the spaniel are numerous . . . A popular distinction made between them by many writers is into springers, cockers and water spaniels.' Used for finding and bustling up game within shot of the gun, also for working cover and for retrieving game; the typical 'maid-of-all-work', as they were known at the end of the 19th century. It was only in the first decade of this century that the Kennel Club recognised the *spaniel* as a special category of gundog. They recognised the following types of spaniel: English and Welsh springers, Clumbers, cockers, Sussex, and Irish water spaniels. It is reasonably certain that most spaniels today originated from the setting breeds of two or three hundred years ago, when all such dogs were used for setting, for falconry and netting, or for close work with the gun. There was at that time little or no distinction between the various breeds of gundog.

speculum   OED: 'from the Latin *speculum*, *specere*, to look, observe; by transference; a mirror'; in ornithology 'a lustrous mark on the wings of certain birds'. Hence of deer; the part of the rump around the tail. This usage is not in the OED.

spellers   OED states 'Aphetic from *Espeler*: obsolete' but it appears to be still in occasional use. Of the antlers of a fallow buck: the points, or tines, along the edge of the palms. In 1576 Turberville wrote: 'In a Bucke we say Burre, Beame, Branche, Aduauncers, Pawlme and Spelers' (p. 238). In 1611 Cotgrave's *Dictionarie* noted: 'Espois d'un cerf; the top of a red Deeres head; of a fallow the Spellers.'

spike buck   OED: 'US. a buck in its first year.' In 1860 Mayne Reid noted: 'In the first year they grow in the shape of two short, straight spikes. Hence the name "spike-bucks" given to the animals of that age' (*Hunter's Feast*). It is also sometimes used of a roe buck having no tines or branches on the antlers and may have crossed the Atlantic. In appearance it is like a *switch* head, and for the same reason should be culled whenever possible. In 1973 Holmes does not term it a spike-head,

but notes; 'The typical six-point roe head is not well designed
to kill. On the other hand the "switch" head (beams without
brow or rear points) is . . .' (p. 66).

splay   OED: 'to spread'. Of deer; the spread of the *cleaves* by
which the age may be estimated.

spoor   the OED gives this as of Dutch origin in South African
use, but also OE *spor.* 'The trace, track or trail of a person or
animal, especially of wild animals pursued as game.' In 1849
Edward Napier wrote: 'Following the "spoor" or tracking the
footmarks of man or beast, is considered quite a science
amongst the border colonists' (*Excursion in South Africa*, i,
197). Hence 'to trace by the spoor' as for example in 1863,
William C. Baldwin : 'We spoored them beautifully into a dense
thicket' (*African Hunting*, 122).

sport   the OED states 'Aphetic form of *disport*. AF' and rather
ambivalently gives on the one hand: n: 'Pastime afforded by the
endeavour to take, or kill, wild animals, game or fish.' Isaac
Walton (*The Compleat Angler:* ii): 'I am . . . glad to have so fair
an entrance to this day's sport.' Also on the other: v: 'To engage
in, follow, or practise sport, esp. field-sport; to hunt or shoot
for sport.' 1812: Hawker (*Diaries*, Sept. 18): 'I hereby give you
notice that you are forbidden to shoot (or otherwise sport) on
the several estates of Earl Manvers.' See *field sports*.

spread   OED: 'the extent, expanse, or superficial area of something' hence of antlers; the maximum over-all measurement.

spring   from OE *spryng*; OED: 'a flock of teal; now archaic.'
'Further out we notice a "spring" of nine teal' (*Cornhill
Magazine*, 2 August 1892). Also a snare, or noose; now
obsolete: Nicholas Breton 'Why, sir, I set no springs for
woodcock' (*Works*, 1879). Also used as a verb: 'v. trans. to
cause a bird (especially a partridge) to spring from cover.' In
1531 Sir Thomas Elyot wrote: 'The men sprange birds out of
the bushes' (*The Governor*).

springe   OED: 'A snare for catching small game; esp. birds.'
The first attestation is in the 13th century and the usage is now
obsolete. See *snare*; *trap*.

spring gun   OED: 'A gun capable of being discharged by one
coming in contact with it, or with a wire, or the like, attached to
the trigger; formerly used as a guard against trespassers, or
poachers, and placed in concealment for this purpose.' Sheridan: 'Steel traps and spring guns seemed writ in every wrinkle'
(*Duenna*, 1775, I, iii). Boswell, in his *Life of Johnson* (1776):
'He should have warned us of our danger . . . by advertising
"Spring guns and men traps set here"' (i, 659). Such guns have

long been illegal and the term is now obsolete. Trip wires
setting off blank cartridges are, however, still used on the same
principle to give warning of *poachers* or intruders in the
coverts.

springer spaniel   probably the most popular breed of working spaniel today. The two types recognised are the *English
springer spaniel* and the *Welsh springer spaniel*.

For *Pheasant Shooting* Spaniels are the proper sort of Dogs
and in Coverts are indispensable. It is to *Sportsmen* this
Assertion is made, and not to those who deem no *Springers*
so good as two or three *fellows* with long Staves, and who
only wish to shoot where the Game is so abundant, that
scarcely a Bush can be struck, but a Bird is seen; to them
Pigeons thrown up from a Trap, *Rabbits* started from a Basket,
or *Swallows* skimming across a Horse-pond, are like Objects
of Diversion; if a certain number of Shots can be obtained
without fatigue, and a certain quantum of *Guineas* be depending upon each discharge. Shooters equipped with only these
steady *Human Mongrels* can neither feel the Ardour nor the
Expectation which gives Spirit to the Amusement and which
the mettled hunting of the *Spaniel* so unceasingly enlivens.
(Daniel, iii, 59)

spurs   OE. OED: 'a device for pricking the side of a horse . . .
attached to the rider's heel.' Also zoological: 'A sharp hard
process or projection on the tarsus of a domestic cock and
certain other fowls and birds; a back claw.' Hence the claws of
a cock pheasant, which grow longer and more pointed the older
the bird.

spy   OF. OED: 'to make observations; (now specially with a spy
glass.)' By transference, to look over the ground for deer, with
telescope, or binoculars, or the naked eye; see *glass*. 'After a
very cursory glance with my own glass, I shut it up and began
talking as Charlie spied' (*Longman's Magazine*, November
1883). In 1963 Tegner recorded: 'From the first spying knoll
we glassed a small parcel of hinds' (p. 39).

squab   the OED gives this as of uncertain origin, varying in
dialect form to *squob* and *squobb*: 'A newly hatched, unfledged,
or very young bird; especially of pigeons.' In 1694 Peter
Motteux wrote: 'Pigeons. Squobbs and Squeakers' (*Rabelais*,
234). The term appears to cover the young until some sixteen
weeks old; the squab is distinguished by its unformed beak and
downy covering.

squeaker   sometimes used in place of *cheeper*. (See quote by
Motteux under *squab*.) Hawker wrote in his Diary for 3

September 1829: 'I actually brought home 24 partridges, 20 of which were old ones, as grey as badgers, and two squeakers, which I killed to encourage a puppy.'

squire   OED: 'in the middle ages, a young man of good birth attendant upon a knight' hence by transference; of deer: a young stag, or buck, in attendance on, or keeping company with, an older beast. This combination is often seen, with the youngster acting as a look-out. See also *fag*; *stooge*.

stag   OE. OED: 'The male of a deer especially of the red deer; specially a hart or male deer of the fifth year.' Now used only of *red* or *sika* deer, the male, and not correctly used of red deer until after the fourth year; see *staggie*. It was also used of either sex when carted deer were hunted and then the term also included *hummels*. *The Master of Game* (*c.* 1400): 'Ye first yere that thei (harts) be calfede, thei be ycalle a calfe, the secund yere a bulloke . . . the thred yere a brokete, ye iiii yere a staggard, ye v yere a stagge.'

stag fever   a less common form of *buck fever*. This is the strange agitation which overcomes many people on taking aim at deer and causes them to miss, often even shutting their eyes as they pull the trigger with the barrels waving around, while totally unable to control themselves. They may even fire several shots, all missing the target, and be unable to recollect doing so while in the grip of this uncontrollable excitement. Mackie observed: 'I have often heard the very best of rifles abused for inaccurate shooting, when the real cause was "stag fever" – a very common complaint' (p. 266).

staggers   of deer; a disease akin to sway-back in sheep, resulting in loss of co-ordination of the hindquarters, hence from the staggering motion, the name.

staggie   colloq. used in the Highlands to denote a three- or four-year-old beast, still not full grown, but beginning to show signs of how it is likely to develop. Never classified as a *shootable beast* unless a *waster*.

stalk   OED: 'An act of stalking game.' In 1470 Malory wrote: 'They were shoters and coude wel kylle a dere bothe at the stalke and at the trest' (*Arthur*, xxi, 764). In 1621 Markham instructed: 'Also you must observe in the stalke to turn that side (of the stalking horse) ever upon the Fowle' (*Fowling*, 53). Also used as a verb: 'to go stealthily *to*, *towards* (an animal) for the purpose of killing or capturing it.' Hence 'to pursue game by the method of stealthy approach.' Speedy maintained that: 'The stalk is far oftener destroyed by the deer getting wind of the stalker than by seeing him' (p. 226). A *stalk* may be a woodland stalk, or still-hunt, or on the hill, after 'glassing' the ground and selecting a shootable beast.

stalker   of a deer forest; the professional in charge of the ground, who will guide the *rifle*, after *glassing* the hill, and choosing the stag to be culled, leading the way in the *stalk* and handing over the loaded rifle when he regards them to be in position either to take the shot, or make the final stalk before doing so. 'Matters being left to the stalker, he will be careful to be a little distance in front, scanning with the aid of his telescope, every bit of fresh ground as it comes in sight' (Speedy, 227).

stalker's law   an understanding, common between neighbouring estates in the Highlands, allowing for mutual use of neighbouring ground to make a successful stalk on a deer on one's own ground and near the *march*. In 1899 Augustus Grimble noted:

> There is usually a mutual understanding known as "stalker's law" on the marches of adjoining forests. The rule is that either party finding deer on his own ground, but so close to the march that they cannot be stalked except by crossing it, may come over on to his neighbour's ground sufficiently far to hide his cap while crawling on hands and knees. At the same time it is best never to follow an injured beast across the march and the usual plan is to send a letter to the owner of the adjoining ground to tell him of the wounded one and ask that his foresters be enjoined to keep a look out for it. (*Encyclopedia*, i, 306)

stand   of a fallow buck; the rutting territory, which it will defend against others. 'In the rut the mature bucks mark out their stands' (Coles, *Stalking*, 142). Also, of a rifle; the position taken to await deer feeding; or at a deer *pass*, when waiting for deer to be driven. Also sometimes used to denote the position or *peg* allocated to a gun in a driven shoot. The guns shooting at the pegs or stands are known as the *standing* guns as opposed to *beaters' guns*. Stanfield employed both usages: 'An answer ... is ... to have five guns standing [. . .] As for spectacular stands providing exceptionally high birds . . .' (pp. 61, 62).

stand at gaze   of deer; to stand watchfully. When disturbed by a scent or sound, or particularly movement, which they cannot immediately identify deer – especially females, hinds, or does – may stand at gaze, looking for some time fixedly at the object which has attracted their attention. If a deer stalker is aware that he has attracted the deer's attention in this way, he must freeze at once and remain perfectly still until she becomes reassured and drops her head to start feeding again. Although the deer's scenting powers are very considerable, their eyesight is not as remarkable and by remaining absolutely still, even when in full view, it is often possible to avoid startling the deer.

step   of a deer track; the distance between one *slot* and another; from which, with the depth of imprint, may be gauged the age, sex and size of the deer.

stern   ON. OED: 'The steering gear of a ship,' thus by transference 'the tail of an animal, especially a sporting dog'. Of a gundog; the tail. In 1677 Nicholas Cox noted 'The benefit of cutting of the tip of a Spaniel's Tail or Stern' (p. 149). In 1881 V.K. Shaw wrote of: 'The Stern or Flag (of the Setter.)' (*The Illustrated Book of the Dog*, 372).

stick   OE: v. to stick; of traps: originally to place sticks in the ground so as to direct an animal towards a trap by blocking the way round it and still used in this sense occasionally: 'placing one or two sticks on the track on either side . . . induces an animal . . . to step . . . in the direction of the trap' (James Bateman, *Animal Traps and Trapping*, 1971, p. 200). More frequently today the converse, e.g. of a *tunnel trap*, to place sticks in the ground at the mouth of a tunnel trap, or alternatively by using stones or similar means, to reduce the size of the entry hole so that only the desired quarry, such as stoats and weasels, can enter easily and protected species such as hedgehogs, or others, such as pheasant poults, which it is not desirable to catch, are prevented from entering by mistake or out of curiosity and cannot be trapped accidentally. In 1985 McCall demonstrated this usage clearly: 'Because the trap site is surrounded by loose earth it may attract birds looking for a suitable dust bath. A pair of stout sticks at both ends of the tunnel should ensure that these do not become unintended victims . . . a restricted entrance may be used as well as, or instead of, sticking the ends' (p. 47). This usage is not in the OED.

still-hunt   of deer; to move extremely slowly through woodland, searching the surroundings at each pace with the binoculars, looking for deer, with the rifle at the ready. Each fresh area of ground must be studied carefully as it comes into view in order to see the deer before it sees or scents the *still-hunter*. Care must be taken to be as quiet as possible, avoiding breaking any twigs underfoot, or otherwise disturbing the deer. The ideal conditions for still-hunting are thus at dawn and dusk when the deer are likely to be moving about and feeding, when the light is reasonable, and when there is a sufficient breeze to mask the sound of the still-hunter's movements. Also sometimes used to refer to sitting in a *high-seat*, waiting for deer, when stillness is obligatory. 'There are several methods of woodland deer-stalking. The first of these is commonly termed the still-hunt, so-termed because the hunter stays in one place [. . .] Somewhat confusingly, still-hunting is also a term often used to describe very slow stalking on foot in woodland' (Brander, *Deer*, 95).

stoat   of obscure origin. OED: 'The European ermine; *Putorius ereminius*, or *Mustela erminea*, especially when in its brown summer coat.' A small furred predator of game chicks, larger than the weasel, with a black tip to its tail, which changes colour to white in winter and is known as ermine. Its kills are usually notable for a wound at the back of the neck, where the blood has been sucked and a small part of the flesh around this eaten. Like the weasel, the *stoat* may be enticed from its hole by imitating the squeal of an injured rabbit and may then be shot. It should be trapped as a bloodthirsty killer and egg eater, although far less of a menace than the *mink*, despite Mackie's tirade:

> The stoat, or ermine weasel . . . is a merciless tyrant, a meaningless murderer, shedding blood from mere wantoness. Both ground and winged game fall prey to his bloodthirstiness. Even woodpigeons are not exempt from his rapacity as I have seen one in a pigeon's nest ten feet from the ground and watched him throw the young birds over the nest and carry them off. The climbing capacity of a stoat can scarcely be credited . . . Their scenting power enables them to track their prey like a beagle and I have seen both rabbits and young hares lie down and squeal through sheer terror, before a stoat was within many yards of them. In an instant the stoat would spring on the back of its victim and with that unerring instinct peculiar to the weasel tribe, seize it behind the ear . . . (p. 127)

The earliest reference is *c.* 1460 in The Porkington MS: 'This byn ye bestes of ye stynkyng fute . . . Ye folmard . . . ye ottur, ye stote and ye polcatte.' It would be interesting to hear both these writers' comments on the mink.

stock   OED: 'The wooden portion of a musket, or fowling piece.' In 1541 an Act of Henry VIII stated: 'Any hangune . . . shalbe in the stock and gonne of the lengthe of one hole Yarde.' Of a shotgun; the wooden section, attached to the *action*, which enables the gun handler for whom it has been made to align the barrels accurately and easily on the target. It is generally made of fully seasoned, walnut, because if the wood is not fully seasoned, shrinkage or swelling may result in interference with the mechanism of the lock, causing the gun to be unsafe: also because walnut is a tough, handsome wood, and readily available

stock dove   *Columba oenas*, also widely known as the 'blue rock'; found throughout the UK, but in far lesser numbers than the wood pigeon. Only about 13 inches long it has no white on its neck or wings, but has two broken black wing bars and is a darker blue-grey than the wood pigeon. Protected under the 1981 Wildlife & Countryside Act, although farmers and land-owners may apply for a licence to shoot them where they are felt to be causing a nuisance.

stooge   American slang, possibly from English slang, a *stodge*: 'a stick-in-the-mud' type of person, hence: 'a straight man to a stand-up comic: one who is subservient.' This form then re-crossed the Atlantic, hence, of deer, a similar meaning to *squire* and *fag*: a young stag, or buck, keeping company with an older beast and acting as look-out. 'He was lying on top of a mound of heather . . . Below him fed his stooge' (Tegner, 78).

stop   MDu. OED: 'Shooting; a person posted in a particular place in order to keep the game within range after it has been started.' In *covert shooting*: a beater posted at a point in the pheasant coverts where it is feared birds may *leak* out during the drive to prevent this happening; see *sewelling, sewin*. Mackie advised: 'Late in the season stoppers are even of more importance than beaters. All stops, should, of course, get into position in the early morning, long before the beaters start and guns begin to fire' (p. 315). Also, a check, or *stop*, squeezed onto a wire fox *snare*, to prevent it closing more than about 8 inches, ensuring that no animals are caught by the foot, or other parts of the anatomy, e.g. sheep, cattle, etc.

strap of the action   the extension of the body of the *action* of a shotgun, along the top of the stock and attached to it by screws. Customarily the safety catch is placed towards the rear.

stride   OE. Of a deer; the space between the impressions of each *slot*. Some idea of the size of the deer is clear from the length of the stride and the size and depth of the slots. The speed at which the deer is moving is also apparent, hence, whether alarmed or moving normally. It is usually also possible to gauge the age, size and sex of the deer. See *step*; *track*.

striker   the pin which strikes the cartridge. 'The Anson and Deeley Lock; it will be noted that the striker, or firing pin, (the peg which actually strikes the cap) is an integral part of the tumbler, although it is fitted separately in some types of box locks' (Burrard, *Shotgun*, i, 58).

stringing   see *shot stringing*; *shot column*.

stripping   of trees; the removal of bark by the teeth of the deer; see also *barking*.

strong on the wing   the term is applicable especially to young game birds, particularly grouse and partridges, which are well grown and able to fly strong and boldly along with the adults, early in the season. In 1845 St John knew what he was talking about when he wrote: 'Although in some peculiarly early seasons the young birds are full grown by the 12th of August, in general five birds out of six which are killed on that day are only half come to their strength and beauty' (p. 28). Speedy also wrote knowledgeably that 'partridges should not be shot until red in the breast, and until the "pecked" appearance in their head and neck has disappeared. . . . when . . . they are strong on the wing and fly off with that sharp and healthy whirr which makes it difficult to distinguish young from old birds' (p. 266). In 1897 Lord Granby declared: 'English grouse are as a rule hatched earlier than those in the bleak North and are therefore stronger on the wing when the 12th of August arrives' (*Encyclopedia*, i, 488). Hare missed the point, that it only applies to young birds which grow stronger as the season advances, when he defined it more simply as 'Applied to birds which fly fast and boldly' (p. 67).

strongylosis   a disease affecting grouse caused by the strongyle worm. Generally affecting birds when they are already weakened by starvation, after prolonged snow, bad weather, or lack of young heather shoots, etc. It may be caused by poor moor management. Another form of the disease affects partridges and is also sometimes fatal, but is not as deadly as *strongylosis* in grouse. Also sometimes termed grouse disease. In 1936 it was noted: 'The real origin, the *causa causans*, of strongylosis is starvation. If an adult grouse can obtain a sufficient quantity of good, healthy heather it remains healthy' (*L L Shooting*, 286).

sub-orbital gland   of deer; the scent gland situated, as the name indicates, by the inner corner of the eye.

Sussex spaniel   a long, low, powerful-legged type of spaniel bred in Sussex, whence its name. It was bred to give tongue while working and a cross of Bassett hound was almost certainly brought into the strain. (See also *noisy*.) Of a golden liver colour it was originally bred at the end of the 18th century and was still popular after the First World War, but is now uncommon as a working strain. The average height of the dogs at the shoulder is 13–14 inches and bitches 10–12 inches.

sute or **sord**   of mallard; a flock. Obsolete.

suture line   of a deer's skull; the demarcation line between the adjacent bones.

sway   not in OED. Of deer tracks; 'the amount of deviation from a central line; particularly seen in wounded deer' (Brander, *Deer*, 1986, p. 163). This is particularly obvious when badly shot and tiring. Even a badly wounded deer may start off at a gallop, but as it loses blood it will soon start to stagger, hence the 'sway'. A useful indication of how badly shot a wounded deer may be. See *tracks*; *trail*.

swing   OE. OED: 'To turn in alternate directions: (usually horizontally.)' Of a shotgun: to move the gun across the body at the speed of a crossing bird or faster. In 1889 Lancaster pointed out that 'it is much easier to swing further and faster to the left than to the right' (p. 83). See also *walk up*.

switch   from Low German *swukse*, a long thin stick. OED: 'A stag having switch horns.' Of a red or sika stag, having a *switch head*, meaning, having beam and brow points only, or just two beam points. Should be stalked and shot whenever seen, as frequently lethal to other and better stags in the rut, hence better culled. An early attestation is in 1912: 'He's nobbut a "switch," he whispered into Lord Donald's ear' (*Blackwood's Magazine*, December, 805). In 1963 Tegner wrote: 'A switch is an adult stag with no points to his antlers except the brow tines; some switches do not even carry these points . . . they are generally shot if possible' (p. 20). It may also refer to a roebuck: 'the mature buck with small and badly shaped antlers . . . the "switch" head (beams without brow or rear points)' (Holmes, 67).

syndicate   a shoot shared by a group of sportsmen who form a syndicate to share expenses of lease, beaters, keeper, etc. Usually organised by a syndicate leader, or organiser, *syndicates* may naturally make their own rules and regulations and will meet at times convenient to them and decided beforehand. Members may have a gun, also a guest gun as arranged, or sometimes may share a gun or guest gun between various members according to agreed payment; i.e. alternate shooting days, depending on the arrangements. Syndicates first became common in the 1920s and 1930s after the First World War, when death duties began to affect the big estates. In 1936 it was noted: 'Syndicates may be large or small. Four is the best number of members, I think, for then each can ask a guest in turn, and part of the pleasure of shooting is being able to ask a guest to share the day. Six is rather a large number except for driving partridges, or for big pheasant days. And with six the number of guests invited through the season must be small' (*LL Shooting*, 266). In 1939 Stephens observed: 'The other notice-able factor in post-War [1914–18] shooting is the rise of syndicate. Actually there is nothing new in a shooting syndicate. They have been known for many years before the War in one form or another. Exactly one hundred years ago the Oakleigh Shooting Code formulated . . . rules for the management of a syndicate (then termed subscribers) . . . But the syndicate as a general rule dates from the post-war years' (p. 26). See also *partnership shoot.*

Tailings OED: 'a name for the inferior qualities, leav-
ings, or residue of any product. . . . Grain . . . of inferior
quality.' Corn tailings are ideal for feeding gamebirds in
a *feed stack* sited on the corner of a *ride*.

tailor OED: 'To shoot at (birds) in a bungling manner so as to
miss or merely wound them; slang.' Also includes: 'wounding a
deer with a rifle.' *The Westminster Gazette* noted: 'One of them
. . . letting birds past him untouched, knocking out tail feathers
and generally "tailoring" his pheasants' (29 September 1903).
From the 17th century onwards *tailors* seem to have been held
in contempt as cowardly and the antithesis of 'gentlemen'. In
the 18th and 19th centuries it was also regarded as 'gentlemanly
behaviour' never to pay a tailor. Hence by transference missing
birds was referred to contemptuously as *tailoring* them.

tallow ME. OED: 'The fat or adipose tissue . . . especially that
. . . about the kidneys of ruminating animals.' Of red or fallow
deer; the fat.

target origin uncertain, but possibly a diminutive of *targe*, a
shield. Colloquial, of sika deer and of roe deer in winter; the
white rump patch. The importance of it in roe in differentiating
the sexes is made clear by Holmes 'The white rump patch
(target) is a reliable guide to sex identification. There is usually
a noticeable difference in shape and size and the anal tush of
the female, a tuft of white hair which emerges from the lower
edge of the target, is the most outstanding point of difference'
(p. 25).

target shooting with a rifle; the target is divided into the
bull's eye, in black, with the inner, as the first circle round it; a
shot outside the bull, but inside the inner circle, counts as an
inner. The circle outside the inner is called the *magpie*; the
remainder of the target is known as an *outer*. At 800 to 1,000
yards for First Class target shooting the bull's eye is 2 feet in
diameter, the inner is $4\frac{1}{2}$ feet in diameter, the magpie 6 feet in
diameter and the target is 12 feet by 6 feet.

teal ME, but possibly earlier. *Anas crecca;* the smallest European duck. The male has an obvious dark chestnut head with a
curving green eye patch, while the female is speckled brown
and buff with paler underparts. Notable for its fast flight and
particularly for its ability to rise abruptly from the water (hence,
springing teal). Often seen in pairs inland and in flocks on the
coast. They are about 14 inches long from beak to tail and
weigh from 11–13 oz. They are mentioned in 1486 in *The Boke
of St Albans*: 'I have sene them made sum . . . to sle the Tele
uppon the Rever.' In 1773 Gilbert White noted: 'I saw young

196

teals taken alive in the ponds of Wolmer Forest' (*Natural History*). Amongst the first to write of them really enthusiastically in 1830 was Hawker:

As a brood of teal, including the old ones, usually amounts to no more than six or seven, they are most commonly seen in very small numbers; unless they have collected on decoy ponds and are driven from them by hard frosts when they will appear on the adjoining rivers in flocks of twenty or thirty together. Of all the prizes that a wildfowl shooter could wish to meet with, a flock of teal is the very first. Independently of their being by far the best birds of the whole anas tribe, they are so much easier of access and require such a slight blow that no matter whether you are prepared for wildfowl, partridge, or snipes, you may at most times, with very little trouble, contrive to get near them; and this being once done, you have only to shoot straight to be pretty sure of killing . . . If you spring a teal, he will not soar up and leave the country, like a wild duck, but most probably keep along the brook, like a sharp flying woodcock, and then drop suddenly down; but you must keep your eye on the place as he is very apt to get up again and fly to another before he will quietly settle. He will frequently, too, swim down stream the moment after he drops, so that if you do not cast your eye quickly that way, instead of continuing to look for him in one spot, he will probably catch sight of you and fly up, while your attention is directed to the wrong place. If the brook in which you find him is obscured by many trees, you had better direct your follower to make a large circle and get ahead of him and watch him, in case he should slily skim away down the brook and by this means escape you altogether. You should avoid firing at random, as this may drive him quite away from your beat. (*Instructions*, 235)

In 1897 J.E. Harting was also enthusiastic:

Although one of the smallest ducks that fly, weighing no more than a partridge, the teal is one of the most attractive wildfowl to sportsmen, not merely on account of the beautiful colours of the male bird, but because of the sporting shots it affords, and its excellence for the table. Teal are generally easier to get at than ducks and as they require but a slight blow to bring them down it matters little what size of shot is used. Instead of rising head to wind like other wildfowl, they have an odd way of springing up vertically from the surface of the water, no matter what their position may be when discovered, and the shooter not aiming high enough, the

charge of shot often passes harmlessly below them. (*Encyclopedia*, ii, 285)
Also known to wildfowlers as a *half duck*. The season is as for other wildfowl.

tealer   from OE *tealzer*, a twig. The cleft wooden stick used as the support for a rabbit snare.
A complete snare is made up of . . . a. the wire noose. b. the short length of cord which is attached to it and the other end of which is fixed to the peg. c. the peg . . . which is driven into the ground . . . d. the tealer, which is a thin stick about 6 in in length, split at one end and pointed at the other, its object being to hold up the snare and cock it at the correct angle. (Sedgwick, *Young Shot*, 88)
On the correct setting of the *tealer* and hence the angle and height of the wire loop depends the entire success of the snare. Not in the OED.

telescope   from Italian *telescopio*, a word thought to have been first used in a letter in 1613 by Count Cesi, head of the Roman Academy of the Lincei (to which Galileo also belonged). OED: 'An optical instrument for making distant objects nearer and larger.' Favoured by many hill-stalkers as the best means of *glassing the hill*, but of little use in woodland stalking where binoculars are undoubtedly more effective. Walsh advised: 'Every deerstalker, whether a principal or an assistant, should be provided with a good telescope . . . it is really astonishing what a difference there is between a first-rate glass and an inferior one' (p. 84). See *glass*.

telescopic sight   sight fixed to the barrel of the rifle providing telescopic magnification of the target. First used before and during the 1914–18 War, but not in general and accepted sporting use until post-1939–45 War. See also *zero*.

territory   OED: from the Latin *territorium*, land around a town. Etymology unsettled; the original form possibly derived from *terrere*, to frighten, whence *territorium*, a place from which people are warned off. Of a deer; an area marked by the scent glands of the male deer on various trees, bushes, stones, etc. to be defended during the *rut*. Holmes wrote: 'A social system of family units occupying fixed territories, frequently the same pair occupying the same territory year after year, has led to the concept that roe "marry for life". . . . the assumption that the species is monogamous is false . . .' (p. 37)

thicket   OE. Of forestry; the stage of growth between the closing of the canopy and the first thinning. It implies dense growth of trees and bushes.

thinnings   of forestry; selective cutting and removal of inferior timber from a plantation, usually required at three to six year intervals. An example of the usage is to be found in the *Journal of the Royal Agricultural Society* for December 1893: 'Thinnings and rubbish should be immediately removed and burnt.'

thrashing   OED: 'Beating, as with a flail.' Of a fallow buck; as when it flays small trees or bushes with its antlers, to get rid of the *velvet*.

three-quarter choke   or modified *choke*; i.e. ten points less than full choke, or 30 points.

tight   of game; sitting *clapped* and immobile, refusing to move until the last moment. Such game may sometimes leave it too late and be *pegged* by over-keen gundogs.

tight pattern   of a shotgun; a pattern which shows all the shot at forty yards well concentrated.

tine   from OE *tind*, or sharp point. The OED gives 'Each of the pointed branches of a deer's horn.' There is an early mention c.1375 in *Scottish Legendary Saints*: 'A gret hart . . . he saw betwen his tyndis brycht A verray croice schenand lycht.'

toe of the butt   see *butt*.

to hand   of a *retrieve*; when the gundog places the game in the hands of the handler, rather than dropping it a foot or so away. The latter is a sign of poor handling, or mismanaged training. See also *hard mouth*; *soft mouth*. In 1924 R. Sharpe wrote: 'One of the worst faults in the part of many trainers is to snatch the game from a dog. This produces the habit of a dog dropping the game instead of delivering it properly to hand' (*Dog Training for Amateurs*, 32).

top lever   see *lever of action*.

top rib   see *ribs*.

top rib extension   that part of the barrels of some shotguns, which projects outwards from the top *rib* and fits into the action providing extra strength. Many shotguns do not have one.

tops   see also *high tops*: the upper regions and summits of the Scottish mountains above 1,500 feet. In 1897 J.G. Millais enthused: 'But a day on the tops amidst the scenes of alternate gloom and splendour such as only Scotland can present, is often more delightful than moor shooting on tamer ground' (*Encyclopedia*, ii, 139). In 1939 Eric Parker wrote: 'I have seen ptarmigan shot "on the tops" when walking up grouse' (*LL Shooting*, 222).

tower, towered bird   OED: n. 'The vertical ascent of a wounded bird.' v. 'to rise vertically, as a bird when wounded.'

A shot bird, usually when only slightly *pricked*, either in the
lungs, causing them to fill gradually with blood, or in the spine,
affecting the nervous system, will occasionally fly almost per-
pendicularly upwards, sometimes almost out of sight, before
finally dropping stone dead. It will almost always be found to
be lying on its back; it is noticeable that such birds frequently
have little or no scent, and gundogs will often pass over them
even when they are lying in plain view in the open. Hence the
importance of *marking towered birds* accurately. I once shot a
woodcock which flew in tight circles upwards almost out of
sight, as if in fact ascending a tower spiral stairway, before
falling dead only a few yards away. Hawker noted in his Diary
'With the exception of one which towered all my birds fell dead
to the gun' (7 September 1812); and again: '8 partridges and a
hare and 4 more birds lost. Never did I lose so many birds as I
have done since I used detonating guns, as they have always
with me proved to hit the birds so weak at long distances that
they get a field or two off to tower before they fall instead of
coming down handsome as they usually did when I used a flint
lock' (22 September 1824). In 1950 Noel M. Sedgwick, editor
of the *Shooting Times*, who regularly wrote under the pseudo-
nym 'Tower Bird' noted:
> If you watch a bird go into a full tower, you will see members
> of the shooting party watching it. They will see it gain
> maximum height, then collapse and fall like a plummet to
> earth. Should that bird have dropped at a distance among
> heather, reeds, coarse grass, or other thick cover, it is doubtful
> whether any member could go and gather it without much
> searching and a good deal of luck – i.e. without the help of a
> dog. Many towered birds are lost in this way. (*Wildfowling*,
> 110)

trace   OF. OED: 'The line of footprints left by an animal.' First
attested in the 14th century. Markham wrote: 'There is more
regard to bee taken unto her traces . . . for the print of the hares
foote is sharpe and fashioned like unto the point of a knife'
(*Farme*, 694). Now superseded by *track*.

track   from OF *traq*; in some senses identical with *trace*. OED:
'a series of footprints, the scent followed by hounds; v. to follow
up the track, or footprints.' Speedy gives a good example of
tracking hares:
> During the heavy snowstorm in December 1882 . . . catching
> a view of one (a hare) we took up its track . . . After following
> the track for about three hours . . . Four times it had turned
> and run back exactly on its own track for a distance of from

one to two hundred yards and then making a bound of eight or ten feet off to the side had started in a new direction. This in all probability would have thrown dogs off the scent . . . young hares a few weeks old often display the power of instinct in this . . . We have . . . ascertained this by following the footprints of small leverets after a snow shower in . . . April. (p. 284)

trail   OED: 'The track or other indication, as scent, left by a person or animal, especially as followed by a huntsman or hound.' In this sense apparently only used since the 16th century. In 1607 Topsell wrote: 'The best manner to teach these hounds is to take a live hare and trail her after you upon the earth; . . . afterward set forth your hound near the trail' (*The Historie*, 120). Of deer; the *slots*, or marks on the undergrowth of its passages, see *sway*.

trap   OE *treppe*; ME *trapp*. OED: 'A contrivance set for catching game or noxious animals; a gin, snare, pitfall.' First attested around 1000. 'She wolde wepe if that she saw a mous Kaught in a trappe' – Chaucer (*c.* 1386, *General Prologue*). See *cage trap*; *snare*; *spring*; *tunnel trap*.

traveller   of deer; one which for some reason moves over a *march*, or marches, and does not stay in one deer forest. This is probably quite common in many deer forests, but such beasts are usually only noted when they have exceptional heads or other outstanding physical characteristics. See also *wanderer*.

tray   OED: '(The same word as trey, three, in dice, cards, etc., re-spelt after Bay; and believed to go back in oral usage to the 18th century at least.) The third branch of a stag's horn; also Tray antler, Tray tine.' In 1812 referring to stag-hunting in Devon, Lord Graves wrote: 'His brow, bay and tray antlers are termed his Rights' (*Letters to Lord Ebrington*)

trigger guard   the protective curved flat bar, which screws to the *trigger plate* and stock of a shotgun to protect the trigger from damage and the danger of its being pulled by accident. The front curve should allow room for the insertion of large fingers. The rear curve should not be too upright or it will cause bruising of the middle finger when the gun recoils. A rubber ring round it will prevent this.

trigger plate   the plate screwed to the bottom of the *action* of a shotgun and projecting in the same manner as the strap. In 1830 Hawker defined it as: "Trigger-plate; Plate in which the triggers work' (*Instructions*, 49). Burrard wrote more fully: 'This is really a steel bar which carries the triggers and which projects from the bottom of the rear end of the action in exactly the same way as the Strap does from the top . . . The trigger plate however, is separate and is screwed firmly to the bottom of the action body . . . this plate strengthens the stock considerably in the weakest place, and so serves a double purpose' (Burrard, *Shotgun*, i, 122).

triggers   the OED interestingly notes that the origin is from the Dutch *trekker*, a trigger and *trekken*, to pull, and states that the original usage was 'tricker', the current usage *trigger* appearing first in 1660, but 'tricker' remaining common usage until 1750 and according to the OED still in dialect use from the Midlands northwards.

Of a shotgun; the curved metal bars, shaped to the fingers, which actuate the firing mechanism. There are customarily two for the simplicity of manufacture, the forward trigger for the right barrel and the left, or rear trigger, for the left, 'Let the Cocks and Trickers be nimble to goe and come' – Francis Markham (*The Book of Warre*, 35), 1662; 'We took a Pistol . . . and ty'd to the tricker one end of a string.' – Robert Boyle (*New Experiments Psycho-mechanical*, 89), 1660; 'The trigger was pull'd' (ibid., 100).

trophy   from Fr *trophee*. OED: 'Anything serving as a token or evidence of victory, valour, power, skill, etc.' hence by transference, of male deer; the head, or antlers.

true cylinder   the barrel of a shotgun completely without any *choke*.

try gun   a gun with the stock adjustable for fit, both for cast-on, or -off, for bend and for length, used by gunmakers to achieve a good fit for the customer. In 1889 Lancaster, himself a famous gunmaker, somewhat naturally advised going to a gunsmith to be measured for a gun by an 'experienced fitter . . . in whose hands the "try-gun" can be adjusted until the length, bend and cast are absolutely right for you' (p. 13). See also *cast*.

tufted duck   *Aythya fuligula:* the drake is black and white with black upper parts and a thinnish drooping crest, hence the name. The duck is browner with a less obvious crest. It differs chiefly from the *scaup* in habitat as it is seldom found at sea, but generally on inland lakes. Size about 17 inches from beak to tail. Season as for other wildfowl

tunnel trap   a so-called *tunnel trap* is nothing more than a trap or traps set in a small artificial tunnel or covering, which may be constructed of any convenient materials that happen to be to hand, such as pieces of wood, straw bales, or slates and stones in stonewall country. The objective is to provide an interesting-

looking pathway and a hole worth investigating for small
predators, such as rats, stoats or weasels, inside which a trap or
traps are concealed. A tunnel may be a cul-de-sac, with a blank
end, or open at both ends. It may be baited, with some suitable
bait such as rabbit liver, or the urine of a female stoat or weasel,
or some similarly attractive scent. In general, however, there is
no real need for bait since it is curiosity that will generally lead
small animals to investigate a well-laid tunnel trap. In the open-
ended tunnel a trap is usually set at each end, with possibly a
bait placed in the middle between them. All tunnels should be
sticked, i.e. two sticks crossed in front, or stuck into the ground
side by side, to allow access for inquisitive small predators, but
preventing access for larger unwanted and unwary beasts such
as hedgehogs (which it is illegal to trap) stray cats or dogs, or
for that matter inquisitive pheasant *poults*.

Turk's head a wire brush, generally of brass wire, with an
attachment for the *cleaning rod*, used to clean gun barrels. So
called from its resemblance to the common plant the teasel, or
Turk's head. The origin is obscure, but probably so named
after artistic impressions of a Turk's head on inn signs, common
from the time of the Crusades onwards, and generally portrayed
with a turban and resembling the plant. In 1930 Burrard noted:
'The most common pattern (of wire brush) is the "Turk's
Head" type' (*Shotgun*, iii, 281).

turtle dove *Streptopelia turtur*: a protected summer migrant
which crosses readily with the *collared dove*. Of similar size,
only 11 inches, it has brownish wings and a noticeably black tail
with white edges. It has a soft, almost sleepy call and is generally
found in open bushy country or orchards.

tush from OE *tusk*. The OED gives 'a canine tooth'. Found in
the upper jaw of red deer, but not normally found in roe or
fallow deer.

Underplanting of forestry; introducing a new crop under the partial canopy of an older plantation. A good system for both shooting and for deer.

uneven head of antlers; where the number of points is uneven on a head it may be referred to by adding a point with the prefix 'uneven'. Thus an eleven-pointer might be described as an uneven twelve-pointer, etc.

under-shot of a beast, having the lower jaw protruding beyond the upper. An undesirable defect in a gundog, but if not too pronounced should not affect the retrieving.

up wind the area of ground from which the wind is blowing, where game or deer are unable to scent the approach of man or dog. See *cheek wind*; *downwind*.

Various from L *varius*. OED: 'Of different kinds, or sorts.' Those species of birds or beasts not specifically named in the columns of game in a *game book* may be included under this heading. This was not in use therefore before the mid-19th century, (otherwise the 'two-legged fox' referred to would certainly have been listed under *Various*). I have in my possession a Scottish game book of 1841. It has columns with printed headings listing Grouse, Ptarmigan, Partridge, Hares, Rabbits, Snipes, Woodcocks, Wild Ducks, Red Deer and Black Grouse, with two columns left blank. Geese, or roe deer, or similar unlisted game might have been included in these columns. Further south another column would clearly have included pheasants. For convenience sake it is obvious that to cover un-listed entries, one such column was labelled 'Various'. The heading seems to have been well-established by the late 19th century, although not often referred to in print. In *The Westminster Gazette* for 30 December 1903 there is included in parenthesis: 'A couple of 'cock, groundgame, and such "various" as snipe, duck, a plover or so.' In 1935 Dawson wrote: 'Some of the most interesting entries in the game-book are found in the "various" column' (p. 54).

velvet the OED gives 'The soft downy skin which covers a deer's horn while in the growing stages.' The delicate skin covering the antlers during growth. While the antlers are growing the deer is said to be *in velvet*. It used to be considered a delicacy for gourmets during the 18th century, perhaps for the same reasons that today it is highly prized in the Far East, where it is regarded as a potent aphrodisiac, similar to rhinoceros horn. Hence the majority of antlers on deer farms are removed while still 'in velvet' and sold for high prices for export. It was first attested *c.* 1410 in *The Master of Game*: 'Hir hornes benn keuered with a softe heer, that hunters call veluetz.' In 1576 George Turberville was more to the point: 'Then they discover themselves going unto the trees to fray their heads and rub of the velvet' (p. 47).

velvet scoter *Melanitta fusca*; distinguishable from the *common scoter*, by its white wing patch and reddish feet, otherwise it is similar in appearance and habitat. Season as for other wildfowl.

venison AF, from the L *venari*, to hunt. The OED interestingly gives: 'The flesh of an animal killed in the chase or by hunting and used as food; formerly applied to the flesh of deer, boar, hare, rabbit or other game animal, now almost entirely restricted to the flesh of various species of deer.' An early example *c.*

1300 in *Havelok* reads 'Kranes, swannes, ueneysun, Lax, lampreys and god sturgun.' From Francis Thynne's *Remedie of Love* (*c.* 1500) comes the truism, 'Venyson stoln is aye the swetter.'

vermin   from AF *vermin* and ultimately from L for 'worm'. OED: 'Animals of a noxious or objectionable kind. a. Orig. applied to reptiles, stealthy or slinking animals, and various wild beasts; now, except in U.S. and Australia, almost entirely restricted to those animals or birds which prey upon preserved game.' This was the widely accepted term for predators of game up to the end of the 1939–45 War, until Aneurin Bevan labelled the Conservatives 'vermin' in the 1950s. Thereafter it became both politically correct and 'greener' to refer to 'predators' of game, and the term *vermin* is now almost obsolete in this sense. An early example is from Chaucer's *Clerk's Tale* (*c.* 1389): 'Youre wofil moder wende stedfastly. That cruel houndes or som foule vermyn Had eten yowe.' The OED also gives 'Varment' and 'varmint' as dialect and US variants of the term, but in 1599 Thomas Dallam wrote: 'We weare sodunly wonderfully tormented with a varmin that was in our pillowes, the which did bite farr worss than fleaes' (*Diary of Voyage in the Levant*). As late as 1830 Hawker wrote of their ratcatcher, Mr Childe, 'who is up to everything from a foxhunt to the killing of all kinds of "warmunt"' (*Instructions*, 152). In the circumstances the survival of 'varmint' in the USA and in dialect form to the present day is not surprising and in this sense it embraces the OED's original form.

vixen   from OE *fyxen*, the female of the *fox*. The OED notes that the word is one of the few in which the southern <v> for <f> has established itself. An early attestation is *c.* 1410, *The Master of Game*: 'Ye fixene of ye foxe bereth as longe as ye bicche of ye wolfe bereth hir whelpes.' In 1605 Richard Verstegan wrote: 'Fixen . . . is the name of a she-fox, otherwise and more anciently foxin' (*Restitution of Decayed Intelligence*). From an early period it also seems to have had misogynist connotations. In 1621 Burton wrote: 'She is a foole, a nasty queane, a slut, a fixen, a scolde.' (*Anatomy of Melancholy*, 636)

W **ad**   origins unknown; of felt, or plastic, used to hold charge in place and expand in barrels when shot is fired, so as to block escape of explosive gases. A faulty *wad* may result in a **blown pattern**. 'There are no less than four wads used in an ordinary shotgun cartridge and these are given the following names, starting from the powder end of the cartridge: Over-Powder-Card; Felt; Over-Felt Card; and Over-Shot Card . . . when a full crimp turnover is used the Over-Shot wad is naturally omitted' (Burrard, *Shotgun*, ii, 101).

wadding   material used in a shotgun cartridge, to seal the bore and prevent the explosive gases of the charge leaking past and scattering the shot pattern. Felt, plastic and other materials are used. Fibre impregnated with a cleansing compound to remove the lead from the barrels is now commonly used for *wadding*.

walk   of snipe; a flock, see *wisp*.

walk up, walking-up   of game shooting; to walk in line with guns and beaters interspersed evenly to flush partridges, grouse, pheasants, etc. On grouse moors *walking-up* went out of fashion with the development of *driving* in the 1890s. It is still, however, practised occasionally on low-ground shootings and even sometimes on moors where neither dogs, nor beaters are available. When walking-up game it is all-important to keep in line, which should generally be taken from the centre. It is vitally important NEVER to *swing* through the line, i.e. to follow a bird or groundgame through the line with the gun. If dogs are worked in front of the line it is important that they are steady and can be relied on not to *run-in* or chase hares disturbing the ground ahead. In 1936 Leslie Sprake warned sternly: 'One of the most annoying faults a man can commit during a walking-up Shoot, is to walk ahead of the line . . . It is most important that a gun should never start to aim at a bird in front and then follow it round to the rear without taking his weapon down from his shoulder . . . in the course of his swing, the shooter will menace the whole line on the side he turns' (*LL Shooting*, 41).

wallow   from OE *wealwan*, to roll. OED: 'the act of rolling in mud.' The first attestation is in the 9th century. Of deer; to take a mud bath, to roll in a muddy patch, peat hag, or bog; alternatively the hag, or bog, where deer are known to take such mud baths. Speedy wrote: 'we discovered (the stag) about four hundred yards off, rolling in a moss-hole. On emerging from his peaty bath he appeared as if transformed into a black stag' (p. 243).

wanderer   of a stag; usually one with a notable head or

features that are easily recognisable, known to frequent two or
more forests. Although many stags, in fact, probably travel
between different forests during their lifetimes, it is only the
more outstanding beasts that are noted and to which the term is
therefore applied.

Warfarin   the trade name for a form of *rat* poison which acts
as an anti-coagulant in the blood. It is easily placed under cover
in drain pipes around *feed hoppers* and *stacks*, to prevent
dogs, cats, or other species of domestic animals from consuming
it. In some areas, however, rats are said to be immune to
Warfarin.

warren   from OF *warenne*, corresponding to the modern
French *garenne* = game park, also (now chiefly) rabbit warren.
OED: 'Now usually a piece of uncultivated land where rabbits
breed wild in burrows.' At one time a *warren* was a place where
rabbits were deliberately preserved and bred; now generally
accepted as an area where there are numerous rabbits living
together, characterised by many holes, *runs* and droppings,
usually also by considerable depredations to the nearby grass,
or vegetation. Warrens in woods, or in cliffs, or broken ground,
near to agricultural land can be a source of trouble to the
farmer. Snaring, gassing or long-netting, especially the *Caldra
system*, are probably the only solutions. In 1784 Fançois de La
Rochefoucauld travelling near Thetford, wrote: 'A large portion
of this arid country is full of rabbits of which the numbers
astonished me ... I ... was told that there was an immense
warren ...' (*Tour of East Anglia*). See *burrow; rabbit.*

waster   from OF *wastere*. OED: 'An animal that is wasting
away.' First attested in the 14th century. Of a deer; a sick, or
emaciated beast, which may be suffering from injury, or disease,
or just the effects of hunger and a hard winter, but generally
descriptive of a beast better *culled* as likely to die otherwise in
any event. See also *piner.*

weasel   from OE, *wesle*. OED: 'A carnivorous animal (*Putorius
nivalis*) the smallest European species of the genus (of the order
Mustelidae). Remarkable for its slender body, its ferocity and
bloodthirstiness.' A furred predator of game chicks and eggs,
similar to the stoat, only smaller and without the dark tip to the
tail. Kills are usually marked merely by a puncture at the base
of the neck where the *weasel* has sucked the blood from its
victim. Weasels are useful around the farm as rat killers, but are
also ruthless predators of game. They may be seen to hypnotise
a rabbit or attract birds by acrobatic performances which attract

their attention and bring them within reach. Once they set off on the trail of a rabbit they seldom give up until their prey is caught and killed. They will also sometimes hunt in small family groups of from six to eight or so, working in unison. First attested *c.* 725. One of the earlier somewhat confusing mentions is in Bartholomew de Trevisa's MSS of 1389: 'The wesell hath a red and a whyte wombe and chaungeth colour.' In 1845 St John noted: 'I have frequently seen a weasel, small as he is, kill a full grown rabbit. The latter is sometimes so frightened of the persevering ferocity of its little enemy, that it lies down and cries out before the weasel has come up. Occasionally these animals join in a company of six or eight and hunt down a rabbit or hare giving tongue and tracking their unfortunate victim like a pack of beagles' (p. 117). Mackie was no admirer: 'The weasel, though smaller in size, very much resembles the stoat. It is also very destructive among young game, and like the stoat bloodthirsty in its habits' (p. 129).

Weimaraner a type of gundog bred in the province of Weimar in Germany. It is claimed that they were bred by the Dukes of Weimar before the revolution of 1840 and were originally a cross with a Great Dane. Like most other similar pointer-retriever breeds, they were subsequently bred by enthusiastic shooters in the latter half of the 19th century when the breed was recognised and established. Known as the 'Grey-Ghost', it is a light silvery grey, short-coated and light-eyed. It is now recognised by the Kennel Club in this country as one of the group IV HPR breeds, grouped with 'German Shorthaired Pointers and those breeds which hunt, point and retrieve'. The height of the dogs at the shoulder is 23–25 inches and of the bitches 21–23 inches.

well-opened of antlers; indicating a wide spread.

Welsh springer spaniel a breed of *springer spaniel*. They are probably as old as any, coming somewhere between the cocker and the English springer in size, but of distinctive colouring, dark red and white. Supposedly originating, as the name implies, in Wales and still common there, they were at one time very popular throughout the country, especially during the 18th century. Smaller than the English springer spaniel and also an excellent all-round gundog the dogs stand 15–17 inches at the shoulder and the bitches from 14–16 inches.

wheel-lock OED: 'A form of gun-lock in which the powder was fired by the friction of a small wheel (wound up with a spring) against a piece of iron pyrites.' The wheel-lock was superseded by the *flint-lock*.

whicker   OED: 'Of a horse: to whinny: also of a sheep or goat, to bleat; of a dog, to whine, etc.' Also of duck; the sound of ducks' wings flying overhead: 'I waited for duck but only heard a faint whicker of wings' (Brander, *Sport*, 197).

whistling   of *sika* deer; the sound made by both sexes, very like a human whistle.

white front   OED: 'The whitefronted goose: Anser albifrons.' In 1830 Hawker wrote: 'Whitefronted, or Laughing Geese; These birds were quite unknown to the gunners on the Hampshire coast, till the last severe winter, when they arrived here. One *Sunday* morning about eighty of them pitched in a field close to the village of Milford . . . the next day . . . a volley from my two large barrels . . . "stopped" about twenty, though I only got twelve' (*Instructions*, 201). In 1845 St John observed:

> The first wild geese that we see here [the Moray Firth] are not the common grey goose, but the white-fronted, or laughing goose, Anas albifrons, called by Buffon, l'Oye rieuse. This bird has a peculiarly harsh and wild cry, whence its name. It differs in another respect from the common grey goose in preferring clover and green wheat to corn for its food . . . Unlike the grey goose too, it roosts, when undisturbed, in any grass-field, where it may have been feeding in the afternoon, instead of taking to the bay every night for its sleeping quarters. The laughing goose also never appears here in large flocks, but in small companies of from eight or nine to twenty birds. Though very watchful at all times they are more easily approached than the grey goose, and often feed on ground that admits of stalking them. (p. 172)

This goose may be distinguished from the **greylag** by its being smaller and darker, also by the bold white patch at the base of the pink bill and by its orange legs. It varies in size from 26 to 30 inches and in weight from 6 to 7 lbs. Season as for other wildfowl.

white stag   one that has not been rutting and is not *run*.

widgeon, wigeon   the etymology is difficult since the form suggests French origin (as in pigeon), but none are as early as the first English usage and the suggestion that it originates from Fr *vigeon* and/or L *vipio*, a kind of crane, is regarded by the OED as 'very dubious'. OED: 'A wild duck of the genus Mareca, esp. M. penelope of Europe.' The male has a chestnut head with a buff crown, a grey body and white belly. The female resembles a smaller version of the mallard, with a smaller beak. Notable for its whistling call, well known to wildfowlers, it grows to about 18 inches. It flights in compact flocks and may be found inland, especially when stormy at sea. Season as for other wildfowl. First attested in 1513 with the spelling 'wegyons'. One of the earliest references is in 1591 in Sir John Harington's *Preface to Orlando*, which spells it with the letter <d>: 'At my Lord Maiors dinner they said he would put up a widgeon for his supper.' In 1767 Gilbert White wrote interestingly, still with the letter <d>: 'We are twenty miles from the sea and almost as many from a great river, but . . . multitudes of widgeons and teals in hard weather frequent our lakes in the forest' (*Natural History*). In 1788 the <d> was missing when it was noted: 'The American wigeon . . . is rather bigger than our wigeon' (*Encyclopedia Brittanica*, 662). The first to write of shooting them in 1830 was Hawker, who also omitted the <d>, giving his reasons: 'Our lexicographers it appears still spell *WiDgeon* with a *d* . . . Mr Bewick spells *"wigeon"* without the *d*. I shall, therefore, take the liberty of following his example, under the idea that lexicographers are not gods but men' (*Instructions*, 237); 'The wigeon for coast night shooting . . . shows the finest sport of anything in Great Britain' (ibid., 238). In 1897 there was a sporting viewpoint given, again without the <d>:

A species of wild duck, Mareca Penelope, best known in the British isles as a visitor during the winter months, when it is extremely common on most parts of the coast . . . A large flock of wigeon is termed by wildfowl shooters a "company"; a smaller number they term a "bunch". A company of wigeon, when first collecting, may be heard at an immense distance by the whistling of the drakes and purring noise of the ducks; but when they are quietly settled and busy at feed, the only sound heard arises from the motion of their bills, which is similar to that of tame ducks. (*Encyclopedia*, ii, 535)

The *Shooting Times* (22 June 1901) made an interesting point on the bird in Ireland, spelling it without the <d>: 'On Lough Neagh the wigeon is known as the "grass wigeon" or the "grass-duck". This may be due to its habit of feeding on the grassy sward along the shores.' Although not entirely accurate, in 1935 Dawson epitomised many views on the spelling when, after noting that wigeon weigh around 1½ lbs, he wrote: 'Why is it I wonder that many people will insist on spelling this word with a quite unnecessary "d" as widgeon, an extremely ugly form to my way of thinking? Etymologists are agreed that pigeon comes through the French from the Latin word pipio. In the same way wigeon comes from vipio' (p. 119). That Lord Mayor's banquet appears to supply the answer.

wig antler   of antlers; another name for the rarely-encountered

malformation of the antlers termed *perruque*, or peruke, after
the 18th century wig so-termed.

wildfowl   as one word or as two; from Ger *Wildvogel* and ON
villifygli. OED: 'Game birds (now especially of the duck and
goose kinds).' A wildfowler would term them: 'Those ducks
and geese and any shore birds, which may legally be shot inland
from 1 September to 31 January and on the foreshore below
the high water mark from 1 September to 20 February.' Hawker
wrote: 'Wildfowl shooting; This amusement is generally condemned as being only an employment for fishermen, because it
sometimes interferes with ease and comfort' (*Instructions*, 305).
In 1870 N.F. Hele wrote: 'Very few wild-fowl shooters frequent
this part of the river' (*Aldeburgh* 8).

wildfowler   OED: 'A sportsman who shoots or catches wildfowl.' One who shoots wildfowl, generally on the foreshore or
salting below the high tide marks.

wildfowling   OED: 'The pursuit or capture of wildfowl.' More
fully: 'The act of flight shooting, creekcrawling, or punt gun-
ning, below the high tide line, or sea wall after wildfowl.' An
early example of the usage is by Henry Folkard: *A Treatise on
Ancient and Modern Wildfowling*, 1859. In 1874 J.W. Long
wrote: 'In no other branch of wildfowling is a breechloader of
more advantage than in teal shooting' (*American Wildfowl*, 193).
See *creek crawling*; *greylag*; *white front*.

wildfowling punt   a shallow-draught, broad-beamed, double-
ended punt with a low freeboard, equipped to carry a large bore
(generally muzzle-loading) gun. It is usually propelled by hand
paddles when approaching wildfowl.

Wildfowlers Association of Great Britain and Ireland
acronym WAGBI. Founded in the 1930s, this Association
changed its name in the 1980s and is now known by the
greener, all-embracing title of the British Association for Shooting and Conservation. It has the largest membership of any
body supporting shooting. Everyone interested in shooting in
any form should be a member. See also *BASC*.

wind   from OE *wind*, pronounced to rhyme with be*hind* until
the 18th century. The OED gives several definitions, but primarily 'Air in motion,' then 'As conveying scent, spec. the scent of
a person, or animal, in hunting.' First attested *c.* 1330.

   Stalking: when the wind is blowing from the deer to the
stalker it is known as 'right'. When the wind is blowing from
the stalker towards the deer it is known as 'wrong'. When it is
blowing from either side, it is known as a *cheek wind*. When it

is seemingly changing direction occasionally, it is known as 'flukey' or 'fitful'.

As wind is the greatest difficulty the stalker has to contend with, we are not surprised that "How is the wind this morning?" should be the first question put to the stalker, when he makes his appearance . . . to make arrangements for the sport of the day. Should the forest not be an extensive one, and the wind in an unsuitable direction, it is advisable not to disturb the ground at all, otherwise there is the risk of the deer being put off the ground to afford sport for the tenant of the adjoining shooting. If the day can be spent in grouse shooting, or angling, so much the better; but if neither of these is available, it is much better to remain in the lodge and wait for a change of wind than to have the deer driven out of the forest, as they may not return for days. It is remarkable how deer, guided by natural instinct, generally travel nose to the wind; and when it is kept in mind that they can detect the presence of man at the distance of a thousand yards, it is easy to see the folly of attempting to stalk down wind. (*Speedy*, 225)

Also a gundog, specially a pointer: this may be said to *wind* game when it is seen to pick up *air scent on the wind*. Speedy wrote of a pointer running downwind: 'She will not get the wind of them and seems almost certain to put them up.'

wing   OED: 'to shoot (a bird in the wing), so as to disable it from flying without killing it.'

winged   OED: 'Shot or wounded in the wing.' 'A partridge which is only "winged" will always try to rejoin his covey the same evening, but a more seriously injured bird creeps away into thick cover to die by himself' (Lynn-Allen, 155).

winged bird   OED: 'Shot or wounded in the wing.' It should perhaps have added 'and incapable of flying', since some birds can still fly at least after a fashion when shot in the wing; see *plane*. It may be the result of inefficient shooting and an ill-aimed shot, shooting at too long a range, insufficient swing on a crossing shot, catching the bird in the edge of the pattern, or a *blown pattern*; also possibly the result of *browning a covey*. Although usually condemned to a certain death at the hands of ground predators such a stoats, weasels, foxes or mink, unless retrieved soon after being shot, this is not always the case. A bird which has only been *wing-tipped*, with the end pinion damaged or broken, can sometimes make a surprising recovery and it is not uncommon to find birds with signs of an obvious mended break of the wing when picking up birds or

when examining the *bag* late in the season. One of the earlier
examples of the usage is in 1810: 'Winged, wounded, or dead
birds' (*The Sporting Magazine*, xxxiv, 149). See also *forward-
allowance*; *pricked bird*; *runner*.

wing-tipped   of a *winged bird*, only just touched by a pellet
or two in the end pinion. Such birds often make a complete
recovery and may sometimes fly a considerable distance.
Dawson noted:

> Sometimes a wounded pheasant will go up a tree . . . A cock,
> obviously hard hit, carried on for a quarter of a mile before
> coming down . . . And there . . . was the quarry sitting in the
> lower branches of a small oak. It was undoubtedly the same
> bird as it could only fly with difficulty [. . .] I saw him [the
> dog] appear at the top of the field, some 300 yards away,
> with the bird in his mouth . . . I . . . found it had one wing
> just tipped' (pp. 61, 64).

wing-trailing/flapping   not in OED. A *winged bird* will often
run with the wounded wing *trailing* and the other wing *flapping*.
Wild birds of many species will instinctively adopt the appearance of a winged bird, running thus in an enticing manner with
one wing trailing and the other flapping, when their nest or
young are under threat from the approach of a possible
predator, such as a cat, dog or man. They will then make a
decoy run, leading the intruder away and skilfully keeping just
ahead before finally taking flight when they decide that they
have led them far enough away. Wildfowl and partridges in the
spring when disturbed will often give a very realistic performance. Either sex may indulge in this performance. 'In the spring
months if an apparently wounded mallard is seen flapping his
way across the water it is always a safe bet, as it is when almost
any adult bird indulges in these manoeuvres, that the young are
somewhere close at hand. A quick search round will probably
reveal the mother hiding with her brood' (Brander, *Sport*, 88).

wipe the eye   slang. Originally of shooting, to 'get the better
of' to 'score off'. Nowadays more frequently used of *field
trials*, especially where a dog performs a retrieve after a
previous dog has failed. This is generally known as *an eye-wipe*.
In 1823 Edward Moor (*Suffolk Words and Phrases*) appears to
have been amongst the first to note the usage as follows: 'In
shooting, if one miss the bird, and a companion, shooting after,
kill it, the lucky, or more skilful, gunner, is said to wipe the eye
of his disappointed friend.'

wisp   OED: of uncertain origin, perhaps OE, meaning: 'A handful, bunch or small bundle.' First attested in the 14th century. A development, first attested in the 15th century, was 'a bundle, or parcel containing a definite quantity' then by transference 'a flock (of birds, esp. snipe)'. In 1806 P. Neill wrote: 'The sportsman will not pass a marsh without starting several wisps of snipe' (*Tour of Orkney*, 56). In 1889 Lancaster referred to 'a wisp of snipe (a flight)' (p. 184).

woodcock   late OE *wudecoc*. OED: 'A migratory bird, *Scolopax rusticola*, allied to the snipe common in Europe and the British Isles, having a long bill, large eyes and variegated plumage and much esteemed as food.' A well-known game bird with a long bill, round wings, grey-brown plumage matching dead leaves, and prominent eyes set well back in a rounded head. There is no difference of plumage between the sexes. Its croaking call is seldom heard except during the mating, or *roding*, flights as they are called. The woodcock pairs early and its nest contains 3–4 eggs, which hatch in April–May. Migratory birds from the continent as well as the native population are to be found. They usually migrate as a 'fall' of woodcock in late October and early November, landing exhausted near the shores in the south and east coasts. Their weaving flight amongst trees often gives rise to dangerous shooting. Season from 1 September in Scotland, 1 October in England, to 31 January. It feeds mainly on worms, larvae and insects. An early mention is in 1486 in *The Boke of St Albans* on hawking: 'The wodecok is comberous to sle; bot if ther be crafte.' In 1768 Pennant noted: 'Woodcocks usually arrive here in flocks' (ii, 348). White observed in his *Natural History*:

> One thing I used to observe when I was a sportsman, that there were times when woodcocks were so sluggish and sleepy, that they would drop again when flushed just before the spaniels, nay, just at the muzzle of the gun that has been fired at them; whether this strange laziness was the effect of a recent fatiguing journey I shall not presume to say. [. . .] No sporting dogs will flush woodcocks till inured to the scent and trained to the sport, which they then pursue with vehemence and transport; but then they will not touch their bones, but turn from them with abhorrence, even when they are hungry.

Daniel was the first to write on shooting them: 'It may save the Sportsman time and trouble to recollect, that after *Spaniels* have flushed *Woodcocks two or three* times, they either pitch in the ditch, upon the Bank of the Wood, or betake themselves the hedges adjoining the Covert. A person who marks well is a valuable Assistant' (iii, 172). In 1830 Hawker gave directions on finding the pin feather: 'The feather of the woodcock, which is most acceptable to miniature painters, is that very small one, under the outside quill of each wing; to be sure of finding which, draw out the extreme feather of the wing, and this little one will then appear conspicuous from its sharp white point' (*Instructions*, 238). In 1845 St John gave an interesting naturalist's observation:

> March 9; A woodcock's nest, with three eggs, was brought to me today. Two years ago a boy brought me a young woodcock nearly full-grown and fledged in the second week of April ... Reckoning from this. I should suppose that the woodcock is about the first bird to hatch in this country. A few years ago it was supposed that none remained in Britain after the end of winter, except a few wounded birds, which were unable to cross the sea to their usual breeding grounds. (p. 251)

Walsh noted the regularity of their movements: 'Woodcock generally take the same line of flight ... even from one covert to another they may always be seen to take the same ride or break in the trees. In beating large coverts ... there are always certain spots where cocks are shot' (p. 64). Mackie advised:

> In the event of woodcock not being in coverts it is well worth trying the open moor for them, especially when the moor lies in the sun. Woodcock as a rule ... are loath to leave any favourite shelter ... and will even fly back to the place from which they have been flushed. Accordingly it is often wise to go over the same ground a second time ... In looking for woodcock in the open it must be remembered that they generally feed on the lee-side of a hill and may be found where they feed ... When there is no wind they choose the brightest or sunniest side. The keeper should remember to draw the leg sinew immediately on picking up; it enhances the eating quality of the leg of the bird. (p. 344)

In 1930 there was an interesting note on the subject of migration:

> Although the woodcock now breeds in most parts of England the birds which supply sport during the winter months are mostly immigrants and arrive during October and November. There is usually a small arrival soon after October 10, another at the end of the month or early in November and ... the largest flight about the middle of November ... followed early in December by the small dark bird which is said to come from Silesia. (*LL Shooting*, 179)

'Woodcock have visited Scotland annually in large numbers and have bred in certain districts in comparatively large numbers long prior to any records . . . being kept' (ibid., 189). In 1963 Sedgwick used the diminutive to make a nice distinction: 'When I shot 'cock (on cock pheasant and woodcock only days) in Derbyshire, it was usually . . . when snow lay on the bracken forming tents, under which pheasants and rabbits sat, and from which sometimes woodcock would jump' (*Waders*, 13).

woodcock snipe   *Scolopax major*; the **great snipe**.

woodcock thighs   the light fleshed thighs of the *woodcock* are regarded as a particular delicacy by epicures. The legs of a shot woodcock should therefore be broken at the knee joint and the sinews drawn at once to enhance their flavour as noted above.

wood pigeon   the OED gives rather sweepingly: 'Any of the species of pigeon that live in woods, as the stock-dove, *Columba anas* and (now especially) the ring-dove *Columba palumbus*.' From a sporting viewpoint at least, the ring-dove, *Columba palumbus*, is regarded as the true *wood-pigeon*. A grey bird with a white collar familiar to everyone in Britain. Rated as a pest, it may be shot throughout the year. Migratory birds from the continent appear in considerable numbers at times. They may rear up to five clutches a year consisting of two eggs. The young gain their familar collar after about 16 weeks. Omnivorous, but greedy feeders on grain and greenstuffs, they are generally shot over decoys or flighting and can provide very sporting shooting. In 1775 W. Hayes noted: 'found in great abundance in Buckinghamshire, there being plenty of beech mast in that county of which they are exceedingly fond. In winter it is generally found in turnip fields, especially those bordering woods' (*A Natural History of British Birds*, 265). In 1830 Hawker wrote 'Ring, Cushat, or Queest, Columba palumbus . . . the most common . . . almost universally known by the name of *woodpigeon*; and if not too much fed on *turnips* and kept till tender, is deservedly esteemed as an excellent bird' (*Instructions*, 220). In 1843 *The Zoologist* noted: 'It was extremely rare in East Lothian about the end of the last century, where it now swarms to a most injurious extent' (p. 132). In 1845 St John claimed that, 'Woodpigeons, blackbirds, thrushes and all the smaller birds, increase yearly in consequence of the destruction of their natural enemies. The woodpigeon, in particular, has multiplied to a great extent. The farmers complain constantly to me of the mischief done by these birds'

(p. 135–6). Speedy was the first to write of flighting pigeons in to roost and shooting over decoys:

> These birds are more prolific than many people imagine, breeding, as a rule, a good many times during the season . . . After the season for killing game has terminated, excellent sport can sometimes be had shooting wood-pigeons. There are few birds more wary and difficult to get near . . . Large numbers can be shot in woods as they fly in to roost, and more especially if there is a high wind as they invariably fly against it and are thus easily killed if the shooter keeps himself out of sight. It is remarkable how indifferent they are to the report of a gun while feeding in the fields, if the party using it is thoroughly concealed. When shooting at them settling beside a decoy, if not struck, we have frequently seen them fly round a few hundred yards and settle down again almost on the identical spot they were shot at . . . (p. 312)

wormburner   of live pigeon shooting; descriptive slang term, possibly originating in the USA, for a pigeon released from the traps which goes away low at high speed. Pigeons can be trained to behave as desired by consistently throwing cinders at the trap in one particular area when they are released until they automatically fly in the opposite direction as required. They can thus be trained to fly directly upwards, or abruptly to the right or left, or in the case of the *wormburner*, very close to the ground. It was customary for each 'side' in a competition to provide pigeons for the other. It was thus possible to study the opponent's form and choose birds trained to exploit any seeming weaknesses. This sort of dubious behaviour is one of the reasons, along with the large sums in wagers involved, that live pigeon shooting fell into disrepute, quite aside from the obvious cruelty involved.

Y **earling** of deer: of either sex, in its second year.

    eld from late OE *gelde*. OED: 'of an animal, barren or that has missed having her young.' Of hinds; one which has not had a calf the previous summer, but is not barren. See *blue-hind*. When *hind shooting*, it is accepted that it is generally not desirable to select *yeld* hinds but even experienced stalkers can be mistaken. Since the chances are strong that a yeld hind will breed again the following season, it is usually very much preferable to shoot first any obviously old or sickly hinds, since in any event they are unlikely to last out a severe winter. Mackie argued: 'It has been proved . . . that 90% of yeld hinds killed would have had stag calves in the following season. Thus every ten yeld-hinds killed mean a loss of nine prospective stags to the forest. On this account yeld hinds should be left alone' (p. 267).

yellow labrador see *Labrador retriever*. It is thought by some to have Chesapeake blood in it, but the breed carries a yellow gene and yellow pups are often born to black parents.

yuppy shooting from Young Upwardly-mobile Person, hence YUP-PY: a term coined in the late 1980s for excessively unsporting covert shooting, where far more birds are reared than can possibly be supported by the acreage concerned; where large numbers of freshly reared birds are released illegally shortly before each day's shooting; where the shooting is commercialised and is regarded by the organisers as a taxable expense classified as 'corporate hospitality'; where the guns are inexperienced and the birds poorly presented and as a consequence badly shot and uneatable. Instances have been reported after such shoots of large quantities of birds having to be buried because they were so badly shot as to be uneatable. Such extremely unsporting shooting can only bring shooting in general and such participants in particular into total and thoroughly deserved disrepute. Somewhat similar complaints have been made about the shooting of reared pheasants in particular, since the early days of driven shooting in the latter half of the 19th century (see *battue shooting; covert shooting*), but this travesty of sporting shooting cannot possibly be defended. Anyone guilty of participating in such activities should rightly be prosecuted and heavily fined and/or imprisoned.

Z **ern** orig. Czech, possibly Hungarian. In its present form first encountered in West Virginia, USA, before the First World War. It became popular in New York in the late 1950s and has since spread around the world. It has successfully crossed and re-crossed the Atlantic, but has remained unchanged: 'That measure of Scotch malt whisky conducive to mellow and pleasurable reflection on the success or otherwise of the day's sport after shooting, fishing or hunting. Hence: a *Zernful.*' (See Brander, *Deer*, 1986, p. 164). So-named after Ed Zern, Editor-at-Large for *Field & Stream*, expert fisherman, keen shot and international all-round sportsman, as well as superb raconteur, on whose eightieth birthday the following lines were penned:

There's many a bottle of Scotch we have shared,
Some better than others, when closely compared,
But even when, maybe, we've thought they had faults
We've tested and tried them against other malts.
For the sake of mankind and the purest of liquor
We've drunk them real slow, then quicker and quicker.
We thus have a right, which took years to earn,
To call a malt measure, what else, but a Zern!
So join us whenever your glasses are raised,
Wherever the pleasures of whisky are praised.
And drink off a Zernful to him, as we quaff,
Whose writing so often has caused us to laugh,
About fishing the water, or out with the gun,
About hunting the dogs, or just having fun.
That tot of fine malt that is drunk at the bar
Also helps us to savour old friends from afar.
So charge up your glasses and keep a clear head,
It's down with a Zernful, Happy Birthday to Ed!'

zero Italian. OED: 'the initial point of a process.' v. to zero: To check the 'zero' of a rifle fitted with telescopic sights, i.e. to *sight-in* a rifle fitted with telescopic sights by firing several times at a target while adjusting the telescopic sights in order to ensure that they are correctly set. When they are correct, the rifle is said to be *zeroed in.* 'If a stalker has a telescopic sight fitted it is obligatory to check the zero of his rifle . . . The zeroing must be conducted in a completely safe location. The following points will assist those wishing to zero their rifle . . .' (Coles, *Stalking*, 190). A *sight-aligner* may be used to zero, or sight-in a rifle. This usage is not in the OED.

References

The place of publication is London unless otherwise stated.

Aflalo, F. G. with the Earl of Suffolk & Berkshire, Hedley Peek (eds) (1897) *The Encyclopedia of Sport*, 2 vols. Lawrence & Bullen.

Brander, Michael (1957) *The Roughshooter's Dog*. MacGibbon & Kee.

Brander, Michael (1958) *The Roughshooter's Sport*. MacGibbon & Kee.

Brander, Michael (1963) *Ground Game*, Shooting Tlmes Library no. 11. Percival Marshall & Co.

Brander, Michael (1963) *Gundogs: Their Care and Training*. A. & C. Black.

Brander, Michael (1965) *The Game Shot's Vade Mecum*. A. & C. Black.

Brander, Michael (1968) *A Dictionary of Sporting Terms*. A. & C. Black.

Brander, Michael (1983) *Training the Pointer-Retriever Gundog*. Swan Hill.

Brander, Michael (1986) *Deer Stalking in Britain*. Sportsman's Press.

Brander, Michael (1986) *Sporting Pigeon Shooting*. A. & C. Black.

Brander, Michael (1989) *The Sporting Roughshoot*. Pelham.

Brander, Michael and Zern, Ed (eds) (1972) *The International Encyclopedia of Shooting*. Pelham.

Burrard, Major Sir Gerald (1930) *The Modern Shotgun*, 3 vols. Herbert Jenkins.

Burrard, Major Sir Gerald (1930) *In the Gunroom*. Herbert Jenkins.

Carnegie, William (1880) *Practical Trapping*. 'The Bazaar'.

Coles, Charles (1964) *Shooting Pigeons*, Shooting Times Library no. 15. Percival Marshall & Co.

Coles, Charles (1983) *Shooting and Stalking: a basic guide*. Stanley Paul.

Collyns, Dr Charles (1862) *Notes on the Chase of the Wild Red Deer in the Counties of Devon and Somerset*. Longman & Co.

Cotgrave, Randle (1611) *A Dictionarie of the French and English Tongues.*

Cox, Nicholas (1674) *The Gentleman's Recreation.*

Daniel, Revd W. B. (1812) *Rural Sports* [1st edition 1801], 3 vols. Longman Hurst, Kees, Orme & Brown.

Davenport, W. Bromley (1884) *Sport.* Alexander Maclehose.

Dawson, Major Kenneth (1935) *Just an Ordinary Shot.* Herbert Jenkins.

Drought, Captain J. B. (1948) *Successful Shooting.* Country Life.

Forrester, Rex (1967) *Hunting in New Zealand.* A. H. & A. W. Reed.

Greener, W. W. (1888) *Modern Shotguns.* Cassell.

Hare, C. E. (1939) *The Language of Sport.* Country Life.

Hawker, Lt.-Col. Peter (1830) *Instructions to Young Sportsmen in all that relates to guns and shooting* [1st edition 1824], 6th edition.

Hawker, Lt.-Col. Peter (1931) *Colonel Hawker's Shooting Diaries* [1811–1853], edited by Eric Parker. Philip Allan.

Holmes, Dr Frank (1973) *Following the Roe: a natural history of the roe deer.* Edinburgh: J. Bartholemew.

Jeffries, Richard (1878) *The Gamekeeper at Home.* Smith, Elder.

Jeffries, Richard (1884) *Red Deer.* Longmans, Green.

Lancaster, Charles (1889) *An Illustrated Treatise on the Art of Shooting.* McCorquodale & Co.

Lynn-Allen, Captain E. H. (1942) *Rough Shoot.* Hutchinson & Co.

Mackie, Sir Peter (1929) *The Keeper's Book* [1st edition 1904], 16th edition. G. T. Foulis & Co.

McCall, Ian (1985) *Your Shoot, Gamekeeping and Management.* A. & C. Black.

Markham, Gervase (1611) *Country Contentments.*

Markham, Gervase (1616) *The Country Farme.*

Markham, Gervase (1621) *The Whole Art of Fowling.*

Parker, Eric (ed.) (1939) *Shooting by Moor, Field and Shore,* Lonsdale Library, vol. III. Seeley, Service & Co.

Pennant, Thomas (1768–70) *British Zoology,* 4 vols.

Purdey, T.D.S. & J.A. (1939) *The Shotgun.* A. & C. Black.

St John, Charles (1845) *Wild Sports of the Highlands.*

Sanderson, C. Mackay (1920) *Breaking and Training of Gundogs.* Our Dogs Publishing Co.

Sedgwick, Noel M. (1939) *The Young Shot.* A. & C. Black.

Sedgwick, Noel M. (1950) *Wildfowling and Roughshooting.* Herbert Jenkins.

Sedgwick, Noel M. (1963) *Wader Shooting, including Woodcock and Snipe*, Shooting Times Library no. 13. Percival Marshall & Co.

Speedy, Tom. (1884) *Sport in the Highlands and Lowlands of Scotland*. William Blackwood.

Stanfield, E. F. (1963) *Pheasant Shooting*, Shooting Times Library no. 5. Percival Marshall & Co.

Stephens, Martin (1939) *Grouse Shooting*. A. & C. Black.

Surtees, Robert S. (1852) *Mr Spunge's Sporting Tour*. Bradbury Agnew & Co.

Tegner, Henry (1963) *Game for the Sporting Rifle*. Herbert Jenkins.

Tennyson, Julian (1939) *Rough Shooting*. A. & C. Black.

Thornton, Lt.-Col. T. (1804) *A Sporting Tour of Scotland*.

Thornton, Lt.-Col. T. (1806) *A Tour of France*, 2 vols.

Topsell, Edward (1607) *The Historie of Four Footed Beastes*.

Twiti, William (c. 1327) *Le Art de Venerie*.

Turberville, George (1576) *The Art of Venerie*.

Walsh, J. S. Stonehenge (1856) *The Manual of British Rural Sports*.

White, Gilbert (1787) *The Natural History of Selbourne*.

White, T. H. (1936) *England Have My Bones*. Collins.